Also by Robert Craft

Prejudices in Disguise: Articles, Essays, Reviews (1974,
    revised edition 1977)
Stravinsky: Chronicle of a Friendship, 1948–1971 (1972)

With Igor Stravinsky

Retrospectives and Conclusions (1969)
Themes and Episodes (1966)
Dialogues and a Diary (1963)
Expositions and Developments (1962)
Memories and Commentaries (1960)
Conversations with Igor Stravinsky (1959)

CURRENT CONVICTIONS

CURR
CONVI

ROBERT CRAFT

NT
TIONS

VIEWS AND REVIEWS

 ALFRED A. KNOPF NEW YORK 1977

THIS IS A BORZOI BOOK
PUBLISHED BY ALFRED A. KNOPF, INC.

Copyright © 1974, 1975, 1976, 1977 by Robert Craft

Because this page cannot legibly accommodate all acknowledgments,
they appear on pages ix–x.

LIBRARY OF CONGRESS CATALOGING IN PUBLICATION DATA
Craft, Robert.   Current convictions.
Includes bibliographical references and index.
1.   Music—Addresses, essays, lectures.
2.   Opera—Addresses, essays, lectures.
3.   Humanities—Addresses, essays, lectures.
I.   Title.
ML60.C89   780′.2   77–74991

Manufactured in the United States of America
First Edition

FOR PHYLLIS AND PATRICIA

CONTENTS

Acknowledgments   ix

MOZART

"A Prodigy of Nature"   3

Salzburg, Mozart, and *Così*   13

Mozart's "Opera of All Operas"   24

Playing with *The Magic Flute*   34

Figaro at the Met: A *Marriage* on the Rocks   49

The Paris Opéra in New York   59

WAGNER, VERDI, STRAUSS

Taking the Wagner Cure   71

Parsifal: The Worship of Wagnerism   82

"Winnie" and "Uncle Wolf"   92

The Giant of Busseto   104

Verdi, Shakespeare, and *Falstaff*   114

A "Beautiful Coloured, Musical Thing"   124

Der Rosenkavalier: "Something Mozartian"?   136

Elektra and Richard Strauss   145

SOME OTHER COMPOSERS

Musical R for a Political Season 159

Lisztomania 168

The Nostalgic Kingdom of Maurice Ravel 184

Towards Schoenberg 195

Ives's World 211

BOOKS

Telling Time 217

Apropos Eliot's Prose 223

In Search of Aldous Huxley 234

A New Interpretation of Hegel? 244

The Discreet Charm of the Bourgeoisie 256

The *Doctor Faustus* Case 269

TV AND THE GREAT WORLD

In the Mouse Trap 285

Hazards of the Fourth of July 298

Elegy for *Mary Hartman, Mary Hartman* 306

Edvard Munch: Self-Portraitist 315

Index of Names 329

ACKNOWLEDGMENTS

The articles collected in this book were written between May 1974 and November 1976 and published in *The New York Review of Books* as follows: "In the Mouse Trap," May 16, 1974; "Taking the Wagner Cure," October 17, 1974; "*Parsifal*: The Worship of Wagnerism," October 31, 1974; "Huxley at Home" (original title), January 23, 1975; "Lisztomania," February 6, 1975; "The Giant of Busseto," March 20, 1975; "Verdi, Shakespeare, and *Falstaff*," April 17, 1975; "The Nostalgic Kingdom of Maurice Ravel," May 1, 1975; "Telling Time," May 15, 1975; "The Discreet Charm of the Bourgeoisie," June 12, 1975; "The *Doctor Faustus* Case," August 7, 1975; "Towards Schoenberg," September 18, 1975; Salzburg, Mozart, and *Così*," October 16, 1975; "Mozart's 'Opera of All Operas,'" October 30, 1975; "Playing with *The Magic Flute*," November 27, 1975; "'A Prodigy of Nature,'" December 11, 1975; "*Figaro* at the Met: A *Marriage* on the Rocks," January 22, 1976; "A 'Beautiful Coloured, Musical Thing,'" March 18, 1976; "*Der Rosenkavalier*: 'Something Mozartian'?," May 13, 1976; "*Elektra* and Richard Strauss," June 10, 1976; "Musical ℞ for a Political Season," July 8, 1976; "Apropos Eliot's Prose," June 10 and July 15, 1976; "Hazards of the Fourth of July," September 16, 1976; "The Paris Opéra in New York," October 14, 1976; "'Winnie' and 'Uncle Wolf,'" November 11, 1976; "Elegy for *Mary Hartman, Mary Hartman*," December 8, 1976; "Edvard Munch: Self-Portraitist," January 20, 1977.

"Ives's World," appeared in *The Sunday Times* of London, November 28, 1976. "A New Interpretation of Hegel?" has not been previously published.

I am especially grateful to Robert Silvers, Barbara Epstein,

Phyllis Crawford, Lawrence Morton, and my English teacher of long ago, Elbert Lenrow, for invaluable aid and advice. I also thank Miss Donna Wright, who typed the manuscript.

R. C.
June 1977

MOZART

"A PRODIGY OF NATURE"

This description by Leopold Mozart of his eight-year-old son might well have said that the boy was also a prodigy of Leopold himself, whose expert tutelage and unrelenting ambition had cultivated and exploited the child's gifts. Leopold's teaching and guidance were a sine qua non, for, without the father's long and omniscient supervision, the son would doubtless have become a different composer from the one whom the world adulates. But this does not imply that a Leopold-father or any kind and amount of education can explain the unfathomable miracle of Mozart.

The father-son relationship determined the development of Mozart's character both in and out of music. Leopold was a composer, a violinist, and the author of a *Violinschule* still used as a treatise on performance practice of his time.[1] For a man holding a humble post in a parochial orchestra, he was remarkable in his broad culture, his accomplishments as a writer, and his worldly wisdom—displaying, for example, in his dealings with royalty, some of the skills of a diplomat. With such abilities, combined with his evident frustrations, he was understandably dazzled by his children and made their careers the main purpose of his life. After discovering that Wolfgang's gifts were greater than his older sister's, Leopold single-mindedly dedicated himself to his son and never willingly let go. The father paraded the youth all over Europe like a performing animal; yet when Wolfgang finally and belatedly emancipated himself, he failed to satisfy Leopold's aspirations, becoming an immortal composer but never obtaining a prestigious and secure position.

———

Mozart's youth was spent in concert tours, playing (harpsichord, organ, violin), composing, waiting attendance on patrons. As is

1. *Treatise on the Fundamental Principles of Violin Playing*, second edition, translated by Editha Knocher (New York, 1951).

evident in an excerpt from one of Leopold's letters[2] written at the start of a three-and-a-half-year journey, the life was hard:

> We arrived in Munich on Sunday evening and on Monday . . . drove to Nymphenburg. Prince Z. . . . saw us from the castle as we were walking in the garden. . . . He asked whether the Elector knew that we were here [and] sent off a courtier. . . . Meanwhile we were to walk in the garden and wait for the reply. . . . A footman bade us appear at a concert at eight o'clock. It was then four o'clock. We walked . . . but were obliged by sudden rain to take shelter. . . . [The seven-year-old] Wolferl was a great success. We did not get home until a quarter past eleven, when we had supper and got to bed late. On Tuesday and Wednesday evenings we visited Duke Clemens. . . . [June 21, 1763]

Leopold's strategy on arriving in a city was to advertise the *Wunderkind* and his sister, call upon prominent musicians, and either give a concert at his own expense or try to wangle an invitation for the children to play at court—with whatever form of remuneration this might bring. In Paris, for example, the daughter received a "heavy toothpick case of solid gold," exactly the thing to delight the heart of a little girl of eleven. But then, few donors seem to have understood that a cash payment would have been more welcome. Wolfgang wrote:

> Just as I had expected, I received no money but a fine gold watch . . . I now have five watches and am therefore seriously thinking of having an additional watch pocket sewn on each leg of my trousers. Then when I visit some great lord . . . I shall wear two watches . . . ; so that it will not occur to him to present me with another one. [Mannheim, November 13, 1777]

2. *The Letters of Mozart and His Family*, 2 vols., edited and translated by Emily Anderson, second edition prepared by A. Hyatt King and Monica Carolan (New York, 1966).

The ill effects of such a life were far-reaching, but most immediately apparent on Mozart's health. With days spent in stagecoaches and nights in inns, and with all of the irregularities of this nomadism, he was undoubtedly more often sick than he would have been at home. In letter after letter Leopold refers not only to his son's colds, fevers, and undiagnosed complaints, but also to near-fatal bouts with smallpox and scarlet fever. Most parents today would regard this price of "fame and fortune" as too high, and though Leopold should not be judged by modern standards of child-rearing, his motives, pecuniary and otherwise, were undeniably selfish. Without the wonder child, the father would never have been able to set foot in the palaces of the nobility, or to boast about it to the burghers back home.

Moreover, Leopold was the one possessed with a *Wanderlust*; Wolfgang, at least in his letters, never so much as commented on the scenery or mentioned such extraordinary sights as those of Venice. Music was the boy's passion, and he could have studied and composed at least as well in Salzburg, while leading a more normal life. True, his native city had no opera house, and his operatic experience was acquired during his travels, especially in Italy. But he could have learned as much from a single tour as from several: it is a mistaken notion that his lengthy immersion in the European musical scene gave him an unmixed advantage. What he chiefly learned from this exposure was the *à la mode*, and in that he was soon a master without peer.

Mozart naturally became aware of his superiority and began to express contemptuous opinions of fellow musicians. Thus he reports on a performance by the Abbé Vogler:

It is much easier to play a thing quickly than slowly: in certain passages you can leave out a few notes without anyone's noticing it. [January 17, 1778]

Of an evening at the opera in Mantua, Mozart wrote:

The prima donna . . . cannot open her mouth. . . . The seconda donna looks like a grenadier and has a powerful voice too, and, I must say she does not sing badly seeing that she's acting for the first time. [January 26, 1770]

No less outspoken about the morals and manners of dignitaries of State and Church, the fourteen-year-old drew a picture of a Dominican monk:

I have had the honor of lunching with this saint who drank a whole decanter and finished up with a full glass of strong wine, two large slices of melon, some peaches, pears, five cups of coffee, a whole plate of cloves, two full saucers of milk and lemon. He may be following a diet, but I do not think so since he also takes snacks during the afternoon. [Bologna, August 21, 1770]

The boy's letters sparkle with such anecdotes, many of them recounted in dialogue form, evincing his affinity for drama. An occasional postscript, such as the one from Rome to his sister saying that he has "not yet seen any spiders or scorpions," both betrays his actual age and brings him closer as a human being— as does the mention toward the end of his life of his fondness for billiards. His intelligence shows in his verbal facility: in parody, for instance, in the invention of conundrums and of names, and in linguistic fluency, for at the Vatican he acted as his father's translator.

—

Mozart eventually became so conditioned to his uprooted existence that it is questionable whether he could have tolerated a settled one, supposing it had been offered to him; throughout his life he continued to move, if only from one Vienna residence to another. In an era when musicians depended for their livelihood on church or court appointments, Mozart worked on a freelance basis, although persisting in the belief that what he wanted above all else was a permanent job, and that this would solve his many problems. After quitting the service of the Archbishop of Salzburg, and thereby, at long last, rebelling against his father, Mozart had to depend on poorly paying pupils, minuscule commissions, and financially risky concert and theatrical ventures for an always fickle public. Leopold's business acumen had not been transmitted to his son, and it would be difficult to conceive of anyone less prepared for such a *modus vivendi.*

The emotional damage resulting from Mozart's peripatetic early life was even further-reaching. He had had very little real childhood, being already at the age of five a precocious and serious young man. His growth was partly inverse, in fact, and in his twenties and thirties he exhibited such symptoms of immaturity as impulsiveness and addiction to juvenile jokes. Forced into premature adulthood in some respects, in others he had not been allowed to grow up at all, never having had enough freedom to learn firsthand. Worse yet, the frequent separations from his mother, and her being overshadowed by her husband, must have hurt him and may account for his later failures with women, as well as for the expressions of scatological adolescent sexuality in his letters—until recently considered unfit to publish except in expurgated form.

Above all, the fact that he was deprived of maternal love would help to explain his disastrous marriage to the totally unsuitable Constanze Weber. Certain feminine types in his operas— the Countess in *Figaro,* for instance—are surely in some measure the idealized fantasy creations of a boy who had longed for greater closeness with his mother. Though he must have grieved deeply when she died (in Paris, during a trip with him), his letters about this event are curiously empty of feeling, as is also true of his remarks to his sister after the death of their father. Nor, on the evidence, was Mozart plunged into inconsolable despair after the deaths of four of his six children. Like his father, he was a fatalist, whether Deistic or some other kind; the philosophy of the Mozart family attributed almost every event to "God's will."

———

Surprisingly, the consequences of the composer's abnormal childhood have never been analyzed in relation to the character and development of his music, and little notice has been given to the effect of the father's domination for almost two decades, which could not help but stifle the son's artistic—as well as every other—independence. During his entire formative period Mozart was indoctrinated with the necessity of mastering not only the traditional but also the *au courant*. At the time, he criticized the quality of both, but his purpose was to improve the forms of music rather than to reconstruct them or to redirect their course.

In other words, he accepted much of the world that he inherited and never deliberately set out to be "original," a concept that he does not seem to have valued. This statement requires explication, of course, since Mozart so revitalized each musical genre to which he turned his genius that he made it new. Furthermore, he was always exploring new possibilities—in combining instruments, for example, in using polyrhythms (the Oboe Quartet), and in employing *scordatura*. Finally, too, he could not help being original, and though repeating the same cadence thousands of times and with the same limited materials (A, B, and C, so to speak), he always introduced variants.

The contention is that originality is possible when working within a traditional frame as well as in the making of a new one. In drawing this distinction it may be useful to compare Mozart and Beethoven, while disregarding the factor of radical political and social changes during the period between the two masters. Mozart, to some extent, seems to have been born to his identity, while Beethoven had to forge his. And at a time of life when Mozart was subject to his father's dictation and had already been much exposed to cosmopolitan musical environments, Beethoven was primarily self-taught and had only provincial musical experience. It is argued, too, that Mozart was trained to supply music according to specifications and on demand, while Beethoven imposed his creations on the world. But this was not always the case; furthermore, the two men's temperaments must be taken into consideration. Whereas Mozart was comparatively conciliatory (if a singer complained of a difficulty, he would remove it), Beethoven never accommodated himself to anyone (and would remove the singer). In such ways we might distinguish the traditionalist from the revolutionary, always bearing in mind that neither term implies a value judgment.

The paradox of Mozart is that music history would not be

greatly different if he had never existed—though obviously music itself would be immeasurably poorer, and classicism more difficult to define. He has been called the founder of German opera, but Weber would have developed that without him, even if from inferior roots; and despite the influence of *Figaro*, Italian opera had its own sources. In instrumental music, Haydn provided Beethoven with the indispensable examples in sonata and symphony. But if the line of succession leads around, rather than through, Mozart, the reason is that his kind of perfection could be neither improved upon nor repeated.

———

The greatest challenge of Mozart's life came from his encounter, in the spring of 1782, with the music of Johann Sebastian Bach, which was strong enough to turn Mozart for a time from his own so-called *style galant.* Today's audiences, accustomed to hearing polyphonic and homophonic music side by side, cannot easily grasp the impact of Bach on Mozart, especially as first experienced in the overpowering form of *The Well-Tempered Clavier* and *The Art of the Fugue.* Mozart's friend Baron van Swieten had received these masterworks in Berlin from Frederick the Great himself, and every Sunday in the months following, a few musicians met at van Swieten's Vienna home to study and perform them. Mozart transcribed some pieces from the *Clavier,* no doubt in order to become even more familiar with the music through the additional perspective of string instruments.

Soon Mozart was composing his own fugues, and, for the first time in his life, coming upon problems that he could not solve. The manuscript of the unfinished keyboard Fugue K.401,[3] with its surprising number of corrections—surprising for Mozart— and the ten unfinished fugues from the same year (1782) reveal the difficulties that he was having. Moreover, some of the fugues

3. The autograph score was on exhibit at the Basle Kunstmuseum during the summer of 1975, along with many other music manuscripts dating from the early 1600s. Several well-known works by Mozart were also included, as well as a newly found letter. This was noteworthy, as very few Mozart letters have come to light since the publication of the "complete" correspondence forty years ago. The catalogue, *Musikhandschriften in Basel aus verschiedener Sammlungen,* can be purchased from the firm of Otto Haas, London.

that he was about to complete, such as the second movement of the Sonata for Clavier and Violin K.402 and the *Gloria* in the C-Minor Mass, belong to unfinished works, indicating that he sacrificed the totality of some of his conceptions because of his preoccupation with fugue writing. Mozart scholars generally describe the fugue in the Sonata as Handelian,[4] though the stretti are in the manner of Bach. But no matter, since the piece is little more than an exercise and seems hardly to have been written for performance, the violin part merely fulfilling contrapuntal requirements without exhibiting much instrumental personality. Also, if the eighths at the beginning are played at a *tempo commodo*, the sixteenths at the end prove to be too fast.

Yet it should not be inferred that Leopold Mozart had neglected to instruct his son in canon and fugue,[5] even though these forms were out of fashion and already had been while Bach was composing them. The technique of counterpoint that Mozart had learned at the age of fourteen not only was remote from Bach, however, but was also dead, an ecclesiastical anachronism practiced only by such pedants as Padre Martini, who became Mozart's teacher in Bologna during the summer of 1770. While in that city, the Padre's illustrious pupil applied for admission to the Accademia Filarmonica and was required by his examiners to complete a composition by adding three contrapuntal voices above a given bass. But Mozart made mistakes and had to recopy the piece after the Padre had corrected it. It was then presented to the jury, and Mozart was "passed," though probably only because of his fame: the shrewd Italians took no chances on being ridiculed by history. Leopold misrepresents the incident (making his readers wonder about possible exaggerations in other cases as well), but the explanation would seem to be that Mozart was simply bored by the whole episode. Certainly if he had had any acquaintance with Bach's music and had been asked to write a fugal elaboration on one of his subjects, the outcome would have been very different.

4. *Wolfgang Amadeus Mozart unter dem Einfluss Georg Friedrich Händels*, by W. Siegmund-Schultze (Leipzig, 1956).
5. The fugues in the Mass K.139, dating from Mozart's twelfth year, are good examples of his early mastery of the form.

Though Mozart's contrapuntal skill had matured in the intervening years—he mentions improvising three-voice fugues—and though he prided himself on being a "learned" composer (that is, in polyphonic art), to construct a fugue in the shadow of *The Well-Tempered Clavier* was a task of a larger order, and the struggle to assimilate Bach's fugue style lasted for over a year.[6] Only once, in the *Qui tollis* from the C-Minor Mass—conspicuously *not* a fugue—does Mozart approach Bach on his own ground and achieve and sustain a comparable intensity in a similarly lofty structure. The monumentality is in fact unlike anything else in Mozart's music, which generally provides relief for the in-between moments of life.

The dramatic aura of the *Qui tollis* is its most familiarly Mozartian feature, and the ending (which recalls the last measures of the introduction of the yet-to-be-composed "Prague" Symphony) would alone identify the music as written by the creator of *Don Giovanni*. Dramatic, too, are the antiphonal choruses, the sudden changes in dynamics, the ostinato accompaniment (inspired by the flagellating rhythm of "Surely, surely He hath borne our griefs" in *Messiah?*), and the separation of the chorus and orchestra (respectively representing Christ and the goading soldiers?). And though the idea of syncopated choruses is at least as old as Monteverdi's *Nisi Dominus,* the use of it here is astonishing. The chromatic harmony, unprepared dissonances, cross relations, and deceptive cadences are no less amazing. As for the remaining movements of the Mass, the best of them are no more than examples of Mozart's usual genius. He knew what he had done, and that it could not be equalled.

———

Mozart's abundance makes virtually impossible the cataloguing of even his most salient qualities, let alone their illustration in individual pieces. Sufficient to mention only one seldom-

6. The Fugue in C Minor, K.426 (December 1783), manifests Mozart's triumph through and over the Bach fugue, every variation and the twelve stretti being derived from the subject, and from the reversible counterpoint countersubject, with a skill that matches Bach's.

noticed habit, that of lavishing great music on what most other composers would consider unworthy mediums. Thus the Adagio and Rondo for Glass Harmonica (K.617) is no mere sound-color étude but a piece of depth and consequence. On the technical side, Mozart amplifies and reflects the "glasses"[7] with a quartet of flute, oboe, viola, and cello. The tone of the flute being similar to that of the solo instrument, Mozart features the former and uses it to complete phrases that exceed the range and dexterity of the latter. The accompanying quartet generally plays legato, in imitation of the rubbing articulation of the "glasses."

Finally, since these sweetly reverberating goblets are in the treble, Mozart provides tenor and bass parts in the strings, which, at the end, play an accompaniment figure suggesting treadle action. The specialties of the contraption are ringing four-part harmonies[8] in slow tempo, and echoing solo lines, conjuring the thought of Pythagorean acoustical experiments or Voices from Other Dimensions. But the composer cared less about "effects" than about music, and, at one point, as if deliberately to draw attention from the novelty of the timbre, he startles the listener with a harmonic progression that turns from what promises to be a modulation to G, into one to the dominant of A flat. Mozart has both dignified a toy and composed an immaculate piece of music.

One of the phenomena of Mozart is his transcendence of temporal boundaries. Like the lives of other composers, his, though brief, divides into early, middle, and late. But as with no other, some of his work confounds by ignoring not only his chronological development but also that of history. The Andante from the Sinfonia Concertante (K.364) is one example. It has been described as "a worthy follower of the introductory movement,"

7. Mozart's instrument apparently had a keyboard, and in any case was more sophisticated than Benjamin Franklin's, which consisted of a series of bowls on a horizontal spindle, rotated by a treadle. In other instruments the pitches were determined by the difference in size of resonating glasses, or by varying the amounts of water in glasses of the same size—thereby subjecting the tuning to the vagaries of evaporation. Some glass harmonicas resemble trays prepared for cocktail parties of about forty guests.

8. It is used to play chords in the closing scene of *Die Frau ohne Schatten.*

and yet the latter is scarcely an adequate preparation for this profound creation. Though written as early as 1779, it shows that Mozart had already felt emotions that are associated with nineteenth-century romanticism. This is not to say that the music actually "sounds like" or "anticipates" the later period but only that Mozart has shared in its feelings. To take the Andante apart and analyze it, however, will not explain how an emotion belonging to a future time can have been projected into a body from an earlier one. Perhaps this reverse transmigration is proof of Mozart's eternalness.

—

From Plato's "essences" to Russell's "resemblances," philosophers have busied themselves with theories of the "universal." Mozart's universality is not a theory, however, but a daily celebration. He had a philosophy of art, nevertheless, and a wise and human one. It was expressed, in connection with some newly composed piano concertos, in a letter to his father:

Here and there are things which only connoisseurs can appreciate, but I have seen to it that those less knowledgeable must also be pleased without knowing why. [December 28, 1782]

SALZBURG, MOZART, AND COSÌ

This summer's[1] visitors to Salzburg discovered every approach to the city, from Autobahn, Bahnhof, and Flughafen, displaying

1. 1975.

a poster of a handsome headwaiter—to judge by the white tie and tails, although he carried no menu, and his transcendent expression exceeded the mystique associated with even the poshest restaurants. In some places the *affiches* stood no more than fifty feet apart—at one intersection almost obscuring the signs for Berchtesgaden—and the arriving tourist must have wondered what this glamorous maître d' could be advertising, with his manner so different from that of the contented consumers pictured on other billboards.

But in close-up the face looked familiar, and the caption and CBS trademark confirmed the suspicion: *"Leonard Bernstein: Wir willkommen Sie bei den Salzburger Festspielen!"* Yet who could deny that the presentation was a triumph of packaging, as well as the launching of a mode, this one ad having sunk the sixties; Ozawa's beads, Previn's hair, Karajan's melodramatic gestures—all became obsolete in a single coup. Moreover, here was an icon to replace that of Mozart, whose image was nowhere to be found among the two hundred glossy-page photos of jewelry and Jaguars, conductors and banks that comprise the Official Program.

———

To the question posed in an article in the program booklet, "Festivals—An Expensive Anachronism?" the answer should be an unqualified "Yes." Festival repertory is no longer distinguishable from that of the regular season, while standards of performance have fallen in inverse proportion to cost (both to producer and consumer), and artistic control seems to be in the hands of airlines and hotel chains. What else could explain the choice for Bayreuth's centenary *Ring* of a producer whose total experience with opera consists of one work by Offenbach and one by Rossini, and of a conductor who has never led the *Ring* or performed any other Wagner in a way to warrant such endorsement? (Carlos Kleiber, the one recent conductor there who *has* demonstrated the temperamental as well as technical qualifications for the undertaking, may not be a marketable name as yet; happily, in the past such considerations did not always take precedence over artistic goals.)

A quotation from the aforementioned article exposes the schizoid confusion of the Salzburg Festival's philosophy:

> Our affluent society offers far more agreeable opportunities to have a good time for lots of money than waiting out five hours of *Tristan*.

This actually suggests that classical music is inherently less enjoyable than the more popular forms of entertainment with which it supposedly must compete. Apart from the oddity of airing such a point of view in an opera program, the statement insults all those who treasure every moment of Wagner's masterpiece. Yet the article goes on to prophesy that

> the so-called classics must capitulate . . . in competition with Frank Sinatra, to say nothing of the possibilities of élite pastimes on the exclusive beaches of St. Tropez. . . .

What, in the name of Neptune, élite seaside pastimes may be, and why such classics as *Tristan* are only "so-called" and doomed to surrender to Frankie, are not explained. But the article seems to defend music festivals in the claim that "according to Franz Kafka, 'Art is to step out from the ranks of the manslayers,' " a dubious postulate even if the translation had been grammatically correct, for has it not been inalterably proven and attested to with human lives—not long after Kafka and not far from Salzburg—that art-loving and manslaying are perfectly compatible?

At least one of the article's observations is beyond argument: Salzburg is expensive. Indeed, it is immorally so! A single good seat for an opera costs ninety dollars at the official price and double that in practice, for the hall is bought out by scalpers months ahead. "Capitalists are not the only ones receptive to artistic experience," the same writer continues, broad-mindedly, but without distinguishing between political ideology and bank balance. In fact a six-digit total in the latter is a requirement for anyone "doing" the festival, while, as far as operagoing is concerned, the difference between the privileged and the deprived is probably greater in our day than in Mozart's. This, at any rate, is the impression made each evening as the Beautiful People arrive on one side of the street for the theater spectacle, while the Third Estate gathers on the other for the spectacle of the audience—like peasants and masters in *Figaro* and *Don Giovanni*.

—

Of the 1975 season, only the three-year-old production of *Così fan tutte* and last year's *Die Frau ohne Schatten* (not reviewed here) were worthy of Salzburg. (The scandalously bad *Figaro*, unless it is restaged and recast, should be discontinued and the money donated to the new Mozart Gesellschaft edition; of this only about half has appeared in almost twenty years, a rate guaranteeing that few musicians of our era will ever see the complete publication.) But a more nearly perfect realization of *Così* would be difficult to envisage. Few productions adequately meet the musical requirements, to say nothing of the dramatic and visual ones, with Mozart's elevated comedy habitually abused as low farce. In every dimension the Salzburg performance sustained the virtuosity which is the essence of the work.

Karl Böhm's tempi were occasionally slow but did not stifle the music's wit, and if his conception of the score was unusually mellow, the quality is implied in the opera's moral: *"Da ragion guidar si fa."* Böhm never italicized by adding a degree to a dynamic, driving an allegro or dragging an andante, or bringing out an "inner voice" that was intended to remain just that. He is not a scholar, and at some places his phrasing and articulation could be questioned.[2] (The study of legato slurs in Mozart's autographs, and the differentiation among his staccato dots, dashes, and wedges—the last indicating more marked separation—is comparatively recent and has had some effect on piano, but very little on orchestral, performances.) Böhm radiated the music, however, and even when the orchestra played raggedly for a measure or two, this evidence of human fallibility was more endearing than Karajan's steely precision. (Böhm, at his curtain call, clasped hands with the singers and graciously redirected the

2. Böhm's cuts are questionable, not in the theater, perhaps, but on records.

applause to the orchestra, while the *Figaro* conductor bowed independently and at a higher elevation than the cast, of which he took no notice.)

Gundula Janowitz, that ideal Mozart soprano, sang Fiordiligi with her customary beauty of tone and flawless intonation. Brigitte Fassbaender, as her stage sister, provided a smooth vocal blend in the many duets, and an appropriate contrast in the dramatic role. Peter Schreier as Ferrando and Hermann Prey as Guglielmo were no less excellent, both individually and as a pair. (For a real appreciation of Schreier, the reader need only listen to the Philips recording of such passages as *"bisogno non ha"* and *"ed intanto di dolore,"* frantically bellowed, below pitch, by Nicolai Gedda.) Rolando Panerai, as Don Alfonso, was vocally pleasing but too benign for the philosophy he preached, and Reri Grist's coloratura, too light for Despina, was more than compensated for however by her superb acting. Having many more ensembles than arias, *Così* requires six singers who complement one another in a variety of combinations. A more satisfying sextet than Salzburg's could not have been selected even by an optimally functioning computer.

Günther Rennert's direction was busy but never distracting. The principals stood still in their big arias, except where a change of tempo or second verse justified a change of position; but faces registered meaning, and the singers were obviously inspired to the full use of their histrionic talents. Rennert replaced the curtain with a panel-drop "tapestry" representing Paradise, an allegorical porcupine being added to the usual serpent; his one mistake was in exhibiting this tableau during the overture, which does not deserve to be treated as background music.

The stage was sparsely furnished, with the Bay of Naples evoked only by fishing nets and by space. The seductiveness of the Neapolitan atmosphere is an important influence on the conduct of the characters, and if the plot is a laboratory experiment—Masters and Johnson, but two centuries ahead of time— then the aura of the South is a part of the chemistry. Period was established by such props as an eighteenth-century swing and a flock of mechanical birds, but some of the sisters' clothing seemed to belong to a later era, a peccadillo that can be readily forgiven, since, for a great rarity, all trace of slapstick was absent from the Albanian disguises of the *amanti*.

———

Richard Wagner, condemning *Così*, spoke for his century and part of ours:

> Mozart's greatness is confirmed by his inability to compose music such as he did for *Figaro* for the dull and insignificant libretto of *Così fan tutte*; otherwise he would have shamefully desecrated music itself.

So far from desecrating music, *Così*, in today's opinion, compounds its glory. Moreover, one of the reasons why the opera is now able to stand with *Figaro*, and has lately become equally popular, is the expertise (whatever else) of the libretto. The changes since Wagner's time that explain this reversal are as numerous as those of an entire century's music—and manners and morals—though this review must confine itself to a few directly related specifics. Wagner's contemporaries despised the story for its immorality and absurdity, and the first impediment to their willing suspension of disbelief was the time element. The sisters' fidelity to their fiancés fails to survive a twelve-hour siege by their new suitors from Albania. Today, of course, a period as *long* as that would challenge the story's credibility—in the opposite direction.

Idealizing Mozart, romantics and Victorians refused to accept the fact that he could have composed such "chaste" music for dramas of illicit sexual adventures: hence the general blindness to the true themes of the operas, and/or pretense that his music could not be related to them. As for the composer himself, who would have believed that music's divine cherub delighted in toilet humor and wrote indecent canons—let alone have considered that this purest of spirits might possibly have been incarnate in a venereally diseased body (and have died from the effects of a mercury cure)? The critic Heinrich Bluthaupt, writing about Mozart's operas in 1887, conceded a certain "warmth" in the music appropriate to characters in the married state, but he ignored or failed to notice the music's sexual ardor when associated with the would-be philandering of Count Almaviva or Don Giovanni.

Ironically, this very difference in sensuousness is what distinguishes *Così fan tutte* from both *Don Giovanni* and *Figaro*. The emotion of *Così* is different precisely because the seducers do not wish to succeed in their conquests: Mozart has delineated veritable and simulated desire. It is an established misunderstanding to think of the stylistic "extravagances" of the music of *Tristan und Isolde* in connection with an unholy eroticism, whereas, on the contrary, this forms the substance of Mozart's operas. In comparison, the passion and voluptuousness of Wagner's music drama are purity itself, portraying a love which is true unto death.

Thus Wagner's judgment, not only on Da Ponte's libretto but also on Mozart's music, becomes more understandable, the composer of *Tristan* being the foremost proponent of operas as drama: for him, music and libretto were wholly interdependent. Nevertheless, the acceptance of the libretto was to come about through the ever-developing comprehension of Mozart in his historical context as well as in his universality, and from this perspective it is obvious that the musician's commitment to the subject matter was as wholehearted as his librettist's. In evidence of this, clues from Mozart's biography might be taken into consideration, such as his transference of affections from one sister to another, his wife's outspoken dislike of the opera, and his concern for her flirtatiousness. But on musical grounds alone, *Così* represents one side of Mozart—as *The Magic Flute* does another, the latter opera coming to mind because the two works share a dramatic device (the protagonists in both undergoing a "test" in order to achieve wisdom, worldly in the one case, spiritual in the other).

———

Analyses of most composers, including Mozart, usually consist of little more than tracing resemblances—recurring melodic patterns, harmonic progressions—between one work and another; thus Osmin's *"O wie will ich triumphieren"* and the theme of the presto of the D-Major Symphony (K.385) are shown to be similar, as are Tamino's *"Der Götter Wille"* and the second theme in the first movement of the Clarinet Quintet. But far more remarkable are those works, of which *Così* is one, that create a world to which Mozart never returned. Such is the case with the slow movement of the A-Major Violin Concerto (which, incredibly, Mozart was to reject as 'too studied," but which is without successor in its idiom while its feeling exceeds in depth that of Mozart's other compositions of the time); with the fugue in the Violin Sonata K.402; and with the Rondo K.494 (both discrete forms, even though not detachable in K.402 as a sonata finale). Each of these pieces (and others) is without sequel, in the sense that the quartets for Haydn form one closely related family, and the last group of string quintets another. This is not to deny either the superficial similarities between *Così* and the other late operas, or the conventions that comprise the containing world of all of Mozart. Yet *Così*'s musical personality is unique and distinct in almost every measure.

Uniquely, too, *Così* is rich in parody, above all of operatic language and of exaggerated romantic sentiment. Thus Fiordiligi's *"Come scoglio"* ridicules most of the staples of tempestuous prima donnas: the bombastic recitative, the showy trill, the rapid scale, the sensationally wide interval, and the ostentatious high note. At the same time, the aria is perfectly "serious" and apt in its dramatic function. Thus, too, Ferrando's *"Un' aura amorosa"* imitates a new, high-flown emotionalism, for the song actually says nothing—in an opera that demands constant attention to the words. But, once again, the music is unquestionably "sincere" and exists happily on two levels. So does a sudden change of key, which musicians hear as a stunning technical feat, but which the audience feels only as a jolt appropriate to the stage action. Jokes, too, are "in," like the reference to Mesmer, who was a personal acquaintance of Mozart's and whose methods seem to have been lampooned in the opera, when the "Albanians," after drinking "suicidal" concoctions and pretending to experience trance-like states, are "revived" by a Mesmer magnet.

The originality of *Così* is manifest in its orchestration, both instrumental and vocal—the greater number of smaller ensembles (duets and trios) than of larger ones. Though by no means the first instance of tone painting in Mozart's music, the rippling muted violins in *"Soave sia il vento"* are as overtly atmospheric as those in *La Mer*. The opera abounds in instrumental effects and, for one novelty, trumpets and violas, ordinarily part of the background, are featured instruments. Trumpets, generally used only in tutti passages, and limited to a few notes in any case, permeate the timbre of the music as a whole; hence it is another of Mozart's virtuoso stunts to be able to give them an important part in a small ensemble, such as the one they share with flutes in the Quartet, one of the opera's most ravishing numbers.

In Mozart's other operas, the rounder, fuller horns would have had the notes that in *Così* are assigned to the more acerbic trumpets, and this, too, is in accordance with the "insincerity" of the sexual pursuit in the opera. Mozart also exploits a new viola quality in several obbligati, but nowhere more beautifully than in *"Di scrivermi ogni giorno"* (a piece that bewitched Stravinsky, and of which he never tired). Commentators have remarked the association of clarinets with the sisters, but the most ingenious employment of this instrument is in a passage in serenade style (with Alberti bass and a pizzicato accompaniment) in the third scene from the end.

The score contains other musical mottoes besides the one, *"Co-sì fan tut-te,"*[3] in the overture. These include the snatches of the songs associated with the suitors when in disguise, and sung by them upon their return to their true selves; the revelations of the final scene are far more immediately effective musically than visually. The March is also a motto, but an almost too obvious one. The most subtle of them all is the link between the melody in slow triplets near the end of *"Per pietà"* and the

3. Most of the many English translations of the title ("Everybody acts like this," "They all do it," etc.) omit the vital identification of gender present in the Italian: "Thus do all *women*."

melodies in fast triplets in the first number of the opera; this connection is underlined by the instance of the same phrase endings in both places to ensure the recognition of the keenest irony in the opera: in the one scene Fiordiligi declares the new-found love that, in the other, her betrothed avows to be his alone.

———

From under-appreciation in the past, the libretto's reputation is at present somewhat inflated. The characters, mere ciphers in a psychological experiment, are limited and not very intelligent, especially when compared to the flesh-and-blood people of *Figaro* —though it may be unfair to say this since in the earlier opera Da Ponte had the advantage of basing his work on a great play. The source of *Così* in Ariosto—the Salzburg program states that none has yet been found!—is no more than a story with cardboard figures; still, Da Ponte might have heightened the individuation of the sisters.

Then, too, the opera changes in mood from light to serious somewhat abruptly and late; that is, not until the second of the two acts. And since Fiordiligi's behavior personifies the adage that "the more they protest, the harder they fall," her second-act excruciations are not easily reconcilable with the precipitate, turnabout ending. In her case, at least, the "happy ending" is unconvincing, the profundity of the music not having prepared for the too simple return to "things as they were." Nor is Don Alfonso's assurance that the lovers will be the wiser for their experience completely persuasive. Women twice mistaken in love cannot be as they were before.

Authorities on the opera are by no means in agreement about how it actually does end:

Whether the ladies pair off with their original lovers or with their new ones is not clear from the libretto, but, as Don Alfonso says, it will not make any difference to speak of.[4]

---

4. *Mozart's Operas: A Critical Study*, by Edward Dent (London, 1913; revised edition, 1947).

But by all of the traditions of the theater of disguise, reconciliation is implicit throughout the opera, and there can be no doubt
that the relationships at the end are the same as they were at the
beginning.

The libretto is more compact, faster-moving, and more circumscribed in content than those of *Figaro* and *Don Giovanni*.
But it is also more artificial. The anatomy of love is a subject
of all of Mozart's operas, but it is the *only* subject of *Così*. The
presence of Vesuvius in the background has been given a tendentious political interpretation. But no revolution smolders in
Così, as it does in *Figaro*, and the impertinent remarks of the
maid have no more social significance than if they were part of
the script for *Upstairs, Downstairs*.

Even the crowd does not seem to be representative of a class as
in the case of other operas; indeed, the chorus might well be
kept out of sight—considering the cost of costuming thirty or
forty extras whose voices are indispensable but whose presences
are not. One absence *is* remarkable, however, that of a family,
or even a duenna, to chaperone the nubile sisters. The most surprising piece of action in the opera is that in which they dress up
in uniforms belonging to their drafted boyfriends. What, one
wonders, are such garments doing in the home of proper young
ladies, and does this not belie their innocence and virtue?

———

Little is known about the first production of *Così fan tutte*, partly
because the death of the monarch closed down the theater after
only four performances. Mozart himself does not mention the
opera by name (except in his catalogue of his works), referring
to it, in two letters, merely in connection with the first rehearsals.
It is comforting to read Michael Kelly's recollections[5] of a rehearsal of *Figaro*, and to hope that something similar might have
occurred at the first reading of *Così fan tutte:*

> Mozart was on the stage with his crimson pelisse and gold-laced
> cocked hat, giving the time of the music to the orchestra. . . .

5. *Reminiscences* (London, 1826; reprinted New York, 1975).

I was standing close to [him], who, *sotto voce*, was repeating "Bravo! Bravo!" for Benucci[6] . . . [when suddenly] the whole of the performers on the stage, and those in the orchestra, as if activated by one feeling of delight, vociferated *"Bravo! Bravo! Maestro. Viva, viva grande* Mozart." . . . The little man acknowledged [their bravos] by repeated obeisances. . . .

Mozart's "OPERA OF ALL OPERAS"

E. T. A. Hoffmann's encomium for *Don Giovanni* attests to a preeminence that has never declined. But in spite of an impregnable reputation, the "opera of all operas" is imperfect in conception, a miscarriage as drama, defective in important features. Yet because the misshapen libretto has been endowed, even overendowed, with some of Mozart's greatest music, the opera continues to occupy its unique position.

Some of the shortcomings are accounted for by the few known facts, such as Da Ponte's simultaneous involvement with two other operas and the necessity of preparing a bowdlerized version of his *Don Giovanni* libretto for the censor. Beyond this, it might be deduced either that the composer was obliged to accept what his collaborator offered, for whatever reasons, or that the subject so appealed to Mozart that he overlooked the unevenness in the treatment of it. Scholarship has unearthed no hard evidence to

6. A baritone for whom Mozart wrote the most elaborate aria in the first act of *Così fan tutte*, which he then removed, believing the piece to be disproportionately large.

substantiate theories that the Don Juan theme had a special attraction for Mozart, but, by the same token, there is no justification for assuming that it did not. The fact of *Don Giovanni*'s existence indicates something, however, and it is not impossible that Mozart could have had a Don Juan fantasy. After all, he was strongly attracted to women, both precociously and throughout his life, and was frequently rebuffed by them. Such speculations are automatically ridiculed, owing to a deification process that forbids attempts to separate the composer's musical genius from his humanness, the sublimity of the one being equated with a saintliness in the other. The Mozart halo outshines that of any other artist.

———

Whatever the reasons why Da Ponte and Mozart chose the subject, they hoped that the new work would repeat the success of *The Marriage of Figaro*. Edward Dent[1] long ago drew some of the parallels between the two operas, though before him Kierkegaard had recognized correspondences between them, including that of Cherubino as Don Giovanni in embryo. Yet the differences between the operas are greater than the resemblances, and the inferiority of the later libretto soon becomes apparent. *Don Giovanni*'s is disjointed, marred by implausible incidents, peopled mainly with one-dimensional figures, and confused in its moral position. This last gives rise to most of the other difficulties: it is because of the absence of a philosophical basis for the character of Don Giovanni that the validity of his destiny is uncertain and the sequence of events is not well ordered.

The stylistic gallimaufry of *opera buffa* and *opera seria* is due to the same morally ambiguous viewpoint. Alfred Einstein, the leading Mozart scholar of his day, argued that the inclusion of *seria* elements within a *buffa* framework is not incompatible, but

1. In *Mozart's Operas: A Critical Study* (London, 1913; revised edition, 1947). The most valuable contribution of this study is a comparison between the Da Ponte–Mozart *Don Giovanni* and another, slightly earlier, opera on the same subject by Bertati and Gazzaniga. Da Ponte helped himself to Bertati's libretto but improved whatever was borrowed.

though this is true as a general principle, the mixture leads to incongruities in the case of *Don Giovanni.* Subtitled *Dramma giocoso* ("comedy"; surely not "gay drama," as Einstein's translators[2] render it), Mozart himself listed *Don Giovanni* in the catalogue of his works as an *opera buffa,* thereby indicating his intentions as to genre even if imprecisely describing the result. "*Opera buffa,*" however, is contradicted by the very first chord of the overture, as well as by the murder of the Commendatore, by the accompanied recitatives of the high-born protagonists, and by the whole of the penultimate scene.

Above all, the stylistic categories determine the musical and dramatic interpretation. In the Quartet, for example, when the pursued Don Giovanni is mistakenly included among his pursuers, the performance may either amplify or mute the humor of the situation. Furthermore, the mere presence of Leporello, an essentially comic character, suffices to undermine the seriousness of a scene such as that of the final confrontation between Don Giovanni and the Commendatore. At this point the spectator identifies with Leporello and his fright, as expressed by his chattering and hiding under the table, but the combination of comic and tragic nevertheless perplexes the audience and provokes conflicting emotional responses. Furthermore, it is unquestionably a miscalculation to allow Leporello, at the opera's most critical moment, virtually to steal the scene from Don Giovanni, unwittingly upstaging him simply through the prominence of the role.

———

Kierkegaard believed that the Don Juan theme was unsuitable for comic treatment, since this destroyed the ideality necessary to the concept of the seducer. The philosopher maintained that Molière's Don Juan was a failure because of the irreconcilability of theme and genre. Yet the comic element is hardly less pervasive in the opera. And apart from that, surely it is a flaw of

---

2. *Mozart,* by Alfred Einstein, translated by Arthur Mendel and Nathan Broder (New York, 1945).

some consequence to cast as the central figure in an *opera buffa* an unrepentant sinner whose crimes include not only deception, exploitation of social advantage, and blasphemy, but also rape and murder. And, finally, how can *any* hero, let alone that of an *opera buffa*, end up permanently in Hell?

That the audience is on Don Giovanni's side may be attributed to his music—which, as Kierkegaard wrote, "lets us hear the power of his seduction"—as well as to the attractions of his hedonism, to the fascination of his reputation as a lover (not entirely justified by the opera, where his amorous forays are failures, Donna Anna having had to be raped), and to a personal appeal that seems to depend largely on charm and audacity; the latter trait, incidentally, has often been misinterpreted as bravery when Don Giovanni accepts the Statue's final challenge, but the Commendatore correctly names the trait: "*audace*." In any case, Don Giovanni's redeeming qualities, if that is what they are, hardly excuse the appalling array of his crimes. Yet his situation is similar to that of Falstaff, who, despite the lying and the thieving, holds the audience in thrall. In the opera, the mind-altering drug is music; in the play, verbal wit.

Audiences react in the same fashion to these popular malefactors' ultimate fates, Don Giovanni's damnation and Falstaff's rejection by the King ("I know thee not, old man"). These two shocks for the spectator are among the least easily absorbed in the repertory of the theater, despite the arguments of Shakespearians that such a reaction betrays a misunderstanding of the play, and of Mozartians that the outcome of the opera, part of whose title is "*Il Dissoluto Punito*," should have been anticipated from the beginning.

But Mozart must share Da Ponte's responsibility for the opera's disturbing dénouement. The composer's "fault" is in having filled Don Giovanni's last scene on earth with such spellbindingly powerful music that to compose still more of it, and of comparable quality, to represent the subsequent triumph of rectitude and social order would have been impossible. Furthermore, this anticlimactic finale replaces the life of the party with his undertaker, Don Ottavio, the most vapid character for whom Mozart ever wrote glorious arias. This opinion is by no means a universal one, however, and Professor Dent actually complains of the "relentless prolixity" of the Statue in the previous scene, though this lasts a mere five minutes. Since in 1780 Mozart had observed that the role of the Ghost in *Hamlet* was too long (letter of November 29), it is unlikely that he would commit the same error in his own opera seven years later—and, indeed, he did not.

———

Mozart's evocation of the supernatural is miraculous. Dent ascribes the "awesomeness" of this apocalypse merely to the use of trombones, but in fact every aspect of the music is extraordinary: the harmony (with its emphasis on the "diabolic" interval of the tritone); the chromaticism; the eerie scales, particularly in the lower strings, presaging Don Giovanni's death and corresponding to those at the beginning of the opera before the death of the Commendatore; the syncopations, dotted rhythms, and explosive accents; the sepulchral octaves; the brooding bass line which finally dissolves into tremolos; and the sheer sound, for the volume of the orchestra is almost Wagnerian. Since this music can still terrify, its impact on Mozart's audience, many of whom believed that Hell had a specific geographic reality, may scarcely be imagined. For the second production, in Vienna, Mozart ended the opera with this scene, probably because of its shattering effect. To do so today is regarded as sacrilege, but it must also be admitted that as a conclusion it compounds the stylistic problem.

Thus the very prodigality of the composer destroys the balance on which his *"opera buffa"* rests. The same abundance is also responsible for further damage to the opera's dramatic cohesiveness. Partly to accommodate and gratify singers, Mozart composed a number of additional pieces for the Vienna production (May 1788), which followed the one in Prague (October 1787). *"Dalla sua pace,"* for example, was substituted at the request of a tenor who could not manage *"Il mio tesoro"*—which is like an actor's asking for a less demanding soliloquy than "To be or not to be." The opera was already overblessed with stellar arias,

however, and did not need a new infusion of masterpieces further
to retard the action and postpone the resolution of the drama.
These Vienna bonuses have now become too popular to be cut,
and the tenor of today insists on singing both arias even though
neither has much relevance.

The inclusion of Elvira's "Viennese" aria, *"In quali eccessi"*
(appropriate title!), is defensible in that it develops the ambiguity of her feelings for Don Giovanni while adding stature to
her role in the opera. Yet this piece inevitably competes with
Donna Anna's *"Crudele?"* (which is in the original Prague
score). But the duet between Zerlina and Leporello, composed
for Vienna, is music of a different caliber—in fact, Zerlina's
part is in the manner of Despina in *Così*—while its dramatic
contribution is no asset.

The opera moves sporadically. An adventure begins but is
soon stalled by an extraneous, though magnificent, aria or ensemble. Thus Donna Anna's Rondo, matchless as music, has
scarcely any dramatic function; it would have had this if the
character of Don Ottavio had been explored, or the idea—on
which E. T. A. Hoffmann based his story—that Donna Anna is
really in love with Don Giovanni. But the lady exists almost entirely in Mozart's music, and, once again, the *embarras de rich-
esses* of his genius overwhelms a drama whose requirements are
too small. A few short pieces such as Elvira's *"Ah fuggi il tradi-
tor!"* help to leaven the grander, more soaring and spectacular
arias, thus quickening the pace. Of these galvanizing numbers, the
most distinctive is *"Metà di voi quà vadano,"* which begins *in
medias res* (as its first word suggests) and is all movement and
suspense achieved by means of syncopation and the switching of
the tonic accent to the middle of the bar.

—

But what was Mozart to do with such characters as Don Ottavio,
as they came to him on Da Ponte's pages? And what *are* these
people besides fixed attitudes—high principle, righteous indignation—or, as Henry James remarked of Donna Elvira, "tone"?
Even Masetto and Zerlina are no more than peasant stereotypes

of the blockhead and the conventional flirt; so far as the lyrics are concerned, those of Zerlina's *"Vedrai, carino"* are lewd enough to be acceptable on Broadway. Yet the very incompleteness of the aristocratic personae is obviously what has inspired so many fantasies about the opera. These begin with Hoffmann, who gives an offstage credibility to Donna Anna, and continue through Shaw to Edmond Rostand in his *La Dernière nuit de Don Juan.* For today, it would be easy to imagine a John Fowles novel, *Elvira, the Wandering Masochist,* or one by Gore Vidal exposing the secret life of vice of that noble nonentity Don Ottavio.

Fantasy has also played an inordinate part in criticism of the opera, which is further blemished by the tendency of philosophical and psychoanalytical interpretations to confound the actual opera with the Don Juan story in its pre-Da Ponte treatment by Tirso de Molina, Goldoni, and others. Fantasy, too, has blinded even the great thinkers to the opera's realities. Thus Kierkegaard's analysis of Don Giovanni as the embodiment of the erotic principle neglects to note that he was a philistine blackguard as well, willing to allow an innocent person to take the blame for him. So much for the "parfit" knight. Today, of course, the Don has been properly unmasked as the archetypal oppressor-class male chauvinist pig.

———

Any re-examination of *Don Giovanni* that ignores Kierkegaard will be the poorer for the philosopher's many valuable insights, though his main tenet, that the subject of seduction was uniquely musical and uniquely Mozartian, is now discounted. Briefly, *Either/Or* differentiates between language as a reflective medium and music as an immediate, as well as abstract, one. Distinguishing the Greek world from the Christian, Kierkegaard argues that the former "lacked the idea of a seducer"[3] because

the whole of the Greek life was posited as individuality. The Greeks did not have the concept of the sensuous-erotic genius [which] in its mediate and reflective character comes under

3. But what about Paris and Helen?

language, and becomes subject to ethical categories. In its immediacy, however, it can only be expressed in music. [Therefore the immediate is] really the indeterminate, and therefore language cannot apprehend it; [this] imperfection . . . is indirectly acknowledged . . . thus . . . we say: "I cannot really explain why I do this or that. . . . I do it by ear."

Whether or not this is the origin of the "play it by ear" *modus operandi*, the statement is the first step in Kierkegaard's attempt to define the "absolute subject" of music. The next, which seeks to establish the relationship between the sensual and the musical genius, involves the philosopher in various conflicts with his puritanism:

the stronger the religiosity, the more one renounces music and stresses the importance of words. . . . It by no means follows that one needs to regard music as the work of the devil, even if our age does offer many horrible proofs of the demoniac power with which music may lay hold upon an individual. . . .

Kierkegaard's incidental observations about *Don Giovanni* are less well known but often remarkably acute. He writes, for example, that

It would be a foolish girl who would not choose to be unhappy for the sake of having once been happy with Don Juan,

that

No power on earth has been able to coerce Don Juan; only a spirit, a ghost, can do that,

that

Leporello's number 1,003[4] is comic and it indicates that Don Giovanni is in a hurry,

4. Kierkegaard seems to consider this figure to be preposterous. He was apparently not aware that King Ismail of Morocco (1672–1727) reputedly fathered 1,056 children, and that Augustus "The Strong" of Saxony supposedly begat well over 1,000 offspring.

and, finally, that

> There is . . . something erotic in Leporello's relationship to
> Don Juan . . . a power by which he captivates him, even
> against his will.

This last statement begs for elucidation, for which the reader may
turn to Otto Rank,[5] though first it must be said that, like Rank,
Kierkegaard believed that Don Juan is "heard through Leporello.
. . . Mozart has . . . permitted Leporello to reproduce Don Juan."

———

Yet to go too rapidly from the depths of Kierkegaard's philosophical fantasies to the superficies of Rank's psychoanalytic
labeling is to risk an attack of the bends, or—when Professor
Winter reveals that Rank identified Don Giovanni's abuse of
Leporello with Freud's mistreatment of *him*—of the giggles. The
editor explains that Rank outlines an

> "Oedipal" interpretation of Don Juan. . . . [The] many se-
> duced women represent the one unattainable mother, and . . .
> the many whom he deceives, fights, and kills represent the
> father.

So far, so bad. Then, regarding Leporello, Rank himself describes the relationship between master and servant as a "psychic
unity," elaborating on this symbiosis to the effect that

> It would be impossible to create the Don Juan figure, the
> frivolous knight without conscience and without fear of death
> or the Devil, if a part of that Don Juan were not thereby split
> off in Leporello, who represents the inner criticism, the anxiety,
> and the conscience of the hero.

5. *The Don Juan Legend*, by Otto Rank, translated and edited, with an introduction, by David G. Winter (Princeton, 1975).

But is it not obvious that Leporello's sole "anxiety" is for his own skin? And certainly Rank is mistaken in claiming that Leporello acquiesces against his will in "the dissolute life of his master." Leporello *is* his master's Doppelgänger, but he is also the most venal of mercenaries, who utters not a word of regret at Don Giovanni's death. Rank further sees Don Giovanni's "behavior with Leporello's wife" as evincing a "deep motive of revenge, clearly illuminating the interchangeability of master and servant." But this "behavior" is no more than hypothetical, since, whatever happened with Don Giovanni, Da Ponte does not say whether or not the woman *was* Mrs. Leporello. Moreover, Rank himself correctly observes that "the action in Mozart's opera portrays anything but a successful sexual adventure."

What ought to have been said about Leporello is that, for some reason, the weaknesses he displays, the corruptibility and the cowardice, endear him to the audience; and, more important, that he alone perceives Don Giovanni's true obsession—as Kierkegaard, and all other writers on the subject except Rostand, failed to do. What the servant recognized and Kierkegaard did not is that Don Giovanni's real satisfaction is not attained in the heat of his conquests—the identity and attributes of his victims being a matter of indifference to him—but from the list of them that he keeps. In short, and as Leporello sings, Don Giovanni seduces *"pel piacer di porle in lista."*

———

A considerable portion of Rank's study is devoted to a discussion of beliefs about the dead who return to avenge their murders. This, he says, documenting his claims, explains the attempt to build indestructible sarcophagi. But the relevance of this background to Don Giovanni seems slight since the Don is extremely hospitable to the man he murdered—or is it to his effigy?

Mozart's father died at the time of the beginning of the composition of *Don Giovanni,* and, accordingly, Rank addresses himself to the coincidence of the killing of the Commendatore at the beginning of the opera:

According to our psychoanalytic experience, the death of the father arouses deeply ambivalent stirrings of affect, especially in the creating artist. These affective stirrings explain the artistic penetration and mastery of the subject matter, an attainment that is made possible only on the basis of a far-reaching identification with the father.

But *how* do these "affective stirrings" explain Mozart's mastery of the subject? To this reviewer the statement is simply so much verbal pollution, still another indication that the time is near for the donning of readers' gas masks.

Yet Rank redeems himself, at least to some extent, by one observation that is worth bearing in mind by all those who plan to attend performances of *Don Giovanni*. This is that the Don is never at peak form during the opera, and that "The happy, gratifying time of the real Don Juan is left to the fantasy of the audience."

PLAYING WITH
THE MAGIC FLUTE

"Explain this riddle, don't deceive me."

—*Tamino, in Act I*, The Magic Flute

The libretto of *The Magic Flute*, once dismissed as absurd and undeserving of serious scrutiny, is today overmined for buried "meaning" and "significance," and often uncritically praised as a "faultless dramatic structure." Nor will a balance between philistine ridicule and sanctimonious approbation be found in the latest spate of books about the opera, which are far more concerned with the interpretation of the libretto than with the musico-dramatic entity. In all likelihood the inadvertent as well as the intentional enigmas of the plot, along with the perennial controversy over the authorship of the libretto, will continue to provide a rich quarry for musicologists. But two other particular mysteries envelop *The Magic Flute*: the question of the representation of Freemasonry, which some believe was more important to Mozart than his Catholicism, and the seeming coincidence of death as a theme of the opera and Mozart's own tragic end after he completed the work.

———

Most audiences for Ingmar Bergman's *The Magic Flute*[1] will come to it as they would to any other film, being quite unaware that the allegorical content has provoked more than a century of debate. Though trying to experience the cinema version through moviegoers' eyes and to judge it on its own merits, the reviewer still must mention from the outset that the film highlights the inconsistencies and structural weaknesses of the libretto. That Bergman also recognizes them is evident in his transpositions of episodes; one of these, the switching of the Papageno courtship scene from the end of the opera to a place immediately preceding the scene of the Ordeals, eliminates a serious anticlimax. The camera also points up illogicalities that may not trouble opera audiences, inured as they are to the conventions of that form, but will disturb Bergman devotees who are accustomed to expect at least a modicum of rational sequence.

The film seems to have been conceived in misunderstandings. Bergman revealed a surprising aspect of his artistic approach in a publicity release:

———

1. *The Magic Flute*, a film directed by Ingmar Bergman, with the Swedish Stage Broadcasting Network Symphony, conducted by Eric Ericson. Sung and spoken in Swedish, with English subtitles (1975).

The most important factor to me was that the singers should have natural voices. You can find artificially cultivated voices that sound marvelous, but you can never really believe that a human personality is doing the singing.

The truth is that only the most highly trained voices can even attempt to sing *The Magic Flute.* Nor, by way of compensation, does Bergman's cast, which is *un*able to sing it, even though the voices are very obviously dubbed, abound in "human personalities." The opera's greatest musical delights can be realized only if the role of Pamina is entrusted to a consummate artist possessing a superior voice—unfortunately not the case here. Musically inadequate, too, are Tamino, whose singing certainly does not suffer from too much "cultivation"; Papageno, whom the film audience might easily take to be the opera's chief protagonist; and the Queen of Night, who sounds extremely harsh in Act Two (a touch of Bergman, not Mozart, realism), and who is uncertain in pitch toward the end, the final B flat of her second aria belonging to some species of unidentified flying object.

If the voices are "natural," Bergman's simulated theater audience, over which the camera periodically and distractingly pans, is too obviously artificial, being a veritable Family of Man, with Swedes outnumbering Indians, Japanese, and Bushmen (though none of these last is actually wearing a bone in the nose). The expressions on the faces in this spurious melting pot are studied, and all are intently watching something invisible to the film audience. Throughout the overture the camera jumps from one blank face to another, and sometimes on the beat, as if Bergman were asking the public to ignore the musical fugue and to watch a visual one on the countenance of mankind. At the changes of tempo, however, the camera offers a glimpse of Lange's portrait of Mozart's inspiring face, then returns to the audience, then, during a measure's rest, shunts back to Mozart, and, finally, in accelerando, settles on the now-transfixed audience.

The illusion of an actual performance is partly established through some preliminary shots of Drottningholm, whose Royal

Theater is contemporary to the Kärntnertor, in which *The Magic Flute* was first played. But the modest stage soon opens out for Hollywoodian "production numbers." The film also uses the eighteenth-century thunder-maker and creaky *deus ex machina* and props—though Tamino's charmed animals look like expensive Christmas toys from F. A. O. Schwarz. The pretense of a live production is further sustained by the sound of an orchestra tuning up, by applause at the ends of scenes and acts, and by backstage tours—on one of which we see Papageno preparing to make an entrance, the Queen of Night's Ladies puffing cigarettes, and a slave of Monostatos reading a Donald Duck comic. Another theatrical, as opposed to cinematographic, device is the occasional display of posters spelling out maxims from such songs as *"Könnte jeder brave Mann."* But almost the only special technique of the film medium that Bergman employs is the close-up; rarely does the camera look at the stage even from the perspective of the Drottningholm audience, and during Pamina's great aria, *"Ach, ich fühl's,"* the lens focuses claustrophobically on her mouth, tonsils, and—that currently overpublicized anatomical feature—jaws.

The scenery and costumes represent a variety of periods that does not include the Egyptian, the only one traditional to the opera. Thus Pamina is dressed like a Hapsburg princess, Monostatos sports a von Stroheim tunic and haircut, and Papagena wears a modern fur-collar coat and matching hat—in the snow, the apocryphal substance apparently being intended to suggest still another Ordeal to add to those of Water and Fire. Except that the flames are very loud, the backdrop for this last might have been adapted from Doré's Dante.

Bergman generally follows the libretto, despite cuts, interpolations, and changes of order, most of which are justifiable. He also alters the spoken dialogue on one major point, making the Queen of Night and Sarastro the mother and father of Pamina, which more clouds than clarifies the subject matter and the story. Scholars have attempted to show that the action of the play is coherent, obscurities and inconsistencies notwithstanding. But their explications usually depend on vague references to "Mozart's genius." Here, for instance, is the argument of a critic for the London *Times*:

> The contradictions make reasonable sense and do not need to be explained away. Chiefly it is Mozart's music that makes scene of the peculiar mixture . . . in the humanity which he found rooted and grounded in every sense and character.

But does this say anything? In truth, the libretto makes so little "sense" that such eminent Mozartians as Edward Dent[2] and Hermann Abert[3] reached the conclusion that the original dramatic theme must have been changed after the first scenes had already been composed.

The crux of the Dent-Abert thesis is that the forces of evil, as they are presented at the beginning of the story, must have been intended to continue as such throughout, but that, later, Mozart and his librettist, wishing to expand the representations of their Masonic rituals and beliefs, reversed the line-up, making the good Queen bad and the bad Sorcerer good. At the beginning, the Queen of Night enlists the spectator's sympathies by saving the life of Tamino, a wandering prince to whom she entrusts the rescue of her daughter, who has been kidnapped by Sarastro. The Queen does not trouble to explain that this supposedly evil magus[4] is actually the girl's guardian and her dead father's deputy.

But when Tamino becomes fully acquainted with Sarastro it is revealed that he and his brotherhood are the virtuous ones and the Queen and her followers the villains. This switch is effected without preparation either in the development of the characters or through dramatic incident, and, as a result, during most of the opera, viewers are confused and unable to identify with one

---

2. *Mozart's Operas: A Critical Study* (London, 1913; revised edition, 1947).

3. *W. A. Mozart* (Leipzig, 1923). An English translation of this book by Robert Marshall has been announced by the University of Chicago Press.

4. In Karl Meisl's amusing *Die travestierte Zauberflöte* (1818), Sarastro is a sybarite, and the Temple of Wisdom the Prater merry-go-round.

side or the other; after being deceived about the first alignment, they naturally mistrust the second.

Professor Chailley[5] and others dispute the Dent-Abert theory, holding that the turnabout in roles is a calculated ruse, and that the ambiguities are resolved by the end of the first act. Chailley commits himself to the postulate that

> Nothing appears in the behavior of the Queen of Night of the legendary change in the subject, no alteration, but instead an altogether normal psychological progression. . . .

In order to account for the Queen's anger and violence in Act Two, he rationalizes that, being thwarted in the "hope of the domination of Woman over Man, [she] becomes deranged." But no "psychological progression" leading to madness has been shown. And if the libretto is to be analyzed in these modern terms, why does the Queen undergo such an overwhelming change, while her daughter, who is subjected to attempted rape, imprisonment, rejection by those closest to her, and extreme mental cruelty, survives unscathed—and all this without the advantage of her mother's supernatural powers? What makes Chailley's thesis even less tenable is that it implies an audience sophistication far beyond that of the popular theater for which the opera was written.

Further blurring of the division between right and wrong is exemplified in the character of Pamina's actual jailer, Monostatos, whose wickedness is manifest and consistent throughout the opera, but who, for some reason, is Sarastro's trusted servant. Here the audience balks, having already learned that Sarastro has the power "to read hearts" and must therefore be aware of Monostatos's evil designs on Pamina. Sarastro is further suspect for his failure to explain to the terrified Pamina that her abduction and captivity were for her own protection. Then, when he states his case against her mother, the charges prove to be

5. *"The Magic Flute," Masonic Opera*, by Jacques Chailley, translated by Herbert Weinstock (New York, 1971).

petty and unimpressive: the Queen is arrogant and too ambitious (for a woman), although these same qualities are acceptable in Sarastro himself, who in addition is self-righteous,
tyrannical, and a slaveholder.

———

Fairy stories—and *The Magic Flute* is one—are based on
Manichaean oppositions; the right side triumphs in the end, and
the moral is made. But in this opera, although the audience is
frequently advised of Sarastro's virtues, he actually shows himself
as vindictive, and both he and the Speaker of the brotherhood
are revealed as rabid misogynists: after condemning her mother,
Sarastro tells Pamina, "You need a man to guide you," and the
Speaker warns Tamino that women are mere chatterers and not
to be trusted. No sharply contrasting character traits are distributed to either side, in fact, and the real contest reduces to one
between the sexes, a war actually fought in the opera's penultimate scene—and predictably won by the men in five seconds flat.

True, when Tamino is ordained into the brotherhood, Pamina
stands by his side wearing the same robes, thereby indicating
that she too has been admitted in at least a limited capacity (as
women were allowed to become Freemasons in Mozart's time).
But this does not gainsay the opera's profoundly anti-female
bias—from which it is not possible to infer Mozart's own views
on "women's place," although *The Magic Flute* does reflect his
well-known idealization of the institution of marriage.

That Mozart was an ardent Mason the opera gives full testimony; he was an active one, too, having induced Joseph Haydn,
among others, to join this fraternity. But Mozart was also, and
supremely, an artist, who understood that Pamina had to be
made the opera's central character. In comparison, Tamino is
without any background, and, for the first part of the action, his
only *raison d'être* is the search for a wife who has been selected
for him by a stranger. (His later quest for Wisdom might be
considered as further evidence of a change in the plan of the
libretto.) Pamina is as loyal and pure as her suitor and may be
even braver, for when he reminds her that they might die during
the Ordeals, she answers simply, "But we will be together."

Mozart wrote much of *The Magic Flute*'s most glorious music for Pamina, yet she is not a real character but a Never-Never-Land Pollyanna. By contrast, Papageno is so human that he seems to belong in another kind of opera. In fact, the Papageno story exposes the "something-for-everyone," multilevel appeal that to some people is a stumbling block. Though apologists refer to a "perfect fusion," in actuality the two incongruous scenarios, Papageno's box-office matinée musical and the Trials of Tamino and Pamina, never blend into a comfortable unity. If the opera had not employed spoken dialogue, Mozart might have provided transitions between the two levels, connecting the Quintet, for example, with the first aria of the Queen of Night; certainly the beginning of the second of these pieces—as it stands, in close juxtaposition—lets the listener down abruptly.

But Mozart could hardly be expected to tamper with the natural limitations of the slow-witted, garrulous Papageno. The composer's logic of characterization required that bumpkins have bumpkins' music. (In one of his letters he uses "Papageno" as a synonym for "ass.") Undeniably the music exactly suits the part, but the repeated verses of the songs are tedious in spite of variations in the accompaniments. This of course has no bearing on Mozart's very evident delight in composing for the glockenspiel—music reminding us that he was a native of cuckoo-clock country himself.

The role of Papageno is disproportionately large, presumably because Emanuel Schikaneder, who commissioned the opera and produced it in his own theater, played the part as well as wrote it. Obviously Mozart had little control over its dimensions and prominence, or over the preferential but misplaced position of the Papageno-Papagena scene so near the end of the opera. Nor is this bird-seller's romance simply a foil, on another social plane, to that of the hero and heroine. Yet it is through Papageno's fibbing and faintheartedness, and the limitation of his world to the satisfaction of bodily needs, that the opera upholds the class prejudices of the *ancien régime*. (Sarastro, incidentally, seems to advocate at least one egalitarian principle when he is reminded that Tamino is of royal blood and replies, "He is a man and that is enough"; but it is evident that Papageno could never enter the brotherhood if only because of his lack of breeding.)

Unlike other Mozart operas, *The Magic Flute* depicts neither a class struggle nor, as in *Figaro*, class hatred. But the opera does contain two truly revolutionary innovations—as distinguished from the much-vaunted but false humanism of the brotherhood. The first is that Papageno's deficiencies are presented as *gemüt-lich*, to the conspicuous pleasure of audiences that share them. The second is that because of its spoken dialogue the opera must be performed in the vernacular. Even though these departures had been tried before, and by Mozart himself, *The Magic Flute* is a kind of turning point in both respects, after which opera ceases to be an exclusively upper-class entertainment.

———

The story of the appalling circumstances of the final months of Mozart's life, during which the opera was written and performed, has so left its mark on the world that to this day his poverty and death are blamed on the neglect of everyone associated with him. Schikaneder has been the principal target of this reaction, partly because he apparently did not share any profits with Mozart when the opera became a success during the composer's last days. Moreover, Mozart's name appears on the original playbill both misspelled ("Mozard") and in a type size indecently smaller than Schikaneder's. Yet the two men had been friends for eleven years, and neither the composer's widow nor her second husband, who was Mozart's first biographer, seems to have accused the impresario of unfairness; in fact, the widow expressed her grati-tude for his gift of the proceeds from the first performance of the opera after Mozart's death. Then, too, Schikaneder himself must have been hard-pressed financially since he declared bankruptcy soon after. (Oddly, no odium has attached to Mozart's prosperous friends, such as Baron van Swieten, a fellow Mason as well as one of the few people who had an inkling of Mozart's genius; but van Swieten's only help was to counsel the widow to order an inexpensive funeral.)

Die Opern in Deutschland, a history published in 1849 by an ex-singer and opera director, repeated a sensational assertion, made in Vienna thirty years earlier,[6] that except for the parts of Papageno and Papagena, the *Magic Flute* libretto was written not by Schikaneder but by Carl Ludwig Giesecke,[7] who worked for Schikaneder at the time that *The Magic Flute* was composed. This story originated with Giesecke himself and was corroborated by some of those who heard it, among them a pupil of Mozart (who was too young in 1791, however, to have been more than a hearsay witness). Support for Giesecke is found in a preface to a libretto by Schikaneder dated three years after Mozart's death that attacks an unnamed literary hack's unscrupulous claims to the authorship of *The Magic Flute*. Mozart's principal biographer, Otto Jahn, who had no direct knowledge of the affair, nevertheless believed Giesecke's story, as have many subsequent Mozart scholars, including Dent, a large part of whose essay on the opera is devoted to this question.

After renouncing his operatic affiliations, Giesecke had a successful career as a mineralogist, working in Greenland for seven years, for the King of Denmark, and later holding a professorship in Dublin. But the story of his collaboration on *The Magic Flute* is unconvincing. Why did Giesecke say nothing about it later in life, since he lived until a time (1833) when the opera had become internationally famous? Dent's answers are that Giesecke might have been reticent about a former association with the stage, and that he may have felt compromised by his early theatrical career; but to have known Mozart was surely never cause for shame, and, besides, Giesecke had already broken the vow in 1819. The real puzzle is in his failure to authenticate his claim while in Vienna at that time, or, earlier, in Copenhagen, where he could have consulted Mozart's widow.

6. 1819 according to Dent, 1818 according to *Die Opern in Deutschland*. In 1822 the part of Sarastro was sung in Schikaneder's Kärntnertor Theater by Johann Nestroy, whose musical career is examined, for the first time in English, in Lawrence Harding's *The Dramatic Art of Ferdinand Raimund and Johann Nestroy* (Mouton, 1974). (*Hello, Dolly!* is based on a play that Thornton Wilder adapted from Nestroy.)

7. Giesecke's real name was Johann Georg Metzler. In Ireland he was known as Sir Charles Lewis Giesecke.

Not until 1941 did anyone undertake a stylistic analysis and comparison between the *Magic Flute* libretto and other writings by Schikaneder and Giesecke. In that year, Egon von Komorzyński effectively demonstrated[8] that Schikaneder was at least the principal author. More recently, Professor E. M. Batley[9] has amplified this conclusion and attempted to rehabilitate Schikaneder's reputation:

> Productions of lesser quality had begun to appear on Schikaneder's stage [by 1791], including the various plagiarisms, travesties and adaptations of . . . Giesecke.

But Professor Batley's book is more valuable for its account of the origins and development of the *Singspiel,* a visual and dialogue genre of theater, popular in tone and moralizing in attitude. He traces the history of this form in Vienna in the half-century before *The Magic Flute* (and earlier than that elsewhere) and describes the form's various categories—heroic, romantic, comic, allegoric, magic—from which Schikaneder drew. This study uncovers the derivations in other works of characters and incidents in *The Magic Flute,* and even of some copied language. Thus the prototype of the Queen of Night is found in Hafner's *Megäras, Die Förchtenliche Hexe* (1763), while Papageno's "suicide" scene was almost commonplace on the Vienna stage.

Professor Batley is neither thorough nor very sound, however, seriously undermining the reader's confidence by such mistakes as:

> *The Magic Flute* was not performed until September 30. . . . Mozart, very ill by this time, died five weeks later on December 5.

The Professor also regards the question of whether the priesthood in the opera

8. *Mozart* (Berlin, 1941).
9. *A Preface to "The Magic Flute,"* New York, 1967.

was specifically intended to portray a Masonic brotherhood [as] by no means satisfactorily resolved.

But since every other writer on the subject accepts the Masonic element *prima facie,* surely some evidence might have been presented to support this dissenting opinion. Finally, in his zeal to establish Schikaneder's influence on the score as well, Professor Batley ascribes to him the suggestion that the entrance of the brotherhood in Act Two should be accompanied by music, and the "clever" idea of introducing the Papageno-Papagena duet by gradually increasing the velocity of the repeated syllable "pa." But Mozart had already fully exploited these plosives at the end of the duet, and the priests' March is a miscalculation, detracting from the chorus that follows by too much resembling it in tempo and character; nor is this March one of those "happy mistakes," like the shadow that fits perfectly in the composition of a great painting though lying in the wrong direction.

———

But the caliber of the literature about *The Magic Flute* is sophomoric. Professor Moberly's essay,[10] for instance, is little more than a line-by-line guide, on this level:

> [T]he strings trip along; they have a message to make: "O, let us to our mistress hurry!"

And even Dent is capable of inanities, such as the following:

> Mozart's religious feelings [are] at their sanest and most exalted [in *The Magic Flute*]. . . . [T]he "sublime" is definitely not a characteristic of Mozart, but if he ever approached the vision of it, it was in this opera, and nowhere else. . . . It is just this sense of freedom and grandeur [on the entrance of Sarastro] that is often wanting in Mozart's church music. . . .

10. *Three Mozart Operas,* by R. B. Moberly (New York, 1967).

In *some* of Mozart's church music, like the merely brilliant *Coronation* Mass. But the remark is wildly untrue of the *Qui tollis* in the C-Minor Mass, which is incontrovertibly "religious," "sane," "exalted," and "sublime." Even more foolishly, Dent avers that the styles of the opera and of the *Requiem* overlap, and that the latter does not

> express primary and elemental religious emotions, but [seeks] rather to reproduce the correct and conventional ecclesiastical atmosphere.

The entrance of the tenor and first two phrases of the soprano in the *Tuba mirum* do indeed evoke the opera, and the *Requiem* is indisputably dramatic. But only the *Dies irae* and the last few measures of the *Rex tremendae* and last fifteen of the *Confutatis* are complete enough to give much indication of what the *Requiem* would have been. If it can be compared at all, it is not to a completed work and certainly not to one for the stage, but to some great maimed masterpiece such as the *Victory of Samothrace*.

Professor Chailley's investigations of the Masonic background and ritual, and his analyses of the ternary versus quinary, and other male and female, symbols,[11] are exhaustive to a degree that will discourage the general reader. Furthermore, Chailley is more concerned with the libretto than with the music, his exposition of the plot being as detailed as anyone could want. Yet his analysis of Masonic symbolism in the music raises questions. Thus the fugue in the overture represents a form of architecture, he says, and hence stands for the craft of masonry. But the publication of the sketches[12] for the overture reveals that Mozart's first idea for the Allegro was not this fugue but, instead, the theme of true love, the upward sixth and descending scale

11. In Masonic ritual, a Brother placed three dots after his signature, and a Sister five dots, in quincunx, after hers. Fire and the sun are masculine, of course, water and the moon feminine. And five is also *Gamos*, the number of Aphrodite. Fives and threes occur in rhythms, chords, and key signatures throughout the opera.
12. See the appendix to *Die Zauberflöte*, edited by Gernot Gruber and Alfred Orel, *Neue Mozart-Ausgabe*, vol. 19, Series 2 (Basel, Paris, London, 1970).

melodic design of Tamino's *"Dies Bildnis"* and Pamina's *"Tamino mein!"* This first idea may have been abandoned in favor of the fugue for the symbolic reason, but even a glance at the sketches shows that Mozart had compelling musical reasons as well. That his deepest beliefs are intrinsic to the music is demonstrable, yet his personal identification with the opera's Masonic philosophy is irrelevant in judging its artistic features.

———

The Magic Flute contains remarkably few resemblances to the music of Mozart's earlier operas. The March for Sarastro is reminiscent of *Figaro,* a phrase near the end of the *"Auf Wiedersehen"* scene recalls the first Terzetto in *Così,* and Monostatos's *"Alles fühlt"* suggests *The Seraglio,* the exotic still being associated in Mozart's mind with things Turkish. (How ingenious to have characterized the Moor's lechery in "nervous" music!) But these few remembrances of things past are minor compared to the cornucopia of new marvels in Act Two: the Queen of Night, Sarastro, the Terzetto, Pamina's aria, the Chorus, and the second Terzetto—a contrast of ensembles and arias, of tempi, moods, and extremes of vocal range, that is unequaled. This diversity is carried too far with Papageno's *"Ein Mädchen oder Weibchen,"* which is a long way down after the others; but the array of separate numbers just before this interruption achieves a continuity as perfectly sustained as that of the symphonic finales in *Figaro* and *Don Giovanni.*

Yet if originality as well as intensity of expression is a criterion, the most stunning music of all is found not in these closed forms but in the two dialogues, Tamino and the Speaker and Pamina and Sarastro. These episodes combine recitative and *arioso* in a manner strikingly similar to Bach, and, in the exchanges between Tamino and the Speaker, to God and the Evangelist in the Bach Passions—except that Mozart blends the older sacred style with operatic figurations. The history of opera reaches a peak with this music, which prepares the path for Wagner—something that can be said only in a lesser degree even of the very remarkable choruses.

The new edition of the score[13] includes the cadenza that Mozart deleted because the singers could not perform it. But the scene is too long anyway. Also, it suffers musically by following the greatest of his overtures, and dramatically because of its content, a confrontation of man and reptile being inherently less promising than one between human beings.

——

The sheer sound of *The Magic Flute* is of an unearthly beauty. This was to have been expected from the title of the opera, perhaps, but the instrumental timbres do have a special intensity, and new effects are discovered with the most ordinary combinations of instruments: in the luminosity of the flute and violins in the Quintet (No. 12), in the Bach-like sonority of the two flutes in Sarastro's aria, and in the wind instruments in the introduction to the C-minor (Masonic key!) Fugato.

These examples are taken from the latter part of the opera, but one of the features of the score as a whole is a delicacy that reflects Mozart's acute aural sensitivity in the last months of his life, when even the singing of his pet canary caused him physical pain. This symptom, together with edema, stomach trouble, vertigo, and spasms of weeping, first suggested a diagnosis of mercury poisoning.[14] If it is true that a stigma increases perception, and that disease, especially one that a sufferer may fear to be fatal, serves to heighten experience, then a purely human explanation can be hypothesized for the ethereality of *The Magic Flute*—though in Mozart's case we are always inclined to suspect a divine one.

13. See footnote 12.
14. See Dr. Dieter Kerner's *Mozarts Todeskrankheit* (Mainz-Berlin, 1961) and *Mozart: Krankheit, Tod, Begräbnis*, by Dr. C. Baer (Salzburg, 1972).

*F*IGARO AT THE MET:
A *MARRIAGE* ON THE ROCKS

Figaro (Marriage of). Another of the causes of the Revolution.

—Dictionary of Accepted Ideas

This epigraph from Flaubert's lexicon would surely mystify most of the audience at the Metropolitan's new *Marriage of Figaro*.[1] Although the reference is to Beaumarchais's play, in which the consequences of prerevolutionary social structure are more accentuated than they are in the opera, the relationship between the classes is an indispensable element in the latter also. Traditional stagings recognize this, but the current one at Lincoln Center minimizes the historical circumstances. Günther Rennert, who directed the new version, believes that

> [There is] little logic in loading Mozart's opera with political portent or emphasizing the class distinctions to make the character of Figaro a personification of the revolution that was to sweep across Europe after 1791. That approach would be right for Beaumarchais but wrong for Mozart. . . .[2]

But any approach to the Figaro story, for Beaumarchais or for Mozart, must "emphasize class distinctions," while to portray the ingratiating valet as the "personification of the revolution" would be ludicrous, no matter what the circumstances. Yet Mozart did choose this "revolutionary" play and naturally would have been attracted to a hero who successfully challenges his "superior" under the cloak of compliance.

1. *The Marriage of Figaro*, by Mozart, libretto by Lorenzo Da Ponte, directed by Günther Rennert, designed by Robert O'Hearn, conducted by Steuart Bedford.
2. *The New York Times*, November 16, 1975.

The opera's continuing supremacy after two centuries testifies to its ability to accommodate a variety of interpretations tending to highlight either the political-social content or the sexual one. But whatever the proportion between them, the two are inseparable. Dr. Rennert's principal error is in too heavily exploiting the latter at the cost of obfuscating the former. This is not to say that his emphasis on the erotic element is unjustified, but only that to blur the social differences of the period is to remove the basis of the plot, which depends on the feudal relationship between master and servant:

> *Countess:* So [the Count] tried to seduce you?
> *Susanna:* His lordship does not make pretty speeches to a girl of my station; he regards it as purely a matter of business.

Rennert ignores this dialogue and places the Count in a cat-and-mouse, Feydeau-type chase of her ladyship's maid. Throughout the performance, moreover, the familiarity between master and servant almost reaches the level of mutual backslapping—or, rather, of fisticuffs; at one point Figaro seems to be on the verge of punching the Count, a preposterous gesture for the late eighteenth century. More important, this betrays Rennert's essential misunderstanding of Figaro's most famous characteristic, his reliance on wit rather than physical strength, for the story is a contest between the power of talent and that of birth. The behavior of the peasants also shows this distorted point of view; instead of presenting their flowers to the Count indifferently or with ill-concealed contempt, as the scene is usually played, the chorus flings them at him like a mob pelting a politician. At this moment and others in Rennert's production the Revolution appears already to have taken place.

Rennert's initial conflict with Mozart, therefore, is in having transgressed the boundaries of class which the composer always scrupulously observes. That Figaro may have egalitarian aspirations, and is more than a match for the Count in native intelligence, has no bearing on the musical delineation of the social positions of the two men. Where Beaumarchais uses verbal idioms to distinguish the nobleman from the notary and the doctor from the dolt, Mozart employs the conventions of his own art. Thus the Count's music, even when he suffers a fit of jealousy, retains a formality appropriate to the aristocrat, while Figaro's music, when he is in the throes of the same emotion, never loses the resilience associated with those who have had to fend for themselves. So, too, when the Count enters the scene during Figaro's and Susanna's *"Pace, pace,"* the musical style of the nobleman's comments is never confounded with that of this rustic, cozy duet.

Similarly, the Countess's music, in arias and ensembles, always befits the noblewoman, just as Susanna's does the maid—albeit one with larger potentialities. And it follows that the music of Bartolo and Marcellina unmistakably marks them, with their pomposities and affectations, as bourgeois. To be sure, this social defining is only one of many means of characterization by which Mozart creates some of opera's most convincingly three-dimensional people. On a more rarified level he even offers glimpses into the subconscious, revealing the true motive that may contradict the one which a character is avowing.

Whether from ignorance or by design the Met's Almaviva lacked all dignity, slouching about, remaining seated when his wife entered the room, brandishing a rapier as if he had never had a fencing lesson. And in her over-enthusiastic response to the advances of the infatuated thirteen-year-old would-be-seducer Cherubino, the Countess behaved incredibly and with unthinkable, if not merely anachronistic, vulgarity. Here again, the more serious fault is the failure to understand that the whole concept of the Countess's character is based on the reality of her love for her husband, which is one of the premises of the opera.

The Metropolitan's costumes also suggest that the times are somewhat later than Da Ponte and Mozart had thought. The peasants look as if they had acquired their clothes from a raid on the *Carmen* wardrobe, or had them copied from Goya's portraits of the nobility. In fact the only protagonist shown as being in a truly wretched condition is the musician Basilio, who is shabby, unkempt, and evidently too poor to afford the tonsorial services of some apprentice of Seville's most famous citizen.

Local 802, in its next strike against the Met, should include among the list of grievances this caricaturing of a musician and his pathetic situation.

As for the sets, Act One perpetuates the built-in inconsistency that requires Figaro to measure a room for the nuptial bed, though a glance shows a space large enough for a dozen such; but this is mandated by the action. Less justifiable is the addition of a corridor visible to the audience, since this eliminates the possibility of the surprise visits that are essential to the plot. The room itself, moreover, is equipped with extra doorways that, despite the Count's obliging, if inexplicable, failure to take advantage of them, obviate the entire dramaturgical problem. Finally, the first-act curtain descends on Figaro alone, as if Act Two were to follow like a second scene—which is the way Karajan presents it, presumably for the sake of the Act Two Finale. But in general, Aguas Frescas, the Almaviva palace, is unattractive both inside and out, the last scene more nearly resembling a cemetery of wire-sculpture tombstones than a garden.

But if the musical performance is reasonably good, *Figaro* can be enjoyed regardless of botched staging. Unfortunately the Met did not offer this compensation. The male leads were passably sung, those of the females not even that. Though superior to the Countess and Susanna, the Cherubino in Salzburg filled the same part much more satisfactorily, which suggests that the Met's unfavorable musical ecology might have been responsible for her frequently sharp notes. But neither of the two other singers possessed the voice for her part, the Countess's lacking purity and warmth, Susanna's the volume for a theater the size of the Met— as well as the range for *anywhere,* a deficiency not offset by a histrionic repertory limited to eye-rolling of the minstrel-show variety. In the letter-dictating scene, where the alternating voices should be perfectly matched, the two women contradicted each other in both intonation and style. But the Met's obliviousness to complementarity in casting is well known, this operation apparently being entrusted to lottery.

Even so, the weakest link in the performance was the conductor. His huge, inflexible beat seldom found judicious tempi, reducing the *presto* overture to an *allegro moderato*, for example, and trailing Bartolo's triplets by a full quarter. Singers and orchestra were rarely together, furthermore, though at the Met ragged ensembles are not always the conductor's fault, since the prompter rules the stage. Apart from these disasters, the musical reading lacked any sense of style, appoggiaturas and ornaments being inconsistently and sometimes incorrectly applied, and articulation left to take care of itself (with, for instance, the habitual mis-playing of portato as staccato).

Whether the conductor or the stage director was responsible for cutting Marcellina's, but not Basilio's, Act Four aria, the decision was ill-advised. Both pieces are pertinent philosophical asides, but expendable ones, since they dissipate the dramatic tension and, arguably, lower the musical caliber; that Mozart was inspired by theatrical situations partly accounts for the superior-ity of the arias in the operas to all but a few of even his greatest ones for concert performance alone. But these two, probably interpolated, numbers are also stylistically alien, Marcellina's *fioritura* and Basilio's "descriptive" chromaticisms being reflected nowhere else in the score. Yet if one of the pieces is omitted, both should be.

Most of the Metropolitan opening-night audience reacted to the performance as if attending a world premiere. Many spectators were more amused by the chair episode than would be possible at a second viewing, and more surprised than either the Count or Figaro at the revelation of identities in the final scene. And each instance of bad singing and jejune stage business provoked applause that betrayed total insensitivity to the music. Yet the audience was not entirely to blame. Mozart's *opera buffa*, with its serious theme disguised in comic conventions, should not have been treated as farce. Who, one wonders, is responsible for hav-ing made pandering a policy at the Met? It does not help the city's claim to artistic pre-eminence as a basis for national sup-port when one of its foremost cultural institutions yields to such standards.

In view of the consensus that *The Marriage of Figaro* is Mozart's most successful opera, it has engendered surprisingly little criticism of any substance. Perhaps the very abundance and obviousness of its virtues explain this dearth. Unlike *The Magic Flute*, for instance, *Figaro* is not encumbered with symbolic meanings, confusing antecedents, and bizarre and supernatural characters, nor is it in need of interpretive theories, such as Kierkegaard's on the erotic in *Don Giovanni*. The story is credible, suspenseful, and well-constructed in spite of loose ends and a considerable dependence on accidents and coincidences. Besides, the play is perfectly fitted to the opera form, and the adaptation is skillful. In *The Marriage* as in *Le Mariage* the characters are so vivid— their emotions and motivations transcending specific time and place—that the audience never questions their humanity.

The one topic that continues to provoke discussion is the extent of the opera's revolutionary subject matter. The British philosopher Bernard Williams argues that the play was not at first recognized as revolutionary at all, and that Beaumarchais's "reputation as a subversive writer increased with hindsight."[3] The first part of this statement cannot be entirely true, since the King banned the play for a time, and the aristocracy repeatedly warned against it, but Flaubert's "definition" attests to the retrospective inflation of the received idea. Williams notes that the explicit political comment in the Beaumarchais play is minute. But surely the implied is as potent as the overt, while even a few words on such subjects spoken in a play have more impact than the same words sung in an opera. Williams proves this and contradicts himself with a quotation from a Viennese newspaper published shortly after the opera's premiere:

> What is not allowed to be said these days is sung, one may say, with *Figaro*—this piece, which was prohibited in Paris . . . we have at last had the felicity to see represented as an opera. . . .

3. "Mozart's 'Figaro': A Question of Class?" *The Listener*, August 15, 1975.

Yet Williams attributes more profound revolutionary sentiments to the opera than to the play:

> Beaumarchais never comes near the depths of . . . bitterness that Mozart uncovered in the recitative *Tutto è disposto* . . . and the snaking aria which follows it.

The comment, peculiar adjective apart, lacks perspective on the opera as a whole, for the essential difference between it and the play is not in the degree of political involvement but in qualities of expressiveness. As Stendhal wrote:

> The true temperament of the French play is nowhere to be found in the opera. . . . [Mozart] converts into serious passion the transient inclinations which in Beaumarchais simply amuse the agreeable inhabitants of Aguas Frescas.

Although the moral edification may come to the same thing in both works—cleverness triumphs, two can play at the same game, fidelity is advisable if only because it is prudent—and although the Almaviva-world is still shallow in whatever medium it is portrayed, Mozart and Beaumarchais have imbued their material with almost antithetical feelings. The play, no matter how expert and ingenuous, and how effective its satire, remains a comedy of manners whose emotional range is inherently narrower than that of the opera.[4] Mozart, by contrast, transfigures the mundane story and less-than-heroic characters in the ardor of his music. *His* theme is romantic love.

The essay on *Figaro* by Edward Dent,[5] still the best-known

---

4. See Georges Lemaitre's *Beaumarchais* (New York, 1949) for a discussion of the difference between the play and the opera. (" . . . Mozart was guided in all the changes he made by a deep sense of the beautiful and the universal. Beaumarchais had faced a world of particular individuals, twisted and tormented behind a deceptive façade of high breeding and gaiety. Mozart, looking at the same human landscape, saw a long and lovely vista of eternal human sentiments, sometimes droll, sometimes sad, never sordid, often enchanting, yet somehow deeply true. . . . ")

5. *Mozart's Operas: A Critical Study* (London, 1913; revised edition, 1947).

criticism of the opera in English, is less than half as long as his studies of *Don Giovanni* and *The Magic Flute*. Moreover, Dent's *Figaro* is useful mainly for its examination of stylistic resemblances between Mozart's opera and earlier and contemporary ones by Salieri, Paisiello,[6] and others. In fact, the critic's one "original" comment about the music, that its highest achievement is the Act Three Sextet, simply repeats Mozart's own preference. Dent discusses this ensemble as a demonstration of the opportunities, unique to opera, for blending different emotions while at the same time keeping them distinct. But he does not offer a musical analysis of the piece, and it was left for Charles Rosen[7] to perceive that its structure is that of the slow movement of a sonata.

Figaro is by no means free of archaic theatrical conventions and of plot inconsistencies, yet the former do not creak loudly enough to distract, and the latter are not really disturbing. Who cares how Cherubino manages to escape from the locked dressing room—or, if the lock were of the one-way type, believes that the Count would not be cognizant of the fact? Also, if the dropping of the pin is too convenient, and the discovery that Marcellina and Figaro are mother and son too outrageous, such doubts might puzzle the audience after the opera but hardly during it. Even Figaro's unlikely marriage contract with the elderly and unappealing Marcellina is forgotten in the music in which this foolish business is exposed.

In one respect the conventional structure of the opera does fail. It is evident that the happy ending will not last long for the Countess. Apprehension and concern for her future arise, of course, because of the depth of feeling suffusing her music, which by the end of the opera has won for her the largest share of sympathy—greater even than that for Figaro and Susanna, who are all too clearly on the way up. After four acts in company with the Count, the audience does not trust him, realizing that

6. It was discovered only recently that Paisiello composed the Mass and *Te Deum* for Napoleon's coronation (1804).
7. *The Classical Style* (New York, 1971).

the one lesson he may have learned is to choose, for future liaisons, more naïve and less shrewdly escorted prey than Susanna. In spite of his final statement of good resolutions, it is obvious that he will follow the pattern of the amorist hero of Mozart's subsequent opera.

The late appearance of Cherubino's partner, Barbarina, has been described as a fault of construction. (She is not introduced in the earlier scenes in order that he can pursue his flirtation with the Countess, which is central to the plot.) Yet the same imbalance in the corresponding role in Beaumarchais's play, that of Fanchette, passes virtually unnoticed. Mozart's "error" is in having given the young girl the opera's most beautiful short piece—one that is further distinguished by tonality (the minor key), color (muted strings), and placement—for to have begun the final act with this delicate lyric was perhaps the composer's greatest surprise. Barbarina's tiny Cavatina makes us regret that he did not enlarge the part.

Da Ponte's preface to *The Marriage of Figaro* warns that

in spite of all the zeal and care on the part of both the composer and myself to be brief . . . the opera will not be one of the shortest that has been performed on our stages.

The librettist's prediction is true: the opera is long. That it does not seem so may be partly due to Mozart's and Da Ponte's avowed efforts "to avoid the boredom and monotony of long recitatives," even though as much as one-fifth of the score consists of this form of dialogue. But the opera's extremely rapid pace gives the impression of brevity, and, incidentally, helps to account for its popularity. Not only are the musical numbers short, but most of them are also in fast tempos. Starting with the *presto* overture, and with the exception of four measures of accompanied recitative, Act One consists entirely of *allegro* or *allegretto* music. As in symphonic tradition, the second act promises to be the opera's slow movement, but after the opening, and apart from three later *andante* passages, music and events resume their rapid tempo. Act Three contains a larger proportion of slow music, as befits the more serious mood of the opera's climax, but even here the fast pieces outnumber the slow, and in the final act quick tempi again predominate.

Other factors contribute to the effect of fluidity. One is that the music is free from digressions. Thus the March and Fandango might well have been extended but, instead, seem to have been written with stopwatch in hand: every note, here and elsewhere, builds toward the dramatic totality. And the same grammar that often seems so confining and rigid in the music of Mozart's contemporaries was for him a challenge to endless invention. His harmonic vocabulary consists of only a few monosyllables—by later criteria—yet he continually renews the music's harmonic aspect through modulation and changes of tonality. Still other causes of the effect of acceleration throughout the opera are the rarity of minor keys, generally associated with introspective moods and slower tempi, the constant varying of meter and rhythmic pattern, and, above all, the succession of ever higher-spirited pieces. As an example of the last element, Mozart manages to top even the effervescence of the "Rossini"[8] *Allegro*, in the Finale of Act Two, with a still more exultant burst of musical joy at Figaro's entrance.

But the fundamental reason for the continual impression of animation is the opera's origin in a play that teems with action, incident, and detail, all of which continue through recitative and aria alike. Further, Mozart creates conversational forms. In the Andante near the end of Act Two, for example, beginning with Antonio's *"Vostre dunque,"* the repartee at first resembles speech more than it does song, each voice being limited to a single pitch or narrow range. And Mozart's tension-generating technique anticipates Wagner's, in the use of ostinato, pedal point, dynamics, and sequences—in Mozart's case, changes of tonal degree corresponding to changes of speakers. The crescendo and switch of key between the Count's *"Su via, ti confondi?"* and Figaro's *"E l'usanza . . ."* are as exciting as the orchestral motif,

8. Verdi also comes to mind at one point, the passage beginning in G minor just before the final Andante.

at successively higher transpositions, that introduces Tristan into the presence of Isolde.

The Marriage of Figaro does not encompass Mozart's most celestial or profound music. Nor should it. His goal was to fit music to character and action, evoke situation, express shades of feeling, convey dramatic meaning. And in these achievements *Figaro* both breaks ground and has yet to be surpassed. Here Mozart reveals himself a master not only of new and greater musical dimensions but also of the understanding of human beings.

THE PARIS OPÉRA IN NEW YORK

During the recent New York visit of the Paris Opéra, the opening-night *Marriage of Figaro*[1] was marked by a real-life incident more dramatic than anything that occurred on stage. Just before *"Vedro mentre in sospiro,"* the Count's Act Three aria, the conductor, Georg Solti, accidentally jabbed his right temple with his baton while trying to evade the glare from a light on the stand. Fortunately his eye was unharmed and the injury slight, though it bled profusely, bespattering the score and temporarily blinding Sir Georg—as sometimes happens to a boxer from a minor cut on the brow. Though failing to stanch the flow of blood with a handkerchief in his left hand, Solti kept going, and, at the end of the number, hurried to his dressing room for first aid, having had the composure to calculate the performance time of

1. *The Marriage of Figaro*, by Mozart, libretto by Lorenzo Da Ponte, directed by Giorgio Strehler, designed by Ezio Frijerio, conducted by Georg Solti.

the recitative which follows and which could be sung without him. He was back in place to lead the great centerpiece Sextet, which cannot be played without conductor, at least in the harrowing acoustics of the Metropolitan Opera House. Before his emergency exit, Solti also had the presence of mind to give a signal to stop the descent of the curtain, which had already begun. These feats of quick thinking and action will undoubtedly be recorded in the annals of opera. No wonder that when Sir Georg emerged to conduct the final act, he seemed to receive a Purple Heart ovation in addition to his usual merely meter-breaking one.

The incident was widely reported in the European as well as American press, with photographs of Sir Georg, patch on forehead. *The New York Times* mentioned the mishap in a news item, but Mr. Schonberg's review did not, thereby disappointing those readers who had hoped that he might include a reference to similar accidents, such as that which (no analogy!) caused the death of Lully. But the word "baton" appeared only in a statement about singers "meshing with one another and with the conductor's baton"—though surely the more noteworthy "meshing" was that of the stick with Mr. Solti.

Mr. Schonberg completely misunderstood the staging, writing that

> In Act I at Figaro's *"Se vuol ballare,"* he lustily thwacked the Count's uniform with a cane. In context this was understandable. Susanna had just told Figaro the facts of life, and he was upset. Mr. Strehler's social commentary . . . stopped here.

So far from expressing a mere "upset" on learning "the facts of life" (which of course Figaro already knew), the blow to the nobleman's coat on its clothes hanger is a gesture of deep and violent hatred. Far from ending the social commentary, this begins it, for the focus of director Giorgio Strehler's interpretation is political. But how could anyone fail to see that the peasants at the end of Act Three, flinging the Count's papers about and seemingly on the verge of seizing the palace, are near to open rebellion? And who could fail to observe that throughout the opera Figaro and the Count address each other virtually through clenched teeth, especially since this is in such contrast to the usual nose-tweaking renditions of Figaro's part? But the two men's detestation is mutual: Strehler's Count would never suffer disrespectful behavior from his servant. The décors also carry out the social message, Figaro's quarters being dingy, the costumes of the *contadini* comparatively drab, and the colors at the end of that "revolutionary" Act Three brownish and foreboding.

Strehler's conception of a more serious Figaro helps to explain why the role itself seems to be less prominent in this staging than operagoers remember it; compared to his betrothed, in fact, he is inconspicuous, at times to the point of being almost a background figure. And because this Figaro is not perpetually playing to the audience, or upstaging the rest of the cast, even aficionados noticed, some of them for the first time, that the part does not have a solo *scena* following Act One until Act Four's *"Tutto è disposto,"* and that Figaro's mood here is the same as it was when he struck that effigy of oppression. Clearly, Strehler means to say that the private Figaro is seditious, no matter how well this is hidden beneath a frolicsome and ingratiating public manner.

Mr. Schonberg views the episode with the uniform as one of the "unconventional" aspects of the production. Another is that "in the last act two cuts were opened—the Marcellina and Basilio arias"—though surely these numbers are more often performed than they are omitted. Nor are they "cuts," properly speaking, Mozart having added them to the original for the same reason that they are included today: good singers refuse to accept such minor roles without the arias. But they intrude, being dramatically deadening and musically alien. In Strehler's version, even more than in most, they spoil the effect of *"Tutto è disposto,"* which, because of them, is no longer set off and so becomes simply No. Three in a roundup of solos.

Mr. Schonberg writes that Margaret Price's *"Porgi amor"* "established her credentials." But it did no such thing, since those roving philanthropists who comprise our gala audiences and who come primarily for the intermissions were straggling back to their seats during this masterpiece, and the disturbance unsettled the singer. Her voice and artistry were not fully revealed until *"Dove sono,"* which deservedly drew the evening's most enthusiastic applause—even more than Mirella Freni's Susanna, to which Mr. Schonberg gave priority, forgetting that while so brilliant a performance of this role is uncommon, a Countess of Miss Price's quality is rare indeed. The *Times* reviewer observed, too, that M. Bacquier "played the Count as a dirty old man," neglecting to add that he should be played as a dirty young one, his wife's melancholy state being attributable to the wandering affections of a youthful, not of an elderly, husband. According to Mr. Schonberg, the Misses Freni and Price sang the "Letter" duet "ravishingly," but in actuality their tone quality did not match—even though, as the critic noted, perhaps anticipating his review of her as Desdemona, Miss Price "throttled down."

The Metropolitan stage is much smaller than that of the Palais Garnier, a fact which literally cramped the singers' style, limiting their space for movement and positioning. So, too, the Met's inferior acoustics marred the perfection of the musical ensemble. Mr. Schonberg found, nevertheless, that

> From the opening measures it was clear that this performance was going to be musically impeccable. The articulation of the fast-moving figurations, so often sloppy, was crisp and detailed.

But so far as the statement concerns the performance of the third and best overture—the one following *La Marseillaise* and *The Star-Spangled Banner*—this sounded remarkably ragged, at any rate from row seven on the right. When the conductor is Georg Solti, such a fault cannot be his but rather indicates that the instrumentalists could not hear one another. The singers, too, were frequently ahead of the beat, which, at one point, Sir Georg had to accelerate to keep the ensemble from going agley.

Balances as well as rhythmic coordination suffered from the acoustics. "... *Di quel labbro menzogner?*" the Countess soliloquizes, and while she briefly pauses, the oboe and bassoon respond. But the two woodwinds were louder than the lady herself, which, when one trusts Solti, can only mean that they did not sound that way at his podium. Solti's reading as a whole was open to reproach only in such paltry matters as the exaggeration of the fermatas in *"Non so più,"* the slight rushing of the Act Three March, and the much-less-than-*presto* overture.

A *Figaro* of such excellence is a lifetime experience. Every phrase was shaped and controlled by a master musician, in contrast to the time-beating, or serving, to which we have become accustomed at the Metropolitan and City Operas. And it would be difficult to imagine a better cast vocally, as well as one capable of so much intelligent acting. Finally, the stage direction was extraordinarily lucid and the philosophy consistent. If Strehler exposes signs of ferment in the lower orders, he also looks for the corresponding moral corrosion within the Protected World. Though the opera may be comic, the *liaisons*, so he seems to say, are *dangereuses*.

Hardly noticeable were the opera's inherent defects—the overly long part of the gardener together with his untoward insistence, and the misleading ubiquity of Cherubino in the first scenes compared to his diminishing importance in the last ones. Strehler almost succeeds in showing that Cherubino's "love" is only his "libido," and that what he really wants is *"coucher avec n'importe qui."* No performance, of course, can obscure the illogicality of this amorous adolescent's return near the beginning of Act Two, and hence almost immediately after his prolonged and elaborate farewell. But in spite of these "inconsistencies," who would exchange a single measure of *"Non più andrai"* for all the logic of Aristotle?

———

The Opéra's production of Verdi's *Otello*[2] inspired Mr. Schonberg to some curious remarks with regard to its visual aspects:

2. *Otello*, by Verdi, libretto by Arrigo Boito, staged by Terry Hands, designed by Joseph Svoboda, conducted by Georg Solti.

The set is highly stylized and severe, largely in horizontal planes. . . . If opera has to have modern sets, this is the way it can be done. . . . [They] created and maintained a mood in their strong, ungimmicky fashion.

Costumes are equally stylized. The soldiers wore futuristic costumes with helmets that covered a good deal of their faces. They were like Martians in a sci-fi film. . . . Officers wore stylized but more conventional uniforms.

But "stylized" means "conventionalized," unless a particular style is designated. If the sets actually were "modern," the description ("severe, largely in horizontal planes . . . strong [and] ungimmicky") fits neither the accepted definitions of the word nor the actual presentation. And if "modern" suggests angular geometrical forms, then the rounded arches and outdoor staircases of this production do not fall within the classification.

Furthermore, to be told that the set is "largely in horizontal planes" is disconcerting to those of us who felt that the emphasis was most definitely vertical. In fact, seldom have the upper spaces of the Metropolitan stage been filled to such vertiginous elevations, and with people—female figures in black, probably Parcae, in eyries—as well as with buildings. Evidently Mr. Schonberg was thinking of the four-tiered white castle of the first act, since the later ones project different architectural forms. "Ungimmicky" says nothing unless the reviewer tells us just which gimmicks the set does *not* have.

In fact the production mixes periods, and the actual one of Shakespeare's play predominates. Those sci-fi Martian helmets (why not try some other planet?) could equally well have come from the Trojan War, while the "Cypriots" and "Albanians" of the Act Two chorus were realistically dressed in an early-nineteenth-century, vaguely Balkan fashion. But the costumes of the Venetian ambassador and his attendants call to mind the cinquecento more than any other era, even if not precisely of the Serenissima. The *Times* itself, as if deliberately to belie its own reviewer, accompanied his observations with a photograph of Othello in the *ropa* of a Renaissance nobleman. The historical setting is also narrowed by the golden Lion of St. Mark that dominates the scene. Mr. Schonberg overlooks another no less important visual element, that of color, the vermilion of the Venetian delegation and Othello's turquoise night robe being especially vivid against white, Arabic-style walls.

"The direction was traditional, for the most part," Mr. Schonberg says. But the use of those silent witnesses in black would seem to be experimental rather than traditional, as would the failure of Othello to make a credible attempt to hide himself from Cassio in the eavesdropping scene. "Acting" is not really expected of anyone who can sing Desdemona or Othello—which may help to explain why Boito left so much of the drama to be expressed by the composer. Overacting is expected of Iagos, and when they avoid the fault, as this singer did, the "motiveless malignity" of Coleridge's description of the character seems even more apparent. Traditional or otherwise, when Desdemona on her deathbed faces away from the audience, she also helps to divert attention from the manifest impossibility of protesting her innocence after her strangulation. Othello, on the other hand, during *his* extremely dilatory dying process, sings his remorse in the direction of the gallery.

———

In the *Times*'s notice of the Opéra's production of Gounod's *Faust*,[3] Mr. Schonberg objects to the transposition of style and period from those indicated by the libretto to those of the year when the work was composed. But this is precisely the director's rationale for the alteration, mid-nineteenth-century French waltzes and military marches being jarringly inappropriate to Goethe's medieval German setting. Many people believe that in the case of B-plus masterpieces like *Faust*, a new approach such as this may not derogate unduly from the original but is legitimate and even necessary if these works are to survive. To tamper with A-plus masterpieces, on the other hand, is more difficult to justify,

3. *Faust*, by Gounod, libretto by Barbier and Carré, staged by Jorge Lavelli, designed by Max Bignen, conducted by Michel Plasson.

for the reason that they are more deeply rooted in the cultures of which they are the supreme expressions. Thus *Figaro* cannot be updated because it depends on pre-1789 social structure, nor can the *Ring* be moved to the nineteenth century because of the lack of enough valid parallels for the Norse mythology and the consequent loss of verisimilitude.

Once the most popular opera in the repertory of the Metropolitan, *Faust* no longer enjoys its high "Nielsen rating." The music is still pretty and well-loved, but its dramatic force has vanished, and what formerly seemed to be strong emotion now appears as mere sentiment. The reasons for the change are that we have learned *Otello* and *Falstaff*, learned *Elektra*, learned *Wozzeck*, and heard other, newer kinds of music in concerts and ballet. Having acquired a taste for *Pelléas*, we now turn away from Gounod's academic cadences, stilted recitatives—a pity that he abandoned the original spoken dialogue!—and banal climaxes, though M. Gedda's high C was not so much banal as terrifying.

The argument against placing *Faust* in a radically different setting is that incongruities between the words of the drama and its realization on stage are inevitable. But the discrepancies, such as the reference to a nonexistent plume in a hat, are trivial. What does matter is that religious and moral beliefs remain the same in the original and in the adaptation, at least theoretically, and that the story, being archetypal, transcends Gounod as it does Goethe.

One feature of this Third Empire *Faust* which seems completely to have eluded Mr. Schonberg is that of irony and parody. One of the least subtle instances of it occurs in the Soldiers' Chorus, where almost all of the returned warriors, singing *"La Gloire Immortelle,"* were maimed, bandaged, and hobbled on crutches. At the beginning of the same scene, the placement of the stage band on a porch of a Vichy-like spa may have been intended to underline the true genre of the music, while in the church scene the crucified Christ is an enlarged specimen of the art sold in "religious articles" shops.

Perhaps the most effective episode in the staging is the *Moulin*

Rouge Walpurgis Night, during which a Bosch-like bubble covers a group of figures in a way to suggest that they are in Hell. But if the time is the 1870s, the chief influence is that of Fellini, especially in the images of purity and redemption—a cluster of white balloons, the white lights on a Ferris wheel, the "garden" of white laundry, the small girl who plays hopscotch in the falling snow.

——

On the Sunday before the Paris company's New York debut, Mr. Schonberg devoted his weekly causerie to some ruminations on the subject of opera, and to the reasons why "There is no such thing as a successful modern [one]," and why "very little viable opera has been written since the great days of . . . Strauss . . . and . . . Puccini." The critic supported these statements by citing Patrick Smith's choice of ten of the more "viable" operas composed in the 1950s: Menotti's *The Consul*, Poulenc's *Carmélites* and *La Voix Humaine*, Britten's *The Turn of the Screw*, Tippett's *Midsummer Marriage*, Dallapiccola's *Il Prigioniero*, Blomdahl's *Aniara*, Moore's *Baby Doe*, Weisgall's *Six Characters*, and Stravinsky's *Rake*. Mr. Schonberg concluded that this is "not a very impressive list," and that "only the *Carmélites* seems to have a chance to survive. . . . Stravinsky's *Rake* never really took hold with any company," he explained (although the Ingmar Bergman production has achieved the status of a classic at the Stockholm Opera).

But the comparison of these works of the 1950s with those of the "great days" of Strauss and Puccini is invidious in the extreme. The fifties composers had not only to compete against the cinema, the phonograph, and television, but also to struggle against a general disbelief in even the possibility of new opera. Nor is a twenty-year perspective sufficient. Only in the 1950s, after all, was the then thirty-year-old *Wozzeck* recognized as the one great modern opera. And who can predict now whether, for instance, Zimmermann's *Die Soldaten*, a slightly later contemporary of the "ten," may "take hold" with a large public as it has already done with a musically sophisticated one? Mr. Schonberg blames

> Serialism, with its strange use of the human voice, [as having] had a good deal to do with the age's dearth of opera. The energies of all advanced composers seemed placed at the service of a terribly mathematical kind of music that was anti-opera. . . . The culmination came with the electronic music and total dissonance [?] of music after 1950.

"Serial" and "electronic" partly describe Zimmermann's opera, while Berg's *Lulu,* the one full-length opera composed in the last forty years that is esteemed as highly by singers as by musicians, is "serial" from beginning to end.

WAGNER, VERDI, STRAUSS

TAKING THE WAGNER CURE

Near Bayreuth the Wagner Theater and the lunatic asylum on the right are conspicuous.

—*Baedeker's* Southern Germany *(1902)*

The 1974 Bayreuth Festival presented continued evidence of the perennial shortage of star-role Wagnerian singers. But even were this not the case, the most remarkable performance at Bayreuth would have been the audience's. Dressed in full evening clothes in midafternoon, the devotees arrive at the Festspielhaus from castles all over the world, especially spiritual Berchtesgadens. Then long before starting time, the faithful file into cramped wooden pews and, because of the lack of both side and central aisles, remain standing to accommodate stragglers. In the mausoleum-like hall (black curtain, Corinthian columns, *Bogenlampen*), and in the absence of any sign of an imminent theatrical event (the orchestra, like the Nibelungs, is subterranean), the congregational standing suggests an act of reverence, preparations for a memorial service rather than a stage spectacle. Carlyle's "lay pulpit" still aptly describes this German theater.

Shortly before curtain time the doors are locked and latecomers turned away, a rule so strictly enforced that, rumor has it, several New Zealanders returned over the oceans and continents bitterly disappointed at having missed *Das Rheingold* by thirty seconds. But all regulations at Bayreuth are rigidly observed, including one which warns that "Tickets Deformed in Any Way Will Not Be Accepted." (Adding "nibbling" and "crumpling" to "do not fold, mutilate, or spindle"?) A minute or two before the performance starts, a total, World War II blackout occurs and induces mass *rigor mortis,* unbroken by a muffled cough or a shift in position. What, one wonders in this inhuman silence and impenetrable dark, would be the punishment for failing to suppress a blasphemous thought? The black-out, moreover, does not end with the final curtain, and since it is impossible to make an exit, one can only join the captive applauders.

The acoustics of the Festspielhaus are its most acclaimed feature, but the differences between the sides and the center, the loges and front parterre, are pronounced. In addition, stage location seems to affect the singers' pitch and rhythmic coordination, suggesting that they, too, are not always within perfect earshot of the orchestra. The voices are never covered, it is true, but that is hardly an unmixed blessing, and, unfortunately, the price of the singer's supremacy is the orchestra's demotion to the role of accompanist. None of the recordings made in the theater reproduces the unique separation between voices and instruments, probably because stereophony and the architecture of the Festspielhaus are incompatible. But the balance within the orchestra is consistently satisfying, the strings predominating and the brass kept at bay. Violin lines scarcely heard in other opera houses come forward, partly as a result of the large number of players (specified by Wagner but employed nowhere but here), partly because of their placement.

The concept of the invisible orchestra is ideological, nevertheless, and only secondarily acoustical. Its purpose is to strengthen, or at least not to detract from, the stage illusion, and to transfer the sound from conscious to unconscious. The sense of participation and the excitement of the "live" that orchestras contribute to the performance of other operas have no place in Wagner's aesthetics. But can the effect that Wagner intended be realized in the electronic age? The first impression of many visitors to Bayreuth is that the orchestra sounds like a recording superimposed on singing. And in the *Ring*, where the frame of the stage picture is shaped like a television screen, the frequent projections of mists and clouds remind the viewer of TV "snow."

Finally, the hidden orchestra pit has provided an excuse for limiting the repertory to Wagner. And, ample though his world is, and desirable as specialization may be, the question remains whether *any* theater should be restricted to the works of a single composer, especially when the theater is controlled by his family. Not that Wolfgang Wagner has been unreceptive to outside influences—the 1972 *Tannhäuser* ballet, for instance, apparently having been inspired by *Hair*. And he is demonstrably grateful for foreign aid. Although in some respects the fortress is still impregnable, to imported vocal talent it is not. Japanese, Maori, and Welsh names, to mention only the more exotic, are now sprinkled among the Ilses and Heinrichs—ominously, perhaps, for was not the admission of barbarians to high posts in the Empire a major cause of the downfall of Rome? But Wolfgang Wagner has arrogated too much of the staging to himself. His *Ring* is not even up to international standards, to say nothing of setting them, as Bayreuth at one time did. And quite apart from his artistic contributions, the inevitable result of control by the Wagner family has been the establishment of a shrine that attracts only an uncritical audience.

Other operas could be given at Bayreuth. The peculiarities of the theater would inflict no damage on either the acoustics or the philosophical bases of *Moses and Aaron*, to name one. Furthermore, comparative mythology—the Vedas and Eddas—has taken over at the new Bayreuth. What, therefore, could be more appropriate than the juxtaposition of Schoenberg's Semitic myths and Wagner's Aryan ones? And this is not to mention the help such an innovation would give in counteracting the picture of the old Bayreuth draped with swastika flags. Useful, too, might be the occasional substitution of the wail of a shofar in place of the end-of-intermission signals intoned by trumpets and trombones.

As it is now, the omnipresence not only of Wagner's music but also of Wagner the man can make the *Ring* itself seem like a vast monologue of autobiographical indulgence. Thus *Das Rheingold* becomes an opera about Wagner's debts and the intransigence of bill collectors, *Die Walküre* turns into an allegory about conventional morality and Wagner's great suffering therefrom, and about elopement, which he proposed to several ladies before succeeding with Frau von Bülow. By similar tokens, *Siegfried* and *Götterdämmerung* become elaborate dramatizations of the worldly fate of a genius (disguised as a folk hero), that is, a man betrayed by the jealous and small, and ultimately stabbed in the back.

Wagner is also inescapable in the town of Bayreuth. Public thoroughfares are called Lohengrinstrasse and Frickagasse, and children are named Brünnhilde and Isolde—though *Tannhäuser* has not yet been commemorated by any "Venusberg" establishment that this writer could discover. On the contrary, dowagers who look like Cosima are everywhere, while the public park is guarded by a copy of a bust of Wagner, of which the original is in the theater's middle-loge foyer; there, also, Wolfgang Wagner can often be seen, a "dead ringer" for his grandfather except that the marble features are sharper than the living ones. All but the most diehard Festspiel fans would be well advised to take rooms outside of Bayreuth, commuting to the theater through the Franconian hills, with their red-roofed villages, half-timber farmhouses, and U.S. Seventh Army missile installations.

A kiosk facing the entrance to the auditorium features the most recent additions to the gigantic Wagner bibliography— along with such perennial sleepers as Adorno's *Versuch über Wagner*, which sells like *The Joy of Sex* at Doubleday's. (Also facing the entrance is a Red Cross station, perhaps to warn of the deadly seriousness of Wagner's operas.) With the 1976 centenary of the *Ring* soon to be realized, and with Wagner's prestige among musicians having reached the highest level enjoyed since the beginning of the century, guidebooks to the plots and musical motives proliferate. But the latest trends in Wagnerology are found in the official program notes, and at present the main topics are the mythic models, the archetypal characters, and the symbolic significances of the gods. Many of these commentaries are based on the Jungian concept of myths as universal dreams; thus it follows that Jungian analysis is employed, and that the conclusions are often expressed in peculiar language.

A comparison of Wagner's Valhalla with the one in the Skaldic poems, for example, may very well contribute to the understanding of the *Ring* dramas, except that the terminology of the scholars undermines one's faith in their learning. Thus the *Ring*

Valhalla is described as a "supermundane transfiguration . . . in which the divinely inspired aggressiveness of its warriors is revealed as paranoia." At the mundane level, "the overcoming of maternal rule" is said to "take place in the fight with the dragon." At that level, too, Siegfried's murderer, Hagen, is no longer regarded as an embodiment of evil but as a victim of heredity—as the son of Alberich, not because of an extra Y chromosome: hence the villain "feels rejected" and needs malice for his self-assurance. Similarly, in the sphere of the submundane, the mining of the gold is now viewed as an ecological problem, while the ring itself is to be understood as "a symbolic compulsion to concentration . . . which can produce . . . destructive ability, and through egocentricity . . . lead to autistic inertia." This last statement proves not only that the realm of mythical speculation is infinite but also that practically anything written about anything can be published.

By the centenary, the linguists should be having their turn, and the program books offering such fare as the etymological origins of "Frigg," Goddess of Marriage. But in fact linguistic analyses of any kind *have* been lacking. Nor is it generally known that Saussure amassed a considerable body of notes on the Nibelungen texts,[1] hoping to prove that the people and events of the legends were based on actual historical personages and occurrences during the dynasties of the Franks and the Burgundians. This aim is contradicted by the conclusions of Max Müller (among others) that "Myth is *not* a transformation of history into legend,"[2] but Saussure's goal is of lesser consequence than his methods. Starobinski, at any rate, speculates that Saussure's search for actual names and antecedent facts in the

---

1. See Jean Starobinski's *Les mots sous les mots: les anagrammes de Ferdinand de Saussure* (Paris, 1971). Saussure's notes, dated 1910, are in the Bibliothèque Publique et Universitaire de Genève, Ms. 3958 (ten books). See also D'Arco Silvio Avalle's *Le semiologie de la narrativité chez Sausurre* (Paris, 1967).
2. See Ernst Cassirer, *Language and Myth* (New York, 1946). For Müller the origin of myth is in "the inherent weakness in language . . . an ambiguity, a paronymia of words." Thus the Daphne myth began in the "etymological relationship between the Greek word for 'laurel' and the Sanskrit for 'dawn.' "

poetic texts may have involved him in the intensification of his study of the synchronic aspects of language.

All of this may seem remote from Wagner, but in fact it touches on the crux of his artistic philosophy. His 1848 essay, "The Nibelungen: World History as Revealed in Saga," a muddle of philosophizing about the political and other history of medieval Germany, is nevertheless indispensable to an understanding of how the *Ring* was made. Even earlier, the composer had written a drama on Friedrich Barbarossa that introduced a mythological element into the life of the historical figure. As a result of these and other literary excursions, Wagner concluded that only poetic myth, not actual historical incident, must become the basis of his musico-dramatic creations.

Wagner's own scholarship was enormous; he is known to have read widely in and on mythology, including, of course, the Eddas, Grimm's *Mythologie, Das Deutsche Heldenbuch*, the *Völsunga Saga, Der Nibelungen Noth und Klage*.[3] For a complete understanding of the creation of the *Ring* it is undoubtedly necessary to compare his borrowings from these sources with the transformations of them in his librettos. But what concerns us here is Wagner's discovery of the renewable power of myths and his realization of the essential truth, in Kerényi's phrase, that "The gods act according to their given characters and not to those invented by the poet."

Among the many mysteries about Wagner—and these include the development of his musical technique—one of the most curious is the period of six years (1848–1854) during which he read prodigiously, wrote essays, dramas, poems, discovered the nature of his own future art work, but composed virtually no music. In fact he seems to have reversed the "usual" sequence of conception, apparently beginning from the outside, with a philo-

---

3. Concerning Wagner's readings in peripheral literature, see Klaus Günzel's essay *Naturkultus und Musikdrama (Bayreuthe Festspiele, Programmheft* VII, 1974) on the probable influence of G. H. Schubert's writings. Günzel argues that Wagner's uncle, the philologist and intimate of E. T. A. Hoffmann, must have drawn the composer's attention to G. H. Schubert's quirky but ground-breaking *Die Symbolik des Traumes (Symbolism of Dreams)* (1814).

sophic, dramatic, or literary idea, and only later developing a musical one. Evidently, too, he could command his musical imagination at will. Thus in the summer of 1857 he worked on drafts of the *Tristan* scenario, versified it, wrote the libretto. Then, within a few days, and apparently with no superhuman effort, he composed the piece that changed the history and language of music, the *Tristan* Prelude.

Still another mystery is Wagner's ability to draft an outline in practically no time, and, after an incubation of twenty-five years, to bring the projected work forth perfectly fulfilled. This was the case with *Götterdämmerung* (1874), the *Siegfrieds Tod* poem having been conceived in 1848. It was also true of *Parsifal*. Wagner wrote to Mathilde Wesendonck in 1858 explaining that she could understand what he meant by "the redemption from suffering in the philosophical imagination" only when she had heard *Parsifal*, which he was not to compose for another twenty years. (Both *Parsifal* and the *Ring* were planned in that six-year hiatus, during which Wagner underwent a phenomenal musical development while composing no more than a few measures of music.)

To return to Bayreuth and to Wolfgang Wagner's *Ring*, all four operas were presented on a tilted disk—Wieland Wagner's innovation—divided at times like wedges of processed cheese, and varyingly textured so that the final scene of *Das Rheingold*, for instance, looked like a large pizza with molten mozzarella. But as the cycle of operas unfolded, this uni-set was more and more exposed for what it was, an inadequately disguised platter. During changes of scene, effected behind a screen that resembled a camera shutter, curiosity mounted, but only about the ways in which the designer might avoid repeating previous camouflages. The lighting was dim, on the whole, perhaps out of charity to the sets and costumes—particularly Brünnhilde's pants suit. Therefore when the moon was turned on in *Die Walküre*, the sudden brightness seemed to alarm the audience, to say nothing of Siegmund and Sieglinde. All of this would have mattered a lot less if the singing had been of high quality, but few of those in major roles were ready for them, and the part of Brünnhilde actually had to be sung by a different soprano in each opera.

The acting, when there was any, fell to an inexcusable low: Richard Wagner's intentions are clear, detailed, and, today anyway, eminently practical. They suppose a degree of visual and histrionic realism, however, that is at the opposite extreme from his grandson's naked and nearly propless production. When will directors understand that the most avant-garde as well as the most effective stagings can be achieved through the rediscovery of a realism based on Wagner's own?

Das Rheingold admittedly does not offer the greatest scope for dramatic action, but in Bayreuth, Loge, not Wotan, was its outstanding performer; when the two of them were in Nibelheim, like Virgil and Dante in Hell, Wotan simply looked on lamely. *Die Walküre* requires some simulation of involvement, yet Brünnhilde's annunciation of Siegmund's death, in the opera's most moving scene, was a study in nonchalance. The first act also lacked dramatic tension, largely because the triumvirate of principals spent too much time seated. Weary though they are supposed to be—and may very well have been in private life— one wonders whether Hunding would have relaxed so completely in the presence of an unknown stranger. And surely Siegmund and Sieglinde would have been able to sing better if at least on their feet.

After all of Siegmund's strenuous invocations for assistance in extracting the sword, he later showed little interest in it; rushing into Sieglinde's arms, he let it fall with a clatter that would have wakened Hunding despite the extra drugs in his sleeping draught. The latter part of the act, incidentally, is more conventionally operatic than any other in the *Ring*: voices are employed traditionally, in arias, and with high-note climaxes and even embellishments. On the other hand, the earlier scenes are remarkable for their use of pantomime, the oboe singing Sieglinde's thoughts, the cello Siegmund's. As for Hunding, he reveals his own, in "asides," no doubt because the quintet of tubas associated with him would be excessively loud; but he does this *sotto voce*, another concession to convention.

Wagner was correct in insisting that the *Ring* should be performed cyclically only, and as an entity. In the perspective of the whole, that which seems to be disproportionate in the individual operas disappears. Thus Fafner's part in *Siegfried* may seem too protracted when that opera is given by itself, but this impression is dispelled when *Das Rheingold* is still vivid in the memory, and, with it, the importance of the Giants as the autochthonous earthlings with precedence over the Gods. The connections and cross-references are also strikingly effective when the four operas are heard in sequence—as evidenced in even so simple a case as the storm music at the beginning of *Die Walküre*, following hard upon Donner's motif at the end of *Das Rheingold*.

Above all, to hear the music chronologically is to follow the composer's amazingly consistent and rapid growth. Each scene —and almost every page—displays greater mastery than the one before. In *Das Rheingold*, for instance, the music still comes to dead ends, Wagner not yet having acquired his great skill in avoiding perfect cadences. His ever-expanding technical resources are not always matched by his dramatic material, however, and since love is generally a more promising subject than dragons and not-very-jolly giants, the first act of *Die Walküre* remains the most affecting in the *Ring*, until the final scene in *Siegfried*. *This* Siegfried, incidentally, gave a remarkable performance on the hammer, striking every blow of his anvil chorus exactly as notated; in fact, his sense of rhythm was so much more highly developed than his sense of pitch that he would have made a better impression in the percussion section.

The difficulty with *Götterdämmerung* is precisely in its infinitely superior musical level. At times the music seems almost too grand for some of the drama, particularly in the second act, where the suspension of disbelief in the story requires a considerable effort, as when Brünnhilde attributes Siegfried's failure to recognize her not to an enemy's wiles but to Siegfried's own treachery. As Wotan's daughter, only recently deposed from demi-godhood, she surely must recall something of the trickery and magic in the world of her past. Moreover, she is, or until very recently was, more aware than anyone else of Siegfried's natural innocence.

As for Siegfried's lack of suspicion about the strangeness in Brünnhilde's behavior on seeing *him,* that is easier to explain, stupidity being a trait of his to which the audience has become accustomed. At Bayreuth, the *Götterdämmerung* staging was unusual in that the Gibichungs, a primitive people, moved in perfectly drilled S.S. platoon formation; and in that the final scene —in which Madame Flagstad departed with a live horse when this writer first saw the opera—is now realized entirely by cinematography (through back-projection), and so successfully as to suggest that film should be employed in a great deal more of the *Ring.*

Unlike the *Ring,* the *Tristan und Isolde* was a new production, although not a deeply memorable one. But if the weaknesses in August Everding's staging outweighed the strengths, without adequate voices in the title parts, what can the visual dimension offer except some diversions? "There is virtually nothing in the Second Act but music," Wagner wrote—in a letter that brilliantly defines the distance between himself and all other opera composers: "I have been criticized for failing to include a glittering ball during which the lovers would hide themselves in some shrubbery, where their discovery would create a scandal." The voice of the Bayreuth Isolde suited her youthful song, *"Das wär ein Schatz,"* but was unequal to the wrath which the part requires. No doubt realizing this limitation, Everding created a girlish princess and a sisterly Brangäne —though hardly a subordinate one, which tends to make the switching of the potions predictable.

The sail on Tristan's ship was obtrusive but of no help even for separating Tristan's and Isolde's quarters, let alone the dramatic levels. The current version at the Metropolitan Opera is far superior in this—as in other respects, including the use of psychedelic lighting after the lovers swallow the potion, and the surrounding of their heads in a medallion of light. At the Metropolitan, too, King Mark heads the procession boarding the ship to greet his bride (as the libretto requires), thus identifying himself to the audience before the scene in which he surprises the lovers.

But *does* King Mark discover Tristan and Isolde *in flagrante delicto?* Not according to Elliott Zuckerman,[4] for whom the music represents a *coitus interruptus.* So it might be in the opera, but the Prelude is music's most unmistakably explicit representation of the fully consummated act. And however that may be, the Prelude remains newer than any music that followed it, at least until *Le Sacre du printemps,* whose novelty is in the different dimension of rhythm. In a letter to Mathilde Wesendonck, Wagner described the baffling effect of the Prelude on a Paris orchestra in 1860: "It was so incomprehensibly new to the musicians that I had to lead them from note to note as though prospecting for precious stones in a mine." But what did those players make of the composition as a whole—if any of them heard it as a whole? And what did they think of this form, which disregarded the right angles, exact duplications, full closes, and rhetorical contrasts of diatonic and chromatic that had comprised the substance of music until that time? Finally, did any of them feel the new ecstasy in it? "Really good [performances] would send people mad," Wagner wrote.

What a relief, after Wagner's Teutonic theology, is his mysticism. How welcome, after the monsters of the *Ring,* are his humans. And how much more haunting is this music. No wonder that when composing the second act he wrote: "I have never done anything like it. I am utterly absorbed in this music . . . I live in it eternally."

4. *The First Hundred Years of Tristan* (New York, 1962).

*P*ARSIFAL:

THE WORSHIP OF WAGNERISM

Si c'est l'amour divin, je le connais.

—*Charles de Brosses on Bernini's* Saint Teresa in Ecstasy

The Metropolitan's 1974 season *Parsifal*, the recent release of a superior recording[1] of the opera, and the publication of a monumental critical edition of the score[2] provoke re-examination of a masterpiece whose music is ever more highly regarded even as a wider audience is beginning to understand that the drama's underlying philosophy is truly repugnant.[3] In no sense is *Parsifal* a decline; on the contrary, Wagner's musical powers are at their pinnacle here. The importance of stage action is reduced, but the musical rendering of the drama is more self-sufficient than ever before—of necessity, given the large part played by transformations that are uniquely within the power of music to express.

During *Parsifal*'s composition (1877–1882), Wagner's musical language continued to evolve and his affective and emotional range to expand. He was still discovering new, more liquescent chord sequences and intensifications of sound colors, fulfilling his promise that the instrumentation would be "like layers of clouds which part and then re-form." The orchestral blends and separations are without precedent. But while the reputation and historical importance of *Tristan* have long been established, it is only recently, and to a large extent through Debussy and Schoenberg, that the profound influence of *Parsifal*

1. *Parsifal*, conducted by Georg Solti, with René Kollo, Gottlob Frick, Dietrich Fischer-Dieskau, Christa Ludwig, Zoltan Kélémén, Hans Hotter. London Records OSA-1510 (5-record set).
2. *Parsifal*, Volume 14 (score) and Volume 30 (documents) of the *Complete Works of Richard Wagner*, edited by Martin Beck and Egon Voss (Mainz, 1972).
3. See Robert Gutman's *Richard Wagner* (New York, 1968).

on the beginnings of twentieth-century music has been recognized. *Verklärte Nacht* and the final Adagio in *Lulu* are inconceivable without the Prelude to the third act of *Parsifal*, as are *Pelléas* and *Erwartung* without other parts of Wagner's opera.

Concerning the performance, the recording, and the publication, the production at the Metropolitan warrants mention if only because it succeeds in imposing the Theater of the Absurd on opera's ranking solemnity. Thus the great bells knelling the death of the king and the hour of the Crucifixion have been replaced at the Met by a species of electric door-chimes in a different key from that of the orchestra, making Gurnemanz's *"Mittag"* sound like first call for lunch on the S.S. *Bremen*. The chorus, too, within moments of most of its entrances, manages to drift into excruciating microtonal regions which it would never have been able to find if demanded by the score.

Yet the jarrings from these and other musical *faux pas* are minor compared to the visual discordances. Klingsor's spear, looking about as lethal as a paper airplane and effortlessly plucked from the air by its intended target, raised titters that turned this dramatic and musical crisis into a farce. And Klingsor's garden, an ithyphallic fantasy at the Met—pistils and stamens like necks and corks of giant champagne bottles—was in radical disagreement with the Pre-Raphaelite tableaux of the rest of the opera. The Flower Maidens' falsies, moreover, worn outside and just above nature's realities, suggested a Jean Genet drag scene with Klingsor as the transvestite madame. (Although Klingsor is self-castrated, his *"Er ist schön, der Knabe,"* with the lip-smacking appoggiatura on the "K," seems to invite a pederastic interpretation of him.) And finally, though the period of the opera is that of the Moorish conquest of Spain, the Met dressed the Grail Knights of the last scene like contemporaries of Velásquez, or so it seemed in the eerie glow of the blood-filled chalice.

The Solti recording far outclasses its predecessors both in the quality of its cast, chorus, orchestra, engineering, and in the performance. The most recent competitor, the DGG album conducted by Boulez, offers compensations in rhythmic precision but distorts the music beyond justification, being shorter by an hour than Toscanini's, and by a half-hour than Solti's—who is never too slow. Boulez's speed record is as pointless in relation to the character of the opera as is his staccato articulation. The woodwind chords in measures 17–19 of the Prelude, for example, are traditionally played with a minimum of separation— and rightly, according to the phrasing in Wagner's manuscript. But Boulez cuts these notes to about half of their written lengths, thus producing a peculiarly asthmatic effect. No doubt this style was adopted in reaction to the usually turgid conducting of the opera, but the antidote simply substitutes one kind of abuse for another.

The new edition of the score, having been sponsored by Volkswagen, may be a penitential offering in atonement for noise and air pollution. But whatever the reason, the publication's technical attributes—print, paper, size, binding, readability—are as commendable as is its scholarship. To illustrate the thoroughness of the latter, Wagner's comments taken down by two assistants during rehearsals for the premiere (July 1882) are reproduced in parallel columns filling sixty-three pages. Some surprising discoveries in the new score await the musician, especially in the revelation of differences between the holograph and the first edition. The strings at the beginning of the Prelude, for example, were *not* muted in Wagner's manuscript, while the all-important horn part in measures 60–64 was added at a later date. This may seem like pedantry, but it is mentioned because alterations of this size indicate the extent to which experience could induce the composer to revise his conception of color and balance.

One other recent publication should be noted, Professor Henry Kratz's monograph, *Wolfram von Eschenbach's "Parzival": An Attempt at a Total Evaluation.*[4] The book is long, and Wagner-

4. Bern, 1973. It should be mentioned that the best-known English translation of Wolfram's early-thirteenth-century classic is by Jessie Weston, author of *From Ritual to Romance* (London, 1904). A more recent version is that by Charles Passage and Helen Mustard (New York, 1961).

ians can skip much of it (including such anachronisms of psychoanalysis as the classification of the twelfth as the most phallic
century because of a prevalence of erect spears). Yet Kratz
illuminates the dramatic structure of the opera. According to
him the main subjects of Wolfram's epic are the problems of
dynastic succession, the transference of power, and the establishment of sovereignty through ownership of the Grail. Wagner
read the sixteen books of Wolfram's poem in 1845, and the
composer's prose and other writings in the years after that
explore these same questions of property (in which Wagner was
a disciple of Proudhon and perhaps of Marx[5]) and leadership
(Wagner's Parsifal, though a man of destiny, becomes the head
of the Grail community by common consent).

At the same time Wagner developed a new dramatic formula
which required the spiritualization of history through legend.
In Wagner's *Barbarossa*, the Christian king's power is sustained
by a mysterious hoard identified with both the Nibelungen gold
and the Holy Grail—which sounds like a subject for Max Weber.
From the beginning, therefore, an essential connection exists in
Wagner's mind between *Parsifal* and the *Ring*, and the transpositions and parallelisms between the works are much stronger
than is generally acknowledged. Whether or not Wotan is reborn
in Titurel, Siegmund in Amfortas, Siegfried in Parsifal, Alberich
in Klingsor, Brünnhilde in Kundry, the ideas of these protagonists—renunciation of love as a means to power, the redemption of the world by innocent heroes—are embodied in both
works. Furthermore, both dramas end with expiations, that of
the *Ring* in pessimism, except for the survival of "immutable
justice," that of *Parsifal* in hope, the wound of suffering humanity having been healed.

Nothing is new about all of this, but what is important to
consider are the musical parallels. In fact, so freely does the
composer of *Parsifal* seem to dip into the *leitmotif* index of the

---

5. In view of Wagner's political collaboration with Bakunin in 1849, it is
unlikely that the composer had *not* read Marx, though it is in their anti-Semitic
writings that Wagner and Marx most resemble each other.

tetralogy that one sometimes wonders if Wagner had thought that he was composing a fifth *Ring* opera. Thus Kundry's awakening in Act Three, especially in the descending thirds in the clarinets at the change of key, could easily be mistaken for a passage from *Das Rheingold;* Amfortas's *"Der du jetzt in göttlichem Glanz"* might have come from the third act of *Die Walküre,* and Gurnemanz's *"Heil der, mein Gast"* from the first act of the same opera; and the resemblance between the music of the Flower Maidens and that of their aquatic, Rhenish sisters, at the beginning of the last act of *Götterdämmerung,* is obvious. But this list could be continued *ad infinitum,* if it were to include symbolisms, such as the one of the spear motive moving upward in the "Christian" drama and downward in the pagan.

With an unerring sense of the anthropological structure in Wolfram's poem, Wagner took from it the concept of the two disabled monarchs, the "Fisher King" dying of old age, and his mortally wounded son.[6] If the anthropological process were *not* of the utmost importance, the composer might conveniently have excluded the dying king, Titurel, and concentrated on Amfortas, his son. By retaining the father, Wagner builds the problem of dynastic succession into the structure of the drama and makes it the frame for the metaphysical subject of redemption through Divine Grace. It is this structure, in which oratorio-like scenes of ritual and pageantry enclose the real opera in the second act, that gives the work its dramatic cohesiveness.

Wagner's instincts for the drama were more reliable than those for its religious subject matter. The latter is vague in *Parsifal,* to be sure, though sufficiently clear to serve the composer's needs in evoking the mystical atmosphere of a sacramental service. The theology of the knights is not Athanasian, no reference being made to a triune God, but it could be that of a sect which had degenerated into heresy as a result of isola-

---

6. Writing to Frau Wesendonck in 1859, the composer described Amfortas as "My third-act Tristan with an unimaginable intensification."

tion. On the other hand, the "pure innocence" of the future priest-king and rescuer of the Grail is, at least in Wagner's context, only partly a Christian virtue. In short, his notion of purity of character seems to be limited to chastity—which by no means distinguishes the Christian from the faithful of other religions—and to a state "beyond good and evil," which is definitely anti-Christian. "What is 'good'?" Parsifal asks, after shooting the swan, and the answer is simply a reflection of Wagner's anti-vivisectionism. So, too, Gurnemanz's discourse before the Good Friday service might have been derived from Schelling's belief that "Oneness with nature was the state of man before the fall." But of the actual tenets of Christian teaching as set forth in the Sermon on the Mount, both the opera and the person are oblivious.

Wagner's knights are Christians by virtue of their belief in the mythology of the Crucifixion, their faith in divine redemption, and their participation in a primitive, nonclerical Mass. This last is "real" only in terms of Wagner's drama, it should not be necessary to say, but after having chosen to depict the principal ceremony of a still-active religion, the composer might at least have prefaced his libretto with the statement that the resemblance was intentional but insignificant. Religious prejudice is one of the reasons that *Parsifal* has not attained the same eminence as *Tristan*—together with a justified bias against the insipid sanctimony that has surrounded the opera since it was first reserved for performance uniquely in the Master's private temple. But "celebration" is a more fitting word than "performance," since applause, considered profane, is still withheld after the first act. The result of this misguided piety is that the opera actually has been regarded as Christian, although the one faith practiced in Bayreuth was and is Wagnerism.

And Wagnerism is the true religion of *Parsifal*. Ironically, it is superior to the opera's sham Christianity, at any rate for the composer's musico-dramatic purposes. Thus his personal *Weltanschauung* provided him with a scheme of opposites offering rich opportunities for contrasts. The difficulty comes because the composer's favorite doctrines are racial purity[7] and male chauvinism, both scarcely more disguised here than in his most odious polemics of the time (*cf. Religion and Art*, 1880). In fact no other work by the musical genius so blatantly trumpets his crank philosophy. And even so, the artist triumphs over the bigot. If *Parsifal* is dramatically weaker than *Tristan*, this is partly because redemption is a state of being rather than an action, partly because the third-act "conversion" of the lover is more convincing than the formal conversion of love's renouncer.

The Knights of the Grail are of course pure, noble, and Aryan, whereas the opera's female population is corrupt, non-Aryan, and menial in class. Klingsor, the archvillain of the piece, is a Jew (as Wagner told Cosima), and so, apparently, is Kundry, his accomplice.[8] These two demonic and supernatural beings also happen to be the opera's most human characters—though the competition is admittedly slight, Parsifal himself having one of the lowest profiles possible to attain and still remain upright.

Kundry, the freak, is one of Wagner's superb creations, and as she herself is timeless, so he almost succeeds in suspending time while she sings. Wagner had already made goddesses, Amazons, and even brides out of women, but none of the others, including Isolde, has Kundry's fascination. In relation to Parsifal she is both seductress and protectress, the latter with a suggestion of Mary Magdalene, for the washing of the feet can only have been intended to evoke a biblical scene, as is surely indi-

---

7. "We must interpret *Parsifal* in a totally different way from the general conception. . . . Behind the absurd externals of the story, with its Christian embroidery and its Good Friday mystification . . . it is not the Christian Schopenhauerist religion of compassion that is acclaimed, but pure, noble blood. . . . The king is suffering from the ailment of corrupted blood. . . ." (Hermann Rauschning, *Hitler Speaks* [New York, 1938], p. 227.)

8. She was Herodias in a previous incarnation, and she resembles some creature in the Hekaloth Books, or the Wandering Jew, having the power to transport herself to any place in no time. Wagner also makes her catatonic, and, if not actually observed from life, this aspect of her behavior is indeed a feat of imagination.

cated by the *zart* music, its beauty bordering on the lachrymose. But there are two Kundrys, the bewitching singer who is Klingsor's slave, and the messenger of the Grail, who is virtually dumb, except for fits of hysterical laughter, a curse for having laughed during the Crucifixion. Her silences and trances increase rather than diminish her mystery.

In comparison, Klingsor is a bit part; he is on stage for less than a quarter of an hour (depending on the conductor), but his music precedes him with such force in the first act, and is so vivid in the second, that he remains indelible. As for the kings, Titurel is too feeble to be very engaging, while the ailing Amfortas poses technical problems, being obliged to simulate constant agony while singing. Vis-à-vis the Grail community, his relationship resembles that of Oedipus to Thebes: both kings are themselves the source of the plagues from which their people suffer. But Sophocles is more practical than Wagner. Not Oedipus but the Theban people are sick, whereas Amfortas is borne on a litter, or staggers about stanching his wound, while the knights appear to be in reasonably good health. This accounts for the brevity of Amfortas's part, at least compared to that of Gurnemanz, who is not really a participant at all but a narrator in disguise. He does not bleed but only bores.

This leaves Parsifal (literally, "poor fool"), whose progress from simpleton to thaumaturge poses the opera's most difficult musical characterization. Wagner casts him in the heroic mold, equipping him with a fanfare motive that is suitably dignifying in slow tempo but when tooted at high speed tends to recall "The Lone Ranger." Boulez's album notes remark favorably on the way in which this motive is "distended" (bloated?) as well as worked into a variety of tempos and meters. But the similar augmentation of Siegfried's horn call in the "Rhine Journey" is a more successful example, and in fast triple-time Parsifal's motive sounds awkward indeed. Wagner overworks this tune. The identity of the hero, decked out like an armadillo at the beginning of Act Three, is supposed to be unknown, but Wagner, who could never keep a secret, announces him at least a dozen times with the motive.

"Too much blood," Nietzsche remarked, and *Parsifal* does seem to be morbidly preoccupied with it, what with a bloodied swan, a bloodstained spear, the incarnadine aura of the Grail, and the bleeding of Amfortas before the audience's eyes. His wound, it should be said, is sexual, punishment for disobedience of the rule of chastity. When Parsifal kisses Kundry at the opera's climax, the implication is that the poison which he tastes, and somehow recognizes as the same one from which Amfortas sickens, is estrual blood. Thus does Wagner signify the uncleanness of Woman. (All except mother, that is, for the Grail is a mother symbol, or perhaps it would be better to say, in this fraternity of knights, a house-mother one.) The Met was once picketed because a monk was shown assassinating Verdi's Don Carlo. By this precedent, Ms. Friedan and associates would be justified in staging a march against any opera house whose repertory includes *Parsifal,* one of the most rabidly misogynistic of all great works of art.

At the same time, any company capable of performing *Parsifal* that does *not* do so should have its subsidies withdrawn. The music is miraculous, more perfectly sustained than any other by Wagner. The contemptible philosophy of the piece offers precisely the dramatic situations that most exactly match his musical language at this summit of his development. Those aforementioned opposites are characterized by, among other devices, an extension and deepening of conventional associations of diatonic and chromatic harmony, except that by the time of *Parsifal* Wagner's language *is* chromatic, the diatonic music in the opera being rarer than one's impression of it; for this reason, no doubt, it stands out in such striking relief.

The other devices are mainly stylistic. Thus the Flower Maidens' scene is a *catalogue raisonné* of the traditional means by which femininity is represented in music, including the *valse* meter, the embellishments (trills, tremolos, curving figurations), the coloration (harp, muted strings, solo violin), and the articulation (staccato and pizzicato), this last to suggest dainty laughter and coquettishness.

Parsifal makes entirely new uses of orchestral color. Debussy

wrote to the young Stravinsky, "You have an orchestral infalli-
bility that I have found only in *Parsifal.*" Surely the Russian
composer remembered the compliment when he later heard the
opera in Bayreuth, and then again in Monte Carlo, after which
he told reporters, "Since *Parsifal* there have been only two
operas, *Elektra* and *Pelléas.*" The instrumentation fascinated
him, and even in the 1920s when he had completely rejected
Wagner—"There is no musical form; Wagner simply submits
the form to the text, and it should be the other way around"[9]—
Stravinsky praised *Parsifal*'s instrumentation.

Without the help of the score, even a very sensitive ear cannot
distinguish the instruments playing the unison beginning of the
Prelude. The violins are halved, then doubled by cellos, a clarinet, and a bassoon, as well as, for the peak of the phrase, an
alto oboe. The full novelty of this color change with the oboe,
both as intensity and as timbre, can be appreciated only after
the theme is repeated in harmony and in one of the most gor-
geous orchestrations of even Wagner's technicolor imagination.
Schoenberg's Five Pieces for Orchestra exploits the idea of varying the sonorities in a unison line, and a whole musical era,
beginning with Webern, annexed this Wagnerian principle.

The heroine of Schoenberg's *Erwartung* owes almost everything to Kundry, dramatically as well as musically, for both
women have mysterious pasts, both are on quests, and both
seek exorcism. Their vocal ranges are the same, and their
laughter, moaning, whispering, and screaming—this last even
on the same notes (a high B to a low C sharp)—are similar.
And *Parsifal*'s influence on Debussy was no less fruitful. Thus
the theme of the first orchestral interlude in *Pelléas* is practically a Xerox of the march theme at the end of Wagner's first
act. More surprising than harmonic and orchestral influences,
however, is that of vocal style. The seraphic music of Wagner's
hero at *"Werd' heut ich zu Amfortas noch geleitet?"* and *"Ich
sah' sie welken"* may well have inspired the *faux moyen-âge*
chanting in *Pelléas.*

9. *Paris-Midi*, January 13, 1921.

Wagner wrote: "The world is taught how to behave itself properly towards all others [*sic*]. But how to behave towards a man of my sort it can never be taught because such a case occurs too rarely." Apart from the question of whether the planet could accommodate more than one Richard Wagner, even this colossal egotism can be forgiven in one who endowed the world with the music of *Parsifal*.

"WINNIE"
AND "UNCLE WOLF"

Not *Winifred Wagner* but *Hitler and Bayreuth* would have been a more appropriate title for Hans Jürgen Syberberg's five-hour film interview[1] with the widow of the composer's only son, Siegfried, the principal subject being not so much the lady herself as her relationship to the Führer during his long involvement with Richard Wagner's Bayreuth. In 1947 a de-Nazification court convicted Winifred of collaboration and forbade her to make public statements, hence this film violates the ruling and breaks a silence of three decades.

Cosima Wagner, the composer's wife, outlived him by forty-seven years, and for about half of this time directed the Bayreuth Festival, which she had revived after his death (1883). Her daughter-in-law, the English-born Winifred Williams, succeeded as director for fourteen more years (1931–1944) of the forty-seven by which she has survived Cosima. Neither

1. Made in April 1975 and first shown at the Cinémathèque in Paris the autumn of the same year.

woman was qualified by experience or talents to undertake the festival's artistic control, though obviously Cosima had the stronger mandate. Siegfried Wagner was nominally in charge during his mother's dotage, but from 1914 through 1924 the festival was suspended, and in the later 1920s (Siegfried died in the same year as his mother, 1930) Winifred's influence seems to have been predominant. The present director, her son, Wolfgang, is married to a woman of scarcely half his age, which would have seemed to guarantee matrilineal rule for at least another generation, except that in 1973 the Bavarian government purchased the Festspielhaus, the family home (Villa Wahnfried), the Wagner Archives, and assumed major responsibility for the festival.

A two-hour version of *Winifred Wagner*, condensed from the original and given English titles, is still so tedious that the prospect of having to see the film in its full Wagnerian dimensions makes one disregard the critics who claim that abridgement means falsification. Ironically, Syberberg's high-minded conditions are themselves partly responsible for the monotony. The camera focuses unrelentingly, and with no pictorial supplementation, on the festival's seventy-eight-year-old former mistress. And instead of following a logical plan of organization—by subject matter, since the same themes disappear and reappear—the film rigidly adheres to the chronology of the five days during which the taping took place.

Clearly Syberberg's aim was to achieve maximum authenticity and candor, but this purpose is defeated by his own tendentious questions and by a moralistic commentary—larded with quotations from Walter Benjamin, Egon Friedell, Thomas Mann, Hannah Arendt, and Erich Fromm—that makes the viewer squirm. At the end, a smiling Herr Syberberg and contented Frau Wagner pose together, signifying that the presentation bears her seal of approval. Yet the film deserves an X-rating, as do all such that lay claim to complete veracity but that, by their very nature, cannot escape the biases of the director.

Despite Syberberg's good intentions and Frau Wagner's sanction, she was nonetheless exploited. For one thing, the filming process at times confuses her. "Imagine keeping those things running like that," she exclaims, indicating the camera and recording equipment, and, once, as if to herself, "I would not say this in public." An inexperienced speaker, especially during a lengthy interview, tends to forget circumstances and to be carried away by a subject. But apart from this, Frau Wagner's life has been so confined to the inbred enclave of Bayreuth—in which, moreover, she reigned supreme for so long—that her views lack perspective.

She is oblivious not only to differing and opposing opinions but also to the outside world. And while not unaware of criticisms of her autocratic management of the festival, and of her flaunting of the friendship with Hitler—"We old Nazis" is one of her favorite locutions—she unquestionably feels that her conduct in both capacities was justified, and that she is not without sympathizers. Though momentarily bewildered by the filming, more often she is consciously appealing to posterity, using the arguments that she was never a political person, and that what Hitler did elsewhere was none of her business. "What was going on in the world did not concern me," she says, bringing to mind a comment by a young German woman in Marcel Ophuls's *Memory of Justice*: "They deliberately did not try to find out."

Yet the "defendant's" position is unfair, if only because the course of the interview is directed by the "prosecutor's" questions, while the commentary looks down on the scene in undisputed judgment. Nor do Syberberg's trappings of "fidelity" —the inadequate lighting, the poor sound, the black-and-white film, the absence of make-up and décors—compensate for the stacked philosophy of the format. These artifices of naturalness might better have been abandoned for a quality of realization and such other alleviating devices as the showing of stills of events and people mentioned by Frau Wagner. A variety of background and some relief from the concentration on her stony face might also have made the film more palatable for its inevitable educational-TV audience.

The preservation of the recorded order of the interviews is obstructively pedantic, Frau Wagner's own time sense being vague and sketchy, while few of her answers depend on sequence or large contexts. When asked for her evaluation of Gustav Mahler—a loaded question, political rather than musical, being wholly unspecific—she strays into an anecdote about a dinner with Alma Mahler and Franz Werfel, quoting a joke by Siegfried Wagner about the paternity of Alma's new baby. But either this child was Manon Gropius, born two years before Werfel became Alma's consort, in which case Winifred's memory was faulty, or else the child was Werfel's premature and short-lived son, in which case Siegfried's tasteless witticism might have been deleted. Or would such tampering destroy documentary validity?

For two hours, and at wart-close range, the camera follows the elderly but robust woman, always alone, usually in an armchair but occasionally standing, once at a desk typing with two fingers, once eating lunch. Her most conspicuous feature is a jutting jaw, emphasized by erect posture and backward tilted head. Her manner is direct, blunt, and, when speaking of Jews, servants, and all social "inferiors" (a not inconsiderable percentage of the population), insensitive to a scarcely credible degree. The voice is husky, and she coughs frequently, but the speech, despite her English upbringing, is without accent. She laughs—at some of Syberberg's questions, at the thought of the "childishness" of such artists as Toscanini—but the audience is amused only once, by her story that after the war she and her friends changed their code name for Hitler from "Wolf" to "U.S.A." The touchiest subjects fail to ruffle her, though she is often stumped for an expression or a way of approach. True to his veristic guidelines, Syberberg does not interrupt, kibitz, correct.

But there is no respite from the woman's dogmatic pronouncements, class and race prejudice, and consuming self-righteousness. She even sees Hitler—"warm-blue-eyed," "kind," "considerate"—only in relation to herself, and when pressed to reconcile these impressions of him with the atrocities of the concentration camps and the realities of the Final Solution, she offhandedly contends that "such things did not come from him but from Streicher and Bormann." Indeed, Uncle Wolf's greatest shortcoming was that "he was too easily influenced by such people." According to Winnie, in fact, Uncle Wolf scarcely appears to have been "anti-Semitic" at all, and

> thanks to his protection, Jewish artists, and the Jewish wives and husbands of Aryan ones, were allowed to participate in the festival even in the late 1930s.

At this point the commentary contradicts her with a horrifying selection from Hitler's own writings on the subject.

Adolf Hitler's spell over Winifred Wagner was cast in the early 1920s. Of his first pilgrimage to Bayreuth, in 1923, she recalls that

> he visited the Master's grave alone, and came back in a state of great emotion saying that "Out of *Parsifal* I make a religion."

While Hitler was in prison she brought food to him, not to mention the paper on which he wrote a best seller, and she invited him to the festival as far back as 1925, when his presence could have had disastrous consequences. These actions alone would seem to indicate what the film bears out: that her interest in him was not primarily for his potential political power, convinced disciple though she was in that sense, but rather that she was in love with him. She is proud and pleased, at any rate, when Syberberg asks about the rumors of a Winnie-Wolf marriage, but she is quick to dispose of a question—thereby suggesting that it might be painful—whether Hitler refrained out of personal consideration for her from ever mentioning Eva Braun. Winnie boasts that Wolf was "a member of the family," an "uncle" to her children—whom he sometimes helped to put to bed at night—and that he stayed in her home. She adds that despite his phobia about women drivers he allowed her to chauffeur him, and that few of her requests were not granted, even during the darkest days of the war. Over and above his dedication to Wagner, it seems indisputable that Hitler came to Bayreuth to see her.

Regrettably, therefore, the film misses an opportunity to fill out the private portrait of Hitler that an expert questioner might have extracted from Winifred Wagner, for it is unlikely that any other living woman knew him so intimately and over so long a period (1923–1945). Although she did not see him after the assassination attempt of July 20, 1944, they continued to communicate, and she was able to recognize when his dosages of antidepressant drugs had been increased. The latter point is an example of an unexplored detail, since it is obvious that she must know more about the subject than appears in her passing reference to it in the film.

But Syberberg fails to pursue even the question of Hitler's musicality, which grew in interest after the war when Heinz Tietjen, Bayreuth's one-time music director, testified that the Führer once complained to him, correctly, that the oboes had played wrong notes (which Richard Strauss, who was conducting, overlooked). When Winnie talks about Uncle Wolf's piano-playing, the audience wants to know just how good it was, as well as what music, other than Wagner's, Hitler may have known and liked—something being indicated about a man who is enthralled by Wagner but perhaps not by Bach, Mozart, or Beethoven. We would also like to know whether Hitler (perish the thought) could sing—anything, that is, besides *Deutschland über Alles*—for if he really was exceptionally musical, perhaps new personality tests and some surveillance should be introduced into our conservatories.

The film reveals how much closer was Hitler's relationship with Winifred Wagner and her family than had previously been known, and how much more profound his association with Bayreuth. In fact, Winnie's son-in-law was the director of the *Kraft durch Freude* organization, which bought up most of the seats during the war and partly filled them with wounded and furloughed soldiers—a sadistic form of rest and recreation, as might appear to some. Near the end of the film Winnie answers the question, "Was Hitler a curse on Wagner and Bayreuth?"

with, "Exactly the contrary"; and undoubtedly she believes in his eventual exoneration, and her own. But when she confesses that "If Hitler were to come through that door, I would be as happy to see him as ever," the feeling is personal, all the more strikingly so because of the absence of emotion during most of the interview.

———

Following the recent reversal of the relationship of genres, the film has been made into a book, and the script should soon be available. Meanwhile, the history of the Wagner dynasty in Bayreuth may be studied in three new volumes of pictures. One of these, *The Wagner Family Albums*,[2] a collection of private photographs, includes views of Hitler with Winifred, and of Hitler with her children. Another, *Richard Wagner in Bayreuth*,[3] is misleadingly titled, little of the book being devoted to the composer and most of it to his heirs and their supervision of the festival. (A reason for the brevity of the section on Wagner may be the imminent publication of the second part of Cosima Wagner's *Diaries*,[4] which center on the Bayreuth period, 1878–1882.) The text, by Hans Mayer, is as intelligent and fair in its analyses of people and events as any that the reader is likely to encounter on the subject, yet silly remarks occur, such as that Siegfried Wagner

> showed a new, freer disposition. The trauma seemed to abate. He died because of this.

Could Siegfried live only when traumatized? And what is the meaning of

> Siegfried Wagner died during the Bayreuth Festival. It was but one of the many ironic setbacks in this seemingly happy and successful life. . . .

2. By Wolf Siegfried Wagner, translated from the German by Susanne Flatauer (London, 1976).
3. By Hans Mayer, translated by Jack Zipes (New York, 1976).
4. The first part, *Die Tagebücher 1: 1869–1877* was published (Munich/Zürich) in 1976.

Admittedly death *is* something of a "setback," but Siegfried's life, on the contrary, must have been profoundly sad, and he was one of the least successful composers of his time.

The documentation by Gottfried Wagner, one of Richard's eleven great-grandchildren, contains new information, but the sources are not identified beyond "The Wagner Archives," and no dates are given for most of the photographs, the choice of which, furthermore, is peculiar. Thus one chapter begins with a reference to the well-known portrait of the loving Cosima looking up into the reciprocating Richard's eyes, yet this picture is nowhere to be found in the book, while the one facing the verbal description is of the widow in old age. Then, too, apart from the cover, only three portraits are offered of Wagner himself: seated, with demonic upward gaze; with his right hand on the shoulder of his young son; and in a Villa Wahnfried "Royal Family" group portrait, in which King Richard, wearing a wide-brimmed summer hat, looks like a diminutive John Wayne. The book does not contain any photographs of Hitler, but Mayer quotes passages from recent publications as evidence that "the new Bayreuth" is by no means de-Nazified. Thus a 1969 biography of Wagner's son actually reproaches Malwida von Meysenbug for her

lack of racist instincts in contrast to the convinced anti-Semite, Siegfried Wagner.

The illustrations that comprise the first half of *Wagner: A Documentary Study*[5] include a generous number in color, of manuscripts, programs, costume designs, paintings, the places and theaters in which the composer lived and worked. The second half of the book is an anthology of writings both by and about the composer chosen by three eminent Wagner scholars. Much less satisfactory is the preface, "Divergences: The Man and His Work," by that more recent arrival among Wagner ideologues and apologists, Pierre Boulez. In an earlier essay,

5. Compiled and edited by Herbert Barth, Dietrich Mack, and Egon Voss, translated by P. R. J. Ford and Mary Whittall (New York, 1975).

"Approaches to Wagner,"[6] Boulez expediently avoided any mention of the composer's controversial doctrines. The subject should have been side-stepped again this time. In any case, readers will be astonished to learn from Boulez that Wagner was "a committed Christian," and that

> . . . Wagner, steeped in the romantic idealism of medieval myths, adds to the political and cultural reaction of the nineteenth century the prejudices of a militant Christian.

The notion of Wagner acting out of Christian belief and principle is patently ridiculous, nor was his anti-Semitism religiously motivated, the earlier brand having been chiefly of the paranoid and scapegoating kind, the latter based on quack anthropology such as Gobineau's *Essay on the Inequality of Races*. Certainly neither manifestation deserves to be dignified by Boulez's term "concept":

> Wagner does represent an amalgam of concepts on which it was only too easy to draw in order to label him the leader of a particularly vicious crusade.

So it was *Wagner*, not "the Jews,"[7] who was maligned and victimized instead.

No less preposterous is the remark that

> a series of misunderstandings converts [Wagner's] work into a narrow-minded symbol of nationalism and racism. . . .

6. *Parsifal* album notes. Deutsche Grammophon, 2713004.
7. A "Letter from Bayreuth," published in *The New Yorker*, September 27, 1976, claims that "Wagner himself hired the brilliant Hermann Levi, a Jew, to conduct the première of *Parsifal* . . . ," but in truth it was King Ludwig who insisted on Levi, against Wagner's wishes, and who would not permit the Munich orchestra to appear in Bayreuth without the Munich conductor. Wagner, for his part, expressed empathic anxiety feelings for anyone having to work under Levi: "[R] remarked to me privately that if he were playing in the orchestra he wouldn't like to be directed by a Jew." (From Cosima Wagner's *Diaries*, July 22, 1882. In *Wagner*, compiled and edited by Herbert Barth, Dietrich Mach, and Egon Voss. New York, 1975.)

But no conversion was possible since the nationalism and racism were already plainly there, even for the broadest minds. The further statement that

> political ideology took hold of Wagner's work and raised it by force as its own banner

implies, of course, that no kindred spirit existed in *Parsifal* or in the composer's contemporaneous writings, such as *Religion and Art*, some of whose tenets, as Walter Kaufmann noted, Hitler was later to enforce by law.

Many comments in the preface on the artistic aspects of Wagner's world are also puzzling. For only one example, Boulez deplores that

> As for architecture, the model of Bayreuth has remained a dead letter—we still live with the Italian-style theater . . . in which . . . the singer's voice attempts to penetrate the wall of sound raised before it. . . .

Which "wall of sound"? Mozart's? Verdi's? Would the acoustical balances and orchestral-vocal rapport of *Figaro* or *Falstaff* benefit from such a subterranean structure as that of Bayreuth?

Incomparably superior to this preface is Boulez's more recent essay, "Time Re-Explored."[8] This deserves to be read,[9] not only for its insights but also as a measure of the evolution of

8. Published in the Bayreuth Festival Program Book, 1976.
9. It is almost unreadable, however, a more clotted, opaque prose being difficult to imagine. Paragraphs, which Boulez does not seem to regard as divisions in the development of his arguments, continue for pages and average about 2,000 words, while almost every sentence is run-on, kept going, so the author must believe, by the insertion of colons and semicolons. But an even worse impediment is Boulez's habit of burying commonplaces in verbal complexities. Thus he writes, "The metamorphoses [of Wagner's motifs] in time depend principally on the moments at which they are employed and on the means of expression of that particular moment" (that is, the composer transforms his motif according to the context). But what can possibly be understood by, "A direct and ineffective proselytism, transmitted by inadequate means, can manifest itself as being thoroughly reactionary"?

Boulez's own views on music. First, however, it must be said that the "re-exploration of time" is simply the familiar idea of a "dialectic" between "the opposition of chromatic and diatonic," which are respectively identified with "fluid and rigid time." Wagner's "re-exploration" is merely a vast enlargement of scale, the principle being as old as the early sixteenth century, thereafter rapidly having been conventionalized. For the rest, some of Boulez's speculations are brilliant, some are highly debatable, and a few are specious, as when he says that

> Wagner has extended the limits of variation well beyond even that [*sic*] which he found in Beethoven.

Obviously Boulez continues to believe that changes in style—though he would not agree that these are such—can be explained as progress.

This new article on Wagner also reveals that Boulez has not changed his mind about the separation of the ideology from the music:

> [T]he dramaturge, the musician Wagner offers a perpetual denial of Wagner the ideologist.

At least the eminent conductor now acknowledges Wagner to have been an "obtuse anti-Semite," and that "his ideological legacy" *was* "adopted by a political power" for whose "tyrannical brutality" Wagner's

> text offered itself as camouflage, [though] his music remained irrefrangible, and that is why his music still lives although his ideology is already no more than a document.

But surely the power of the ideology is reflected in the music, which cannot be entirely dissociated from the dramatic and verbal meaning. If the ideology of *Parsifal* is pernicious, so too, in some degree, is the music, which is not to deny its greatness.

[He] considered himself a genius. He was [a leader], and he believed that by virtue of his special gifts he could command subordination and allegiance. He considered himself removed from the realm of rational criticism by reason of his self-appreciation.

Thus Walter Scheel, President of the Bundesrepublik, in a speech inaugurating the Bayreuth Festival of 1976. Was he referring to Richard Wagner or to Adolf Hitler? It was to the latter, in fact, which contradicts the President's further claim—the fallacy of most apologias for Wagner vis-à-vis Hitler—that it was hardly Wagner's fault that Hitler liked him. For to some extent it *was* Wagner's fault, so long as things equal to the same thing are also equal to one another. And there is truth in Satie's *bon mot* on being told that Ravel had refused the Legion of Honor: "But he should not have done anything to deserve it." To name only one of the charges against Wagner's operas, they are accused of glorifying nationalism and the power of arms.

Like Wagner's grand- and great-grandchildren, Scheel hopes to de-Nazify the festival. But it is doubtful that this can be done. On the other hand, Winnie's *pro*-Nazi confessions could conceivably save Bayreuth. The film unleashed an unexpected reaction among German audiences, some members of which admired her honesty in saying what she and many of them felt, preferring her forthrightness to the rationalizations and ambiguities of the politicians and "intelligentsia." As an instance of this, Syberberg concludes his sermon: "It is easy not to be a Nazi when no Hitler is around."

Winifred Wagner's continuing loyalty to Hitler is totally misplaced, of course, as well as evidence of a seemingly unbalanced mind; otherwise the revelations of 1945 would have compelled her to deplore her former blindness. Yet by exposing Bayreuth as the spiritual center of Nazism, her interview invalidates the argument that Wagnerism and its unfortunate heritage are "divergences." The moral of the film is that the wisest course would be to tell the whole truth and to acknowledge that even the worst of it is an integral part of Bayreuth history. Men and institutions carry the past with them, after all, and to pretend that it is possible to make a new start which is not laid on old foundations is foolish. The acceptance of the full story might at last afford an objective view, and perhaps even transform Bayreuth's oppressive atmosphere of uncritical worship into one of free and intelligent appreciation.

THE GIANT OF BUSSETO

Most creators of Giuseppe Verdi's stature have altered the language, the substance, and the direction of their art. But the giant of Busseto was himself something of an exception to this rule. Nurtured in a popular and regional tradition that he never completely outgrew, he nevertheless fashioned operas with a universality that has been rivaled by only two other composers. Yet his work is self-contained, and his path leads down a cul-de-sac.

For better or worse, contemporary music would be much the same if the composer of *Aida* had never lived, his influence being evident only in exceptional cases such as Stravinsky's *Oedipus Rex*. But Verdi's isolation from the post-Wagner, Debussy, Second Viennese School "mainstream"—if that is what it should prove to be—can be explained by the nature of his genius, that fusion of prodigious lyric and dramatic gifts expressed in a melos so indigenously Italian as to be untranslatable. Nor are the other dimensions of his music (formal, harmonic, rhythmic, coloristic) innovatory in a way that could be readily transmitted. Yet Verdi's circumscribed universe has never seemed more appealing and the cultist progressivists never more ineffectual in their efforts to extirpate his pre-Boito work by treating it as a joke. The last laugh, and not only the one which is set to such glorious music in *Falstaff*, would seem to be Verdi's.

———

Perhaps the inattention paid to Verdi is at last beginning to be repaired. But not a single one of his operas is available in an accurate, let alone a critical edition, and many of the countless mistakes in his scores remain uncorrected since the first printing. Worst of all, only nine of the operas are obtainable in full scores, as if the orchestral role—the textures and colors, dynamics and volumes, doublings and interactions with voices—were of no importance. This need for proper texts is especially deplorable now that recordings of a majority of the early operas are available, a phenomenon that can be explained only by the proliferation of recordings of the later ones. Had Verdi been German, a *Gesamtausgabe* would long since have appeared, together with facsimiles of sketches, variorums of changes and revisions, complete scores of alternate versions, and a *Kritischer Bericht*. As it is, the German editions of the orchestra scores are superior—if one overlooks such introductory comments as the following to the Philharmonia pocket *Partitur* of *Rigoletto*:

> The work achieves true dramatic expression notwithstanding the typically Italian character of its music.

Insofar as English editions are concerned, Verdi's correspondence has been more disgracefully neglected than his scores, although it is among the most illuminating of any by a great composer about his art. Only a few hundred of the letters have been translated,[1] and despite the fact that some sixty years have passed since the publication of his letter copybooks—that indispensable source covering all but the first years of Verdi's life as

1. The dust jacket of Charles Osborne's *Letters of Giuseppe Verdi* (New York, 1972) calls it "the first book in the English language to be devoted to Verdi's letters," but the English edition of the Werfel-Stefan selection, which is larger than this one, appeared more than thirty years ago (1942).

a composer—apparently no English version is even contemplated. The same is true of the *Carteggi verdiani,* of the Muzio-Barezzi correspondence, and of those classic and compendious Italian biographies that include firsthand material. Surprisingly, even the Verdi–Boito correspondence, outlining the story of one of the most fascinating collaborations in the history of music, has not yet been fully published in English.

Nor is this a matter of mere quantity enlarging insignificant biographical detail. Alessandro Luzio, editor of the *Carteggi,* characterized the letters to Ghislanzoni,[2] the versifier of *Aida,* as "a marvelous course in musical aesthetics in action"—although a more comprehensive description would be "a course in opera construction, words-and-music, and music history." No less absorbing are the letters to the other librettists, Piave, Cammarano, and Somma—the might-have-been co-author of *King Lear,* that masterpiece *dis aliter visum*—as well as those to publishers, impresarios, and performers. Yet even the Italian editions of the correspondence include only Verdi's side of it. Luzio had not based his observation on a reading of all of Ghislanzoni's letters, without which many points in Verdi's are not completely intelligible.

———

Yet some new and forthcoming publications, together with studies presented at the International Verdi Congresses, indicate that a more just appreciation of the composer and his work may at last be imminent. The most eagerly anticipated is Hans Busch's documentation of *Aida,*[3] a work-in-progress that will include more than eight hundred letters relating to the opera. Professor Busch is exceptionally qualified for this challenging task, being at the same time an imaginative stage director, a cultivated musician from a renowned musical family, and a Verdi scholar with few peers.

2. Twenty-five of these, of a known thirty-five, have recently been acquired by the Pierpont Morgan Library, New York.
3. To be published by the University of Minnesota Press.

Among the other good omens, meanwhile, are William Weaver's translations of the seven most popular librettos.[4] His versions seem to be the first to avoid the stilted style and inverted word order usually associated with opera translations. An odd publishing idea (who would think of encumbering himself in the theater with a heavy volume that includes the texts of six operas *not* being performed?), the book might be useful to buffs of opera recordings seeking painless methods of increasing their Italian vocabularies. Mr. Weaver's non-singing versions consistently improve on earlier ones. To give a single example, he renders Aida's *"Pietà ti prenda del mio dolor"* as "Have pity on my grief," which reaches the point more directly than the standard version's "Let pity for my sorrow move you."

Another hopeful portent is Julian Budden's study of the early operas.[5] In fact this book towers above all others in English on any aspect of Verdi. Budden is an erudite expositor not only of Verdi's own growth and distinguishing qualities but also of the structures, contents, and conventions of opera in general during the years when he was learning his art. It is to be regretted, however, that the author has not published his second volume together with the first, since a large book devoted entirely to the lesser-known operas may not find the readership it deserves.[6]

Budden's knowledge is impressive, and his insights about the dramatist and the musicians are equally acute. He keeps the larger perspectives of his subject in sight, furthermore, as in the chapter on *Rigoletto*, where he notes:

One looks in vain in Verdi's writings for any consistent statement of his dramatic ideals. They varied according to the

4. *Seven Verdi Librettos*, with English texts (New York, 1975).
5. *The Operas of Verdi: From "Oberto" to "Rigoletto"* (New York, 1973).
6. Charles Osborne's *The Complete Operas of Verdi* (New York, 1970) offers plot summaries, biographical contexts, and matter-of-fact descriptions of musical data. One novelty is that the Requiem is listed as an opera and treated as such stylistically. But Osborne overlooks the outstanding feature of this, namely the way in which Verdi sometimes introduces his vocal soloists like characters on the stage. A striking example is in the orchestral build-up to the bass's entrance at *"Confutatis maledictis."*

needs of his developing creative personality, which is one
reason why as he grew older he repeated himself less and less.

Comparing the sketch for Gilda's *"Tutte le feste"* with the
finished version, Budden both contributes a valuable statement
about Verdi's music as a whole and identifies a derivation:

> [The incidence] of F minor instead of E minor proves yet
> again the absence of large-scale key-systems in Verdi, and at
> the same time makes clear the source of Gilda's melody as the
> duet between Raoul and Valentine in Act Four of *Les
> Huguenots*.

A deduction or two of this quality would have been welcome
in Mr. Wechsberg's popular-style biography,[7] in place of such
remarks as, "There was no pretense about Verdi, nothing
phony." In fact the evidence seems to indicate that Verdi *was*
guilty of pretense, if unconsciously—for example, in the legend
he sought to establish about his youth.[8] But the composer was
more complex and ambivalent than is generally supposed or
than his biographers have wanted to explore. Mr. Wechsberg's
is yet another portrait of Verdi as the wise and honest peasant,
but it is time for an investigation of the conflicting motives, the
"inexplicable" vindictiveness, the domestic tyranny, and the
other manifestations of an almost morbidly secretive personality.
Certainly a clearer understanding of the man would not reduce
his heroic dimensions as an artist.

Two of Mr. Wechsberg's most mystifying statements must be
quoted. He writes that *"Un Ballo in Maschera* should be heard
in Sweden"—is it not?—"where the details are historically and
visually accurate." (!!) And he says that "in Cremona, the
Amatis, the Guarneris and Antonio Stradivari created the magnificent instruments which later sang the beautiful melodies of

7. *Verdi*, by Joseph Wechsberg (New York, 1974).
8. See the article by M. J. Matz, "The Verdi Family of San' Agata and Roncole:
Legend and Truth," in *Atti del Primo Congresso Internazionale di Studi
Verdiani* (Parma, 1969).

Verdi." But one wonders how many poor fiddlers in the opera orchestras of the world have even so much as held a Stradivarius. In Verdi's time, as today, these treasures would have belonged to wealthy collectors or to Heifetzes, who were most unlikely to be using them to play arrangements of *"la donna è mobile."*

Philip Gossett's recent essay on *Aida*[9] is important, both for its analysis of the use of cabalettas in that opera and for a convincingly argued thesis:

> It was largely through his own doing [that] Verdi was faced with a totally conventional text, and it is hardly surprising that his musical response was dependent on earlier models.

Verdi's attitude toward operatic forms in *Aida* was more conservative and more ambiguous than has been recognized by any scholar before Gossett. The composer starts by confiding to his librettist:

> When the action demands it, I would demand rhyme and stanza immediately, using irregular verses in order to say clearly and precisely everything that the action demands.

Before receiving the libretto for the last act, he writes to Ghislanzoni:

> Make the characters say what they must say without concerning yourself about the musical form.

And at another moment in the same correspondence Verdi lets it be known that he is

> open to free recitatives, in preference to stanzas with single metrical patterns.

9. "Verdi, Ghislanzoni and 'Aida': The Uses of Convention," *Critical Inquiry*, Vol. 1, No. 2 (December 1974).

Yet Verdi did not always say what he meant. On the one hand he asks for novelty and originality, exhorting Ghislanzoni to provide "new forms, something different," and inveighing against the regularity and monotony of the conventional in music and verse, even proposing changes of meter and stanzaic length himself. Then, on the other, when actually given more standard structures, he often accepts them, belying his statements and revealing that he feels more at ease with the familiar. The most obstinate of men about other matters, in this one he acquiesces more often than not, making do with what Ghislanzoni sends. Moreover, Verdi himself initiates compromises, sometimes hinting that he prefers the older, established form. Thus he says, in one of the very same letters proclaiming his desire for originality: "Perhaps [the piece] should be changed to make a little cabaletta at the end." Gossett shows that Verdi was responsible for further conventionalizing an already standard Radames-Aida duet, persuading Ghislanzoni to add a parallel stanza for the hero. But Verdi's own comments evince his recognition of the weakness of this piece:

> Perhaps the cause of the failure is in the situation, or maybe it is in the form, which is more common than that of the preceding [Aida-Amonasro] duet. In any case, this succession of eight-verse cantabiles sung by one and repeated by the other will not keep the dialogue alive.

Nor was the composer surprised after the first Milan performance, when a Wagner-minded reviewer criticized the cabaletta as no longer in fashion. Verdi answered, "They scream against conventions but abandon one only to embrace another"; yet he tried to improve the offending number by revising its instrumentation.

As for the words themselves, Verdi insisted that they be "*parole sceniche* . . . carving out a situation or a character." He is forever pretending not to interfere with his librettist's vocabulary but at the same time proposes his own and writes a draft which Ghislanzoni scarcely modifies. Some of the musician's specifications are extremely precise:

Give me four beautiful eleven-syllable verses, and, to make them singable, place the accent on the fourth and eighth syllables.

He was also quick to reject any word or phrase that he found awkward or unsuitable, and in this his instincts were more reliable than those of his librettists. Thus he deleted Ghislanzoni's couplet at the end of the Aida-Amonasro scene, immediately seeing that the heroine's decision for her father over her suitor at this point would weaken the effect of her immolation at the opera's end.

———

If Verdi had collaborated on *Aida* with Boito, the opera would have been less conventional, but would it have been as successful? Whatever the answer, part of the explanation for Verdi's succeeding fifteen years of silence as an opera composer was his dissatisfaction with librettists. His sense of dramatic situation was superior to that of Ghislanzoni and Camille du Locle, who drafted the original scenario. It was Verdi's idea, not his librettists', to insert the reprise of Aida's *"Numi, pietà,"* as well as to involve Amneris in the final scene, thereby injecting an irony that lifts the situation from the level of mere melodrama.

Yet Verdi was slow to institute reforms. For all of the immense broadening of his dramatic scope in the operas preceding *Aida* (*La Forza, Don Carlo, Un Ballo in Maschera*), he was still addicted to such out-of-date devices as those of mistaken identity and of the slave who is really a princess. The principal weakness in Verdi's operas as a whole—until Boito—is in the strain they put on credulity. Shrewd as the composer was in diagnosing mistakes in plot and construction, he seems to have been myopic in this other respect. But Verdi's first concern is subject matter, the suitability of the story for music. Next in importance is character, and he visualizes every gesture of his people as well as the most minute details of external appearance. Plot and structure are last to be considered, and in spite of the attention he gives to them, here he is less successful.

Verdi's greatest power is in the creation of melody. "This entire scene can and must consist of nothing but pure melody," he once wrote to Ghislanzoni, and attempted to distinguish "melody *sui generis*—a declaimed melody, sustained and lofty—[from] the melody of romances or cavatinas. The meter can be as you wish. . . ." But this ignores the origin of the melodic form in the verse form, and of the verse form in the dramatic situation. Thus at one place Verdi recognizes that metrical regularity is unsuited to Aida's "mental state," and he insists that her words be cast in a dramatic recitative. In a letter to Ghislanzoni, the composer observes, "I do not abhor cabalettas"—quite an understatement!—"but wish only that an appropriate subject and pretext be found for them." The subjects and pretexts would become rarer, obviously, with the development of more psychologically sophisticated music dramas.

In this sense *Aida* is simply a good "penny dreadful," whose plot develops not from character but from an accidental situation. In fact the characters are the most uni-dimensional in any of Verdi's operas, with little life apart from their music. If Verdi seems not to have been aware of this, one explanation could be his love for Teresa Stolz. Whatever the extent and truth of their relationship, the most convincing proof that it was a profound one is the intensity of his inspiration in *Aida,* in which his lyric genius sustains him from beginning to end, and at such heights that the shallowness of the characters makes little difference.

With his every resource Verdi attempts to disguise the conventional basis of the opera's construction. Thus the duets are made into dialogues; at any rate the personae sing in rotation more than they do simultaneously. Duets, moreover, are the opera's chief ensembles: it has no fewer than five. Another factor is that although *Aida* is an action-packed spectacular, Verdi moves from event to event with almost cinematographic speed, as if he were in a hurry to dispense with the De Mille aspects of the script in order to reach the intimate drama of the last two acts. But even in the final scene, which more than any other by Verdi invokes his greatest epigone, Puccini, the drama does not linger.

In the same way, the music is no less remarkably tight, and the continuity and unity are greater than ever before in Verdi. Repetition is virtually eliminated; in fact the listener would like *more* of certain melodies (of Amneris's great sweeping "*Voi la terra*," for one), but Verdi's melodic prodigality is evidently such that he can afford to throw these jewels away. No wonder he was never a *leitmotif* composer—which is not to ignore the powerful effect of the returning themes, especially the one at the beginning of the Prelude,[10] as pregnant with anticipation as the first phrase in *Tristan* and always subtly varied on reappearance; he would have found it unbearable to limit himself to reiterations of the same motives.

If the ballet is one of the weakest episodes in the opera, it is nevertheless enjoyable, especially the *Ballabile*, to which Tchaikovsky's *Nutcracker* is surely indebted. But the fault lies in the limitation of the *Kismet* genre. Only in Mozart's time, and perhaps only by that master himself, would it have been possible to compose dances for serious rituals in a temple; by the second half of the nineteenth century the subject was beyond the typical "light" music associated with ballet.

———

Much writing about Verdi is devoted to his employment of voices, both solo and in every kind of combination, and though in this area he had to reform before he could originate, he became the greatest of innovators. Finally, his use of voices is so personal and so inseparable from the roles in his operas that the Verdi singer at his or her best never quite suits any other music except that from which Verdi derived. (In the superb new Angel recording, [11] Fiorenza Cossotto and Placido Domingo are

10. This successor to the *Traviata* Prelude is so marvelous that no one would suggest replacing it with the original overture. But the latter deserves to be heard, at least, and bringing this about should have been one of the first orders of business at the International Verdi Congresses.
11. Recorded in London, 1974, Riccardo Muti conducting, with the Chorus of the Royal Opera House and the New Philharmonia Orchestra (Angel SCLX 3815).

true Verdians; Montserrat Caballé, with her spun-sugar high notes, is not, but she sings with great beauty, nevertheless.)

One seldom-mentioned but distinguished attribute of *Aida* is its instrumentation.[12] The inadvertence can be explained by Verdi's stand against the contemporary tendency toward the expansion of the orchestra and the creation of larger and more complex combinations. His instrumentation is discreet rather than massive, making novel use of solo instruments. Thus the flutes and oboe in *Aida* and the basses in the introduction to the *"Giudizio"* scene are as memorable as the voices they introduce and embellish. Yet Verdi was no less a master of mixed orchestral colors of extreme delicacy. The flute and string sonority in the Prelude to Act Three, for instance, is as "exquisite" as any effect in Debussy, though Verdi's "sensibility" as an instrumental colorist has not been considered even comparable to that of the French master. But then, that aforementioned post-Wagner "mainstream" misses many of the varied beauties of musical art.

VERDI, SHAKESPEARE, AND *FALSTAFF*

Falstaff is not only a masterpiece of opera but, *sui generis*, both a comedy of pure fun and a great work of art. According to Bergson, who considered the function of comedy to be the

12. The same can be said of all of Verdi's operas. One thinks of *Giovanna d'Arco*, for example, with its association of harmonium and percussion with the devils and of the accordion and harp with the angels.

criticism of society and social conventions, such a combination is an impossibility. Other philosophers argue that the principal targets are human deformities, either moral, as in the case of Molière's hypocrites, or physical, the misfit or freak (Cyrano de Bergerac). It is implicit in most comedy that the audience should feel superior to its prototypes on stage, thinking itself less prone to vice, less vain, less stupid.

The exceptions to these definitions are found in certain plays by Shakespeare, and, supremely, not in any play but in the character of Falstaff. It may even be that some of Shakespeare's comedies are the only ones that do not rely on ridicule, in which the humor is free from malice, the irony untainted by bitterness, and the purpose entertainment rather than instruction. Instead of exposing the follies of his characters for the scorn of the audience, Shakespeare offers a variety of amusing scenes with no other aim than the viewer's delectation.

———

But "fun" for its own sake is not usually held in high esteem, nor have many philosophers taken laughter seriously. Studies of it are rare, in fact, and some of the best-known fail to comprehend more than one or another aspect of the phenomenon. Thus Hobbes's much-quoted description, "sudden glory," begins loftily, even suggesting a metaphysical dimension, then disappoints by attributing the exalted effect to a demeaning cause, hypothesizing that laughter arises from a "sudden conception . . . of some eminency in ourselves, by comparison with the infirmity of others." And another observer on the subject, George Meredith, trips conspicuously over his thesis that "Larger natures are distinguished by the greater breadth of their power of laughter." Dante, for example?

Laughter, like most other innate behavior, is culturally determined. Homer's gods are allowed to laugh, but Plato's Republicans should not. Though Aristotle may have composed a poetics on comedy, none survives, and though he discusses comedy in connection with tragedy in the *Poetics*, he does not seem to have given much consideration to the cathartic value of laughter. But where early Greek comedy is ritualistic and political, the Roman brand farcical and pornographic, the medieval moralistic, the comedies of Shakespeare do not fall into any single category. (Certainly *The Merry Wives of Windsor* does not aim to propound a moral truth; Falstaff upbraids Pistol and Bardolph for robbing Dr. Caius, not because it is wrong, but because the manner of the theft was so unaesthetic.) Shakespearian comedies divide, instead, into the serious and the light, according to theme and to whether all's well that ends well. That the light ones are less highly valued today may be owing partly to a prejudice in twentieth-century criticism, over which Chesterton lamented: "A light touch is a mark of strength and not of weakness."

——

According to John Dover Wilson, "In studying the character of Falstaff,[1] *The Merry Wives of Windsor* may be left out of account." The real Falstaff is the one in the *Henry IV* plays, and the most perspicacious analysis of him is still Samuel Johnson's:

> The man thus corrupt, thus despicable, [makes] himself necessary . . . by the most pleasing of all qualities, perpetual gaiety . . . an unfailing power of exciting laughter. . . . [His] wit [is] not of the splendid or ambitious kind. . . . Falstaff is stained with no enormous or sanguinary crimes, so that his licentiousness is not so offensive but that it may be borne for his mirth.

This is also the character of Verdi's Falstaff, and it is created as much by the music as by the words.

The libretto of the opera is an adaptation of the *Merry Wives* play, as is most of the operatic Falstaff's dialogue. Boito drew only slightly from the great historical plays, but his selections are crucial. In the opera, the latter part of Falstaff's monologue on honor comes from *Henry IV*, Part One, while other interpola-

1. See also Morgann's essay *On the Dramatic Character of Sir John Falstaff*, London, 1777.

tions include: the image of Falstaff as a slender youth in the old, fat Falstaff's courting song to Mistress Ford, this from *Henry IV*, Part One; Falstaff's third-act encomium on wine, borrowed from *Henry IV*, Part Two; and, in the opera's final scene, the line "My wit creates the wit of others," derived, in essence, from *Henry IV*, Part Two.

Boito's libretto deletes more than it adds, and telescopes, concentrates, simplifies to meet the demands of converting spoken to musical drama. In reshaping the structure he reduces the number of episodes as well as the number of characters. One reason for these changes was to match each role with another in the same vocal range; thus Falstaff and Ford are baritones, Fenton and Caius tenors, Mistress Ford and Nannetta sopranos, Mistress Quickly and Mistress Page mezzos.[2] Since Falstaff's exploits in the *Merry Wives* took place in a five-act frame, awkward for operatic purposes, Boito fashioned a classical three-act Italian comic opera. No doubt the story lent itself so easily to its new form because it was originally derived from Boccaccio situation comedy. But as Boito wrote:

To make the joyous comedy live from beginning to end, to make it live with a natural and communicative gaiety, is difficult, difficult, difficult, though it must seem simple, simple, simple.

Boito, moreover, adapted as well as translated Shakespeare's language. Verbal humor is a part of the merriment in the *Wives*, and the play brims with current phrases, puns, neologisms, malapropisms—such as Mistress Quickly's "she's as fartuous a civil modest wife," which anticipates not only Sheridan but Joyce. Some of Boito's linguistic adaptations were made merely to improve the sound of the corresponding words in Italian, as when he changed the hour of Falstaff's assignation with Mistress Ford. But, at another extreme, Boito takes the liberty of reversing the view that a man's corpulence causes him to sink. In the

2. Curiously, Mistress Page's husband is never mentioned, nor is it made clear that Mistress Quickly is Doctor Caius's servant.

play Falstaff says that he was saved from drowning only by the
shallowness of the water: "You may know by my size that I have
a kind of alacrity in sinking." Yet in the opera he asserts that
"If this puffed belly didn't float me, I would surely have
drowned."

In at least one place Boito successfully rivals Shakespeare's
wordplay. This is in the opera's final scene, where Falstaff answers
the wives' prayer, *"Domine fallo casto!"* ("Lord make him
chaste!"), with *"Ma salvagli l'addomine"* ("But save his abdomen"). Verdi embroiders the joke by having the wives intone a
taunting chant that overtly refers to the *Hostias* in his Requiem,
and by accompanying the tune with an imitation of an organ in
the woodwinds. But making fun of himself provides Verdi with
some of his sliest humor. Bardolph and Pistol sing their mock-
penitential *"Falstaff immenso!"* in the same rhythm and key as
Aida's *"Immenso Fthà"*; Mistress Quickly's *"Povera donna"* obviously alludes to Violetta's self-pitying scene in the first act of
La Traviata; and Ford expresses his jealousy in an aria reminiscent of *Otello*.

In adapting the *Wives* to opera, Boito supplied the basis for
these and other parodies partly by renewing certain features of
the Rossini tradition. *Falstaff*, in fact, is a virtuoso's treatise on
musical style, spanning Italian musical history from fifteenth-
century antiphon to canon, fugue, and baroque instrumental
forms. By the time he wrote the opera, Verdi's range was so
great that he could even celebrate such a deity as Mozart, in the
revels of the last scene. Elsewhere, Beethoven's boldness of
imagination is recalled in the swaggering music expressing Falstaff's elation at the prospect of his conquest of Mistress Ford.

———

For many years Arrigo Boito, poet, composer, librettist, ardent
reformer in art and politics, and, above all, Verdi's angel, must
have seemed to the giant of Busseto more like his demon. When
the two men first met, in Paris in 1862, Boito was only twenty,
and since Verdi immediately commissioned him to write the text

of a cantata, the older man surely had a profound intuition of the younger one's gifts. But two years later Boito, writing for a French periodical, issued a manifesto that Verdi must have interpreted as a personal attack. The document advocated:

1. The obliteration of formula.
2. The creation of form.
3. The employment of the most comprehensive tonal and rhythmic development possible at present.
4. The highest incarnation of the drama.

But is it not probable that in some degree Verdi recognized Boito to be right? After all, the author of *Il Trovatore* complained that he was a prisoner of the most debased operatic traditions, that some of his greatest efforts were flawed and even ruined by outlandish plots and inane dialogue. Perhaps Verdi may also have sensed that his own liberator might be this same Boito. But that could hardly have seemed conceivable during most of the fifteen years after *Aida*, when Verdi produced no operas but did spend time sparring with his future collaborator, although indirectly, through publishers and friends. When Boito's *Mefistofele* failed at La Scala, Verdi was not above remarking that he had nothing against the "Music of the Future" providing its composer had some music in him in the first place.

The story of the way in which Verdi and Boito eventually became opera's greatest team is well known, but the "dynamics" of the relationship remain an enigma. Despite Verdi's artistic refinement, and his knowledge of music, literature, history, and the visual arts, especially in relation to the world of opera, he retained some of his peasant traits. Boito, on the other hand, was a cosmopolite, a linguist, and, though partly Polish, a German-minded intellectual who wrote a book about Mendelssohn (with whom, strangely, he identified) and translated *Tristan* into Italian for Wagner. To have inspired Verdi, Boito must also have had a forceful personality, and his work as a librettist, at least of *Otello* and *Falstaff*, is *sans pareil* and worthy of the originals. In the following description of the composer on his deathbed,

Boito even appears to have been infused with some of Shakespeare's power:

> [Verdi] looked downward and seemed to weigh with his glance
> an unknown and formidable adversary and to calculate mentally
> the forces needed to oppose him.

———

The *Falstaff* audience must grasp the meaning of every word. Of all operas, it is the least able to be appreciated by simply reading a synopsis, so perfectly do the words and the music complement each other. An example occurs in the monologue on honor. Being sung without accompaniment, Falstaff's *"l'onore"* and all of his inflections are easily understood. But the musical setting invests the verbal expression with levels of meaning beyond the spoken word. Falstaff sings *"l'onore"* in his upper register, which shows his indignation at Bardolph and Pistol for having used and sullied a term reserved for knights like himself. His voice falls an octave and grows softer out of shame as he curses them: *"ladri"* ("thieves"). But the relationship between the notes and tonalities for the two words says more than the words themselves, and in this respect the music adds articulateness even to Shakespeare.

This is not to question the "pure music" concept but simply to say that the listener who fails to understand the words will miss important aspects of the music's dramatic purposes. He may also misconstrue meanings in a way that is not likely in any other Verdi opera. Thus Mistress Ford and Mistress Page, reading aloud their identical love letters from Falstaff, match their suitor's most florid language with a "grand" melody. It is not blatantly parodistic, and it is a good tune, yet Verdi clearly intends a burlesque, as the exaggerated concluding trill of the female singers confirms.

The musical and verbal pace is swifter than in Verdi's tragic operas. Arias are compressed into a few measures, recitatives condensed so that a few lines of text are given in a rapid repetition of notes on a single pitch, as if the composer were eager to be done with them. But, in the first place, the opera begins *in medias res*—as well as on the second beat, which immediately creates the requisite atmosphere of turmoil and does so even more vividly than the antics on stage.

The listener must also hold in abeyance his preconceptions about the nature of melody, for nothing could be further from the truth than the pronouncement of an eminent German musicologist that "in *Falstaff*, the purely melodic element is set aside in favor of declamation." The amount of expansive lyric music is naturally smaller than in Verdi's earlier operas, but that may be attributed as much to the requirements of the genre as to an old man's shortness of ardor or breath. The lengths of the set pieces for Nannetta and Fenton, who provide the romantic interest, are, in context, perfectly proportioned, even though the listener would like to have had more of their music.

———

The melodic element is omnipresent, in fact, being determined neither by length nor by the characteristics of Verdi's earlier music but by fragments of tunes and the relationships of a few notes; thus Mistress Quickly's cadential *"Povera donna"* suggests an entire aria and is used as a refrain throughout the opera, where it serves to identify and to unify. But Verdi, the musical Midas, can turn even a single note into melody, as the latter half of the monologue on honor illustrates. In this one-man catechism, Falstaff asks the questions and then answers them: "Can honor set a leg?" "No." Et cetera. The "no" is melodic in that it resolves the harmonies to which Verdi has set the questions. These, incidentally, demonstrate one way in which words suggested rhythm and melody to Verdi, although our musicologist would undoubtedly label the result "declamation." The first question becomes an important tune with which Verdi ends the first act.

The music of *Falstaff* dances as well as sings. Mistress Quickly's *"Reverenza,"* for example, is one kind of minuet, the wedding pantomime in the final scene another. The music of the "Fates" is subtitled *Danzetta* in the score, but all of the midnight revels, beginning with the entrance of the "Nymphs," are ballets. Much of the remainder of the opera could be choreographed, too, including the women's trios, some of the orchestral preludes and vocal ensembles, and even Sir John's Act One exit piece, bespangled with brass as it is and moving with an elephantine grace. The heritage from Rossini is evident in some of the music's kinesthetic impulses, but the balance between tradition and invention in this instance is heavily tipped on the side of the latter.

Verdi transformed his language in his final opera even beyond the exigencies of the new comic style. True, he was never a harmonic experimenter and was apparently unaffected by contemporary developments in the use of a palette of newer chords and chord progressions. But the rate of harmonic change in *Falstaff* is rapid, the chromaticism of some of the music is intensified, and the movement from one key to another is free, with little or no preparation. An instance of this last occurs shortly before the exit of the three women at the end of the first scene of Act Three, in a section of descending sequences which pass through nearly a dozen parallel triads—an effect, though all Verdi's own, associated with French music of a slightly later date. But if Verdi is not interested in stretching the bounds of tonal harmony, he created dissonance by other means. In Falstaff's Act Three wine-drinking scene a flute trill is imitated first by more woodwinds and then, one at a time, by other sections of the ensemble until the entire orchestra is whirling "drunk." Here the dissonance is not only in the simultaneous trilling but also in the appoggiaturas with which each one begins. At the opera's first performances this effect left some listeners unhappy, but no one seems to have analyzed the reason.

———

Verdi added to the vocabulary of comedy in music as his work on the opera progressed, though it should be remembered that the first part to be composed was the fugue at the very end. Trills, both vocal and orchestral, become a feature of the opera's comic style in Falstaff's monologue on honor, but embellishments of all kinds abound throughout. And yet these are less subtle than the rhythmic artifices, the most striking of which is the superimposition of one quartet singing in 6/8 meter on another singing in 4/4. The rhythmic patterns themselves, the rapid scales and so forth that had been staples of comic opera from Rossini and before, are additional ingredients. Verdi's most ingenious stratagem in the rhythmic dimension is no part of the comedy, however, but a device for controlling it. This is the use, in part of Act Three, of a single beat through fast and slow music and music of different meters, in order to intensify the effect of continuity.

The numerous tricks of Verdi's musical humor extend from Falstaff's falsetto to Ford's mockery of opera singers' never-ending final cadenzas. Even so, the orchestra is the largest reservoir for the composer's wit. Examples are endless; if only one is to be mentioned, it should be the eerie effect of a piccolo doubled by violins and cellos two and four octaves below, as a terrified Falstaff contemplates the possibility of growing thin and of therefore no longer being himself. One other effect, an ascending chromatic scale in the horns, evokes the world of Richard Strauss; Verdi introduces it when Falstaff envisions his belly swollen by drowning. But the most spectacular orchestration is in the opera's final scene, where the sonorities are muted and the articulation *"en pointe."*

———

One fundamental criticism of *Falstaff* cannot be avoided since it concerns the opera's dramatic perfection. In the matter of Ford's jealousy, the audience is asked to suspend its disbelief. But belief in the sincerity of his feeling is essential to the plot. Once Ford has seen Falstaff, however, it is quite impossible for the audience to accept Ford's fear of the Fat Knight as a threat to Mistress Ford's hymeneal contract.

A second question arises, at least in this listener's mind: Are the limits of the opera's comic conventions overstepped in the music's unanticipated depth of emotion at the striking of midnight? Falstaff counts the hours out loud and on the pitch of the bell, whose note is also common to each of the ever-changing accompanying chords. The harmony resolves at the final stroke, but Falstaff's part does not and moves instead to an inverted position of the triad, conveying his fear. Although he is a ludicrous figure to behold, in his mantle and Wotan-like hat, his pathos is touching. The importance that the aged Verdi gave to this music suggests that the scene meant much more to him than a routine piece of stage business, for which, after all, a few sound effects would have sufficed. Did that final *"Mezzanotte"* remind him of the lateness of the hour in his own life?

The continuation of the scene, the last in the opera, is as joyful as any in musical drama. And the words from *Henry IV*, Part Two that Falstaff echoes at the dénouement could also be applied to Giuseppe Verdi: *"L'arguzia mia crea l'arguzia degli altri"* ("My wit creates the wit of others").

A "BEAUTIFUL COLOURED, MUSICAL THING"[1]

In all likelihood Oscar Wilde would not have chosen these same words to describe his *Salomé* as transformed by Richard Strauss. Yet despite substantial cuts the opera follows the play and its two major deviations from the Bible: Salomé acts not on her mother's behalf, but on her own, and is put to death at the end. And while the play is seldom given today, the popularity of the opera, attested to by an epidemic of new European productions, is greater than ever. In New York, too, *Salomé* is in the repertories of both houses, the Metropolitan and the Rudel, though the

1. Oscar Wilde, from an unsent letter, Reading Gaol, 1897, to Lord Alfred Douglas.

former is not offering it this season, perhaps because the roster already includes three Strauss operas and a fourth would acknowledge him, at least in number of works performed, as the peer of Mozart, Wagner, and Verdi. But then, Strauss *is* the only other composer whose dramatic pieces, in quantity, currently hold a place on the world's stages.

The sensational elements in *Salomé* have not interfered with its appeal, of course, but the position that the opus enjoys in the by no means crowded company of operatic masterpieces requires another explanation. Not that everyone would agree with this high estimate, yet even the most severe critics concede the pre-eminence of Strauss's creation in the vanguard "expressionist" music of its time. Compared to *Elektra* (1909), with its superior dramatic structure and more compact and consistent score, *Salomé* (1905) is a mere narrative, uneven in musical quality —that of the "Seven Veils," for instance, coming perilously close to *Samson et Dalila*.

Salomé, all the same, is musically a more abundant creation than *Elektra*, and the last scene, its impossible dramatic situation notwithstanding, is the most gripping that Strauss ever composed. The emotional involvement here—Strauss's as well as the listener's—is difficult to account for since the stage tableau, super-ficially if not facetiously regarded, would seem to be no more than "hair-raising." But this is the anomaly of *Salomé*: while the plot and characters are far below the level of tragedy, the music, at the end, provides both tragic feeling and catharsis.

Writing to Strauss after the first Paris performances, Romain Rolland,[2] the composer's confidant, refers to "the pity which you try to feel for your unfortunate heroine." But "pity" is the very last emotion that Salomé inspires, whether or not Strauss sought to evoke it. Nor does the audience feel that she is "unfortunate," at least not in the sense of provoking personal sympathy, though like other dangerous psychopaths she may arouse

2. *Richard Strauss and Romain Rolland: Correspondence, Together with Fragments from the Diary of Romain Rolland and Other Essays*, edited and annotated with a preface by Rollo Myers (Berkeley, 1968).

compassion for her troubled state. In fact Salomé's death is morally and dramatically necessary, and hence a relief. This is not to deny that the tale and the character could be interpreted to make her behavior excusable "by reasons of insanity," but that would require the dramatization of the destructive effect on the young girl of her father's murder by his brother, who later became her stepfather and would-be seducer. The libretto, however, which is little more than unthinking action, makes nothing of this. Salomé is apparently motivated solely by lust and the desire for revenge, a woman spurned, overreacting, and, at the end, exulting in the triumph of her will. Yet the music is full of shadows that suggest what the libretto ignores.

Wilde's characters are scarcely developed to the point of self-awareness, let alone to tragic stature. This may be illustrated by comparing Salomé and Lady Macbeth, who comes to mind because she also dominates and misuses her power over a weak man. But the crucial differences between the two women are that Shakespeare's acts within a moral frame, struggles with her conscience, and, though rationalizing her deeds, survives to experience their consequences. Wilde's, by contrast, lacks even the concept of any principle higher than the gratification of her own desires, while the likelihood that she would ever be disturbed by conscience seems remote. Obviously the ethical development of the two women was largely determined by their different historical circumstances. Lady Macbeth lived in a society whose values were nominally Christian, while Salomé was the product of conflicting cultures and a "mixed marriage," the daughter of a Roman tetrarch and the Queen of Judea. No less important, Shakespeare's villainess is multi-dimensional, Wilde's a mere silhouette. In fact, Salomé is simply a personification of wickedness, and in this respect the drama resembles a morality play.

Why, then, unlike other embodiments of evil, is the Salomé of the opera believable? One answer is that the biblical tale is a part of our culture, consecrated by two thousand years of religion and history, and made vivid by art. Josephus, in the *Jewish Antiquities* (A.D. 93–94), is the first to mention her by name, the Gospels—Mark (6: 16–28), probably writing before the fall of Jerusalem, and Matthew (14: 3–11), who copies him—referring to her simply as the daughter of Herodias. As for Salomé's familiar role in the death of John the Baptist—which doubtless still has significance for some audiences—this was established by Jerome and other fourth-century Fathers. Salomé has been portrayed by artists from Giotto to Caravaggio, Donatello to Titian, the mosaicists of St. Mark's to Moreau, but her greatest fame followed the adoption of John as the patron saint of Florence, even though the city's sculptors and painters who depict his martyrdom reduced her prominence in the story.

In the nineteenth century, Salomé was reinterpreted by, among others, Delacroix, Flaubert, Mallarmé, and Laforgue, this last introducing the idea, of the greatest importance to Wilde and Strauss, of Salomé's kissing the slain prophet's mouth. When Salomé in her terrible soliloquy asks whether the bitterness of this osculation is the taste of love (thereby revealing that she has never experienced the emotion), Strauss succeeds in turning the *mauvais goût* of Wilde's feeble irony into true "redemption through love," the theme of a century of German romanticism of which the composer was perhaps the last exponent.

The Salomé of the opera is also believable in her obsession, so convincingly expressed through the music. But while Strauss could not have been conscious of her aberration as symbolism in any Freudian sense, contemporary audiences can hardly escape this aspect of the opera. First of all, the nocturnal setting suggests the thought that the events are not actual but dreamed. And, second, the cistern in which Jochanaan (John the Baptist) is confined has also been the prison of Salomé's father; it is a symbol for the tomb, therefore, and Jochanaan's emergence from under the ground is a "resurrection." But Salomé's violation of the grave, the breaking of the taboo, requires that she be punished, and, mythologically speaking, her death is necessary as much for this reason as for her part in Jochanaan's murder.

"*J'aime l'horreur d'être vierge. . . .*" Hérodiade[3]-Salomé's

3. Mallarmé first uses the name in *Fleurs*. As Henri Mondor makes clear (*Mallarmé plus intime*), Hérodiade *is* Salomé: ". . . *quand Hérodiade commença sa danse enivrée, elle cueillit quelques roses de cette couronne, les effeuilla et, y mêlant les pistils de la royale rose rouge avec laquelle elle avait conservé son père . . .*"

ambiguousness toward her virginity, the essential question of her psyche, apparently arises from her unresolved Oedipal relationship with her murdered father. In any event, her infantile libido has taken a necrophiliac form, whose object is not only dead during the love scene but corpselike at her first view of him. Finally, she has both wanted and feared her dead beloved's now inextrusible tongue. ("Viper" is her word, and in Mallarmé she wishes to be a *"reptile inviolé"* herself.) In other versions of the story, Jochanaan's decapitation, or castration, is his punishment for beholding Salomé's nakedness, the crime of forbidden knowledge in symbolic form, but in the opera he is punished for the opposite transgression, that of ignoring her.

If Salomé has little dimension, apart from her case history and her thralldom, none of the other characters has enough to stir up the slightest interest in what becomes of them. Jochanaan might have been a figure of tragic proportions, as he is elsewhere. But though he is imprisoned as a fatidic nuisance, and loses his life for his beliefs, his death amounts to little more than a bizarre incident, partly because, like Salomé, he is no more than a personification—of virtue in this case. The main part, however, is that his musical characterization is inadequate: his "heroic" motif belongs to a genre more appropriately associated with the good pioneers in a Western than with a mystic, a type for which Strauss admittedly felt no sympathy. But the audience's indifference to Jochanaan's fate may also be attributed to his infrequent appearances. Since he is no more than a disembodied voice during much of the opera, a disembodied head at the end of it, and all in one piece only at the beginning, the role is unusually fragmented.

Herod's part is larger, and his struggle of wills with Salomé supersedes hers with Jochanaan. Though the outcomes of both confrontations are predictable, the one with Herod is the more suspenseful, the feeling being conveyed that, just conceivably, he could change his mind and avert the catastrophe. He is complex, too, and the audience cannot tell whether the strongest of his motives in ordering Salomé's death is revulsion, fear, or jealousy, all three being intricately combined in his well-drawn musical characterization. Yet he, not Salomé, has compunctions. In contrast, Herodias and Narraboth are practically featureless, and even the suicide of the latter goes unnoticed, not only by Salomé and the holy man but also by the audience. Human sympathy is not the theme of this opera.

———

We have been conditioned to regard the "progressive" aspects of many composers as the most important ones, and *Salomé* makes that thesis difficult to disprove. (Whether the same can be said of *Elektra*, with its formal introductions to "set" arias, depends on the listener's perspective vis-à-vis *Der Rosenkavalier* and *Ariadne*.) Certainly *Salomé*'s most exciting moments are in such "expressionist," "free-association," and new and unrepeatable passages as the orchestral swirling during Herod's final dialogue with his wife. But Strauss continually surpasses himself in this scene and in a way that transcends these categories. No doubt believing that his heroine, like Elektra after her, has gone mad, he translates her to a plane beyond communication. *"Ich habe deinen Mund geküsst, Jochanaan,"* she whispers, and muted violins moan an echo under an aura of woodwind trills, an unforgettable effect that isolates her as completely as if she were in solitary confinement.

"Progressive," too, if that is the direction of Schoenberg and Berg,[4] are some of the opera's thematic metamorphoses. For one example, at the moment of Jochanaan's first awareness of Salomé —*"Wer ist dies Weib?"*—her legato initial motif is transformed into a choppy ostinato figure and placed in a clashing counter-rhythm to his music, thus conveying her threat to the Prophet, even though the listener may not recognize the motif as Salomé's. The same pattern returns when Herod invites her to drink wine with him, and this time the suggestion of "dripping" in the staccato figure suddenly becomes evident, for although she refuses him, the music belies her thirst, or, rather, bloodthirstiness.

———

4. Berg, like Mahler and Schoenberg, was profoundly impressed by *Salomé*, both in score and at the first Austrian performances, in 1906.

———

The debt to *Salomé* in Alban Berg's *Wozzeck* is immense and ranges from the simple borrowing of instrumental devices to the incorporation of stylistic ones. But Berg and his generation, twenty years after *Salomé*, had long since regarded its composer as a lost leader and forgotten that he had ever been a real one. The two operas differ from each other as much as they are alike, *Salomé* being a single, sustained symphonic act, *Wozzeck* a series of brief, self-contained units. But Berg's orchestral interludes, a feature of his opera, were clearly modeled on those in *Salomé*, especially on the one which escorts the soldiers to the cistern to carry out the execution, and in which the explosive dynamics, the brutal lower brass and the alarum in the horns, the repeated major seconds, the chromatic harmony and wide intervals, and the combining of different rhythmic patterns might actually have come from *Wozzeck*.

Among the many instrumental inventions which Strauss's opera seems to have suggested to Berg's are the contrabassoon obbligato (in *Salomé*'s fourth scene, *Wozzeck*'s first) and the high solo bass notes (before the decollation in *Salomé*, and, in *Wozzeck*, to represent the snoring in the barracks). No less apparent is the effect on the Hauptmann's music in Berg's opera of Herod's nervous vocal style—*"Es ist kalt hier," "Es weht ein Wind."* Yet the point about these and other innovations is not so much their "influence" as their contribution to the most thrilling passages in *Salomé*.

The opera's minor weaknesses include the lapses into inappropriate styles, such as the Viennese waltz at Herod's table and the Danubian lilt of the Sea of Galilee, and the literalisms—every reference to dancing, for example, being marked by a flick of the tambourine, or to lions by a roar in the trombones. But "Straussian orchestration," a pejorative term suggesting a diapason of doublings and over-rich textures, is comparatively rare. True, Strauss always prefers the many-hued to the pure, seldom using the strings or woodwinds or brass alone, as Wagner does so tellingly in the Prelude to *Parsifal*. Yet the most striking effects are obtained from solo instruments, small combinations, or even from the sudden *removal* of a doubling—as when the first part of the "kiss" motif is played by violins and clarinet, the last part by the clarinet alone (*cf.* 320), its timbre skillfully exploited by a harmonic turn.

———

Anyone in search of enlightenment about *Salomé* should stay well away from the two leading authorities in English on Strauss.[5] Although "critical" appears in the titles of their books, "appreciative" would be a more apt word for these potpourris of biographical information, anecdotes about the backgrounds of compositions and their premieres, résumés of plots, and impressionistic descriptions of the music. Attention to "technical" aspects of composition is limited to the identification of tonalities, time signatures, and instrumental combinations—including, in the latter case, some that are *not* heard:

> one expects organ and harmonium here [but] Strauss does not need them at this moment. [Mann]

Many examples in music type are also included, twenty-eight for *Salomé* in Mr. Mann's book, thirty-nine in Mr. Del Mar's. Since harmonic contexts are provided in only a few of these extracts, however, and tempi in none—is it of no importance that the beginning of the second scene is in a fast "one" rather than a slow "three"?—these scraps of music are as useless as the words that they are intended to supplement. Some of Mr. Del Mar's examples, moreover, are printed not as they are heard but as the player of the "horn in E" or the "clarinet in A" sees them, which is to say, untransposed. Considering the density of the music at certain of the places where these motifs appear, Strauss himself would have had difficulty in recognizing them.

5. William Mann, *Richard Strauss: A Critical Study of the Operas* (New York, 1966), and Norman Del Mar, *Richard Strauss: A Critical Commentary on His Life and Works*, 3 vols. (Philadelphia, 1962–1973).

But a more important objection to both studies is their assumption of an all but absolute literalness of verbal meaning in Strauss's treatment of motifs. In fact Mr. Mann's analysis translates the music into words in a way which tends to imply that the composer scarcely thought in musical terms at all:

> [When the prophet] rejects Salomé's advances . . . Ex. 14 [Jochanaan's motif] in diminution marks Salomé's change of instinct.

Even if Strauss did modify his materials with such precise literal intent, which is doubtful, to approach the music in this way is to detract from it.

But in fairness to Mr. Mann, it must be acknowledged that his own intentions are often obscured by his style. Thus he writes that

> the music sinks into a timeless B major while Salomé cries the Prophet's name, and first horn with oboes and clarinets drag out Ex. 1 as from a sluggish chest of drawers.

Meaning that "Ex. 1" was reluctant to leave its place among the shirts and socks in an unlubricated chiffonier? Or is the allusion anatomical, a complaint about possible respiratory ailments in wind players? (What actually happens at this place is simply that Salomé's first motif is heard in a rhythmic form whose momentary effect is to dissolve or suspend the metronomic beat.) Also, the reader who has followed Mr. Mann's elucidations of motivic usages up to this point may justifiably ask why Salomé's, rather than Jochanaan's, motif is played, since his name, not hers, is being called.

To confound the Strauss lover even further, Messrs. Mann and Del Mar disagree on everything from the import of motifs to the question of Salomé's purity. For Mr. Mann "Ex. 24 gives voluptuous expression to the action of biting," while for Mr. Del Mar the same example is simply "a vulgar tune." And whereas Mr. Mann refers to the "passions that are welling inside Salomé's untutored heart," Mr. Del Mar believes that "passions run high in the East and Salomé was no innocent child at the time of these events." But the subject so disturbs Mr. Del Mar that it must have been a great strain on him to write about it:

Strauss . . . failed to do justice to a horribly important section of [Wilde's] work . . . [and] Salomé's Ex. 15 combines with her mother's Ex. 34 in a horrible display of hysterical triumph. . . .

In fact Mr. Del Mar appears to identify with the victims since he writes that

After a performance of *Salomé* one is left with a very nasty taste in one's mouth.

Romain Rolland, though mistaken about *Salomé*, is nevertheless a keen observer of its composer, noting that in Strauss's presence

One falls underneath a pride that is cold, self-willed, indifferent or contemptuous of the majority of things and people.[6]

Strauss conducting a rehearsal, Rolland remarked,

looks bored, sulky, half-asleep, but lets nothing escape him. His music stirs me [but] one always wonders how *that* can have come out of *this*. . . .[7]

Rolland was not afraid to challenge Strauss on the suitability of *Salomé* for opera:

The sensual ferocity of the ending may frighten an Opéra-Comique audience; and I do not know how the ending can be staged. As it is impossible in the theater to give an impression of the true horror of it, there is a risk that it may arouse irony.[8]

6. Diary, April 1899.
7. Diary, March 25, 1906.
8. Letter, November 5, 1905.

But these fears were unfounded, and *Salomé* has been an enduring success in the land of the guillotine.

After becoming familiar with the opera, Rolland wrote that

> When you speak in your name, as in the *Domestica* or *Heldenleben*, you attain a matchless intensity and fullness of feeling.[9]

But the exact opposite is true. Strauss is at his most unbearable when he speaks in his own name, and the *"coeur mis à nu"* in those two orchestral works is shallow and banal indeed compared with the "fullness of feeling" when he speaks in Salomé's. Rolland also wonders "if music gains as much as the theater does in this victory" and assures the composer that "nervous tension . . . is not the best . . . that you have to give." But the theater rescued Strauss, and rescued "pure" music *from* him, while that "nervous tension" is the very secret of *Salomé*'s power.

Preparing the libretto for the Paris performances, Strauss explained to Rolland that

> as Wilde's . . . text . . . is in French, I would like to achieve a quite special French edition of my opera, which does not give the impression of being a translation, but of being a real setting of the original.[10]

But just as Wilde had submitted his manuscript to Pierre Louÿs, and then accepted only his grammatical corrections, refusing to alter unidiomatic expressions, so Strauss showed his French version to Rolland, yet ignored some of his advice. And Strauss's French seems to have been rudimentary. For example, he allotted only one syllable for *"crié"* (*"De celui qui a crié"*) and, in writing *"Comme est belle la princesse"* (for *"Comme elle est belle, la princesse"*), seemed to be trying to preserve German word order. Worst of all, he insisted on remaining faithful to Wilde's *faux pas* of having Herod repeat the phrase *"Je suis sûr*

9. Letter, May 14, 1907.
10. Letter, September 13, 1905.

qu'il va arriver un malheur à quelqu'un," for though Herod is not thinking of Jochanaan, the audience would do just that, and, of course, be most inappropriately amused.

———

Rolland, like Hofmannsthal after him, occasionally talked down to Strauss, though both writers were aware that the composer's instincts as a dramatist were at least as acute as theirs, and that his musical genius included other kinds of intelligence. But Strauss is the most puzzling of composers—to say nothing of human beings. While he was as sensible and shrewd as these two literary friends, unlike them he often seemed unprincipled as a man, and as an artist quite incapable of understanding music as a moral realm. He also, as Hofmannsthal put it, "tried to escape from all of the higher standards of intellectual existence."

Thus Strauss's neo-classicism, initiated a decade before Stravinsky's or Schoenberg's, cannot be compared to their struggle to reshape an age. Not that Strauss's "Lully" (1912) is less skillful than Stravinsky's "Pergolesi" (1920), but whereas the former work turns an indifferent and even philistine back on its own time, the latter helps to create it. Thus, too, the songs which Strauss wrote at the end of his life, and which are among the most beautiful of their kind, could have been written nearly a century before. On the other hand, fifty years of "modern music," the years of Stravinsky and Schoenberg, have produced only two or three musico-dramatic creations that can compete with the most popular operas of Richard Strauss.

DER ROSENKAVALIER: "SOMETHING MOZARTIAN"?

I was tied down by the metre [of the final duet] which you prescribed for me, but in the end . . . I felt something Mozartian. . . .

—Hofmannsthal to Strauss, June 6, 1910

The Metropolitan Opera's productions of *Der Rosenkavalier* and *Ariadne auf Naxos* seem to reflect a new endeavor and spirit. The casts are superior, the sets and costumes better than the standard of recent years, and the stagings as good as those of any opera in this season's repertory. *Ariadne* received the better performance of the two, both because its success is less dependent on the conductor and because Tatiana Troyanos's voice is more suited to the role of the Composer than to that of Octavian. (It must be said that having the same person in the *travesti* parts of two operas of the same period and place makes them smack of a television serial.) Montserrat Caballé's Ariadne could hardly be improved upon and was perfectly complemented by Alberto Remedios's Bacchus. Ruth Welting as Zerbinetta may have been at a disadvantage, however, in that her stage movements appeared to be almost as taxing as her vocal ones. Of the minor characters, the commedia dell'arte quartet, the trio of nymphs, and the Hofmeister were irreproachable. But the dramatis personae of the Prologue inevitably obtrude in the opera, a stock complaint against all performances of the piece. On the question of the intermingling of styles in the two parts, the composer *in*—not *of* —the opera seems to have been right.

The Metropolitan's *Rosenkavalier* was also well staged and furnished, though the appointments for the *levée* scene ranged from the too rich (Pavarotti as the Tenor looked like the best dressed and fed of noblemen) to the too poor (the animal seller's merchandise consisting of a single spaniel, a reincarnated

"Flush"). The weakness of the staging was due to the disparity in the histrionic performances. Walter Berry's masterful realization of the difficult part of Baron Ochs mercilessly exposed the shortcomings of the Octavian, the Sophie, and the Marschallin, with their three or four stereotyped poses. Berry made Ochs believable by never overplaying his egregiousness, and even managed to win a measure of sympathy for him during the revelation scene, when, fitting the pieces together and discovering that the girl is a boy, the Baron finally sees what his refined cousin the Marschallin has been up to. But Berry's acting skill was evident in every gesture, from frothblowing hand flourish to courtly bow, and this in addition to singing of an equally high caliber. Of the three female leads, Teresa Zylis-Gara's Marschallin was the most suitably cast and most pleasingly performed, Troyanos's Octavian being somewhat too heavy for Judith Blegen's Sophie, at least in their duets. The conductor, James Levine, must share the responsibility for allowing Miss Blegen to distend the music at *"Wie himmlische, nicht irdische"* and to ruin it a little later with a fermata on the high C sharp.

Elsewhere, Mr. Levine charged through the score, failing to give the curves of the melodies their natural play, and to hesitate on upbeats in waltzes, or delay resolutions—in short, stripping the music of the stylistic traits that Strauss was so proud of having embodied in it. But Mr. Levine also neglected balances within the orchestra, as well as between it and the stage. And, astonishingly, he implemented Clemens Krauss's mistaken "corrections," which substitute E natural for E flat, for example, in the initial trumpet statement of the *"Wo war ich schon einmal"* motif during the presentation of the rose—a thorn in one of the opera's most beautiful passages. Mr. Levine's shortcomings have been overlooked in the past because of talents that merited encouragement and because of his inexperience, but such criticisms must now be made. After all, he holds one of the most important posts in the musical world, in which he is apparently conducting more operas than anyone else.

—

Der Rosenkavalier recently received its 199th performance at the Metropolitan, a record number for any opera written after the first decade of this century, and so far outdistancing its nearest competitor as to seem like the last of a dying breed. This popularity can be partly attributed to its encompassing most of the ingredients of a Broadway musical: hit tunes, mixtures of comedy and romance, a costume extravaganza, a setting in travel-poster Never-Never Land. Apart from its instant success, the opera represents the most significant and unexpected turn in direction in Strauss's entire development, one, so some critics believe, that diverted him from the fullest realization of his genius. In their view he should have continued, in the vein of *Salomé* and *Elektra*, to explore new musical frontiers inspired by even more gory biblical and classical atrocities.

But did he have a choice? The dimensions of the two earlier music dramas could hardly bear enlargement, while to achieve a greater degree of intensification would have required a compression that was not in Strauss's nature. In any case, a radical change was inevitable after *Elektra*, partly because the same road could not be pursued any further, but also because of the composer's long-gestating ambition to write a comic opera *à la Figaro*: "*Das nächste Mal schreibe ich eine Mozartoper,*" as he said at the time. Therefore it would seem that Strauss's "backsliding" from his obligations as a leader of the modern movement was not a defection but a step in sequence.

Hugo von Hofmannsthal has been blamed for the "turncoat" musical position that Strauss adopted in *Der Rosenkavalier* and was to maintain thereafter. But is it reasonable to suppose that the librettist, whose musical knowledge was unremarkable, could have had such an influence on this powerfully self-willed composer? To be sure, Hofmannsthal had quickly recognized the "mixture of the burlesque with the lyrical" as a feature of Strauss's personality and had even offered one suggestion for the *Rosenkavalier* music: "An old-fashioned Viennese waltz, sweet and yet saucy, which must pervade the whole of the last act." But the librettist could scarcely have been aware of Strauss's potentialities as an opera composer, nor would anybody but a skilled musician have perceived the tendency in *Elektra* toward the restoration of traditional structures. One wonders what species of music Hofmannsthal did actually anticipate when, on April 19, 1909, he sent the first scene of his eighteenth-century situation comedy to Strauss. And it is even hard to understand the librettist's belief that Strauss *could* compose suitable music for a play set in Maria Theresa's Vienna and using some of the period's conventions of social hierarchy, character types, and plot.

Whatever the answers, luck must have played a large part in the creation of *Der Rosenkavalier*, for the libretto made its appearance at precisely the right moment and was the catalyst for Strauss's dormant wish vis-à-vis comic opera. At an earlier date, he might have felt the need to write one more work in a similar mode, and have asked himself whether his musical language had been so conditioned for tragedy that a change might be premature. Successive creations by any artist contain links to one another, of course, and many such are easily discernible between the first act of *Der Rosenkavalier* and the latter part of *Elektra*. Thus Elektra's aria, *"Von jetzt an will ich deine Schwester sein,"* and her waltz before the murder of Aegisthus resemble the Marschallin's music. Nor are portents of a general kind lacking in Strauss's early music. He had composed burlesques before, to be sure, and the "humor" in his tone poems is as conspicuous as the sentiment. Yet even the closest observer of Strauss's development before *Elektra* could not have foreseen the transformation of its composer into the one of *Der Rosenkavalier*.

The libretto has the reputation of being among the most nearly perfect of any opera; what is more, it has been praised for a psychological subtlety and wisdom seldom found in the comic genre that it imitates. But is this accepted opinion justified? To begin with, having introduced perspectives anachronous to the ethical codes of eighteenth-century comedy, the plot wavers in sustaining a moral basis. Not only is adultery condoned, but when an impoverished nobleman, Baron Ochs, uses his title to contract a marriage for money—an accepted practice of the age—he is rebuked for what modern, democratic thinking considers a venal action. But contrariwise, Faninal, the father of the unwilling bride and Ochs's partner in the transaction, is rewarded, despite social-climbing motives as despicable as the financial ones of the Baron. What Hofmannsthal seems to say—without making a particular point of it—is that morality equals expediency, and even follows no certain course. With Strauss it has to be said, regrettably, that the moral question never arises at all.

Even when compared with other operas demanding a large tolerance toward the illogical, *Der Rosenkavalier* is full of inconsistencies, loose ends, obscurely motivated behavior. But apart from unexplained details, the plot is mystifying in two important particulars: Valzacchi's and Annina's shift of allegiance from Ochs to Octavian, and the Marschallin's appearance in the inn, in Act Three. The first is not clear to the audience in dramatic terms, though the explanation—money—is given; hence the plot function of these two intriguers from Italy seems to be arbitrary. So too, the nocturnal visit to a lowly tavern by one of the great ladies of the realm is both implausible and dramatically unaccountable, although Ochs's natural son and body servant, Leopold, has ostensibly fetched her in order to rescue his father. But this is unconvincing, the Marschallin having up to this time shown no interest in the welfare of her cousin, and now treating him unfairly when she does arrive. One commentator on this *dea ex machina* conclusion has written that

it does not really matter why . . . she is there . . . but come she must to resolve the situation.[1]

But though no one would disagree with the second part of the statement, who could agree with the first?

1. See "The Characters in *Der Rosenkavalier*," by Rodney Blumer (London Records OSA-1435; part of album notes). Mr. Blumer mixes his metaphors ("Those who look no further than the end of their nose where Hofmannsthal is concerned miss a great many interesting scents"), describes impossible phenomena ("You can tell without hearing who is speaking"), and provides

The most crucial and immediately evident weakness in the libretto is its failure to reach a decision as to who is the central character; and this, in turn, is responsible for inchoate mixtures of moods and emotions. The original title, *"Baron Ochs auf Lerchenau,"* indicates that the "villain's" role was considered to be the leading one, as indeed it is so far as Ochs's time onstage and share of action are concerned. In the exposition, however— in the first act, which is the only satisfyingly constructed one of the three—Ochs's part is merely incidental to the love affair of the Marschallin and Octavian, the principal subject of the opera both before and after Ochs's escapades. Yet the Marschallin does not reappear until the dénouement, which Ochs dominates. Meanwhile the audience's sympathy, which should be on the side of Ochs's adversaries, Sophie and her new protector Octavian, does not follow in this direction, for the reason that Ochs, in spite of his vanity, grotesque manners, and general obnoxiousness, is incomparably more engaging than are the two young lovers.

The opera's greatest puzzle, in fact, is in the contradictory responses provoked by Baron Ochs. Hofmannsthal and Strauss clearly thought of him as exceedingly droll, both in himself and in the adventures in which he is involved. It seems obvious that he was intended to be another Falstaff, with similarly ingratiating vices, but, if so, the attempt to make him one was a failure, and the authors were badly misled. Ochs has little of the appeal of Sir John, and without it the role is too long. The Falstaff hypothesis gains support on other grounds, too, for the scene in the inn, with figures emerging from the dark to frighten Ochs, must have been suggested by the midnight episode in Windsor Park. Furthermore, the ruse of the letter inviting Ochs to an assignation may well have been borrowed from the older play, since two examples of conceit and gullibility on this same scale

unreliable character analyses. Thus he finds Faninal "engaging and sympathetic . . . a wonderfully rounded study," though by other criteria this parvenu who pushes his daughter into Och's arms instead of protecting her from him would be considered the very personification of a cad. Nor is Faninal consistently drawn, being presented in his final line, totally without dramatic justification, as suddenly "understanding" his daughter's feelings.

are too much of a coincidence. Finally, whether consciously or otherwise, stage directors appear to recognize the parallel, wrongly making Ochs, who is thirty-five years old, both elderly and obese.

Apart from the music associated with him, Ochs is nearly devoid of endearing qualities. Even as a seducer he lacks skill, which is surprising in one who is as lecherous as he is greedy, and his dullness of mind in failing to suspect the traps that are set for him strains the audience's credulity. Yet most of his crimes prove to be peccadilloes, which would be forgiven if, like Falstaff, his powers of intelligence were greater—and this, of course, is the vital difference between the two men.

Still another reservation about the characterization of the Baron is the pratfall humor of which he is the target. Doubtless some of the audience is amused when Ochs, slightly wounded by Octavian's sword, agonizes out of all proportion to his injury. Nevertheless, he does shed blood. So, too, in the scene of his humiliation in the inn, he must suffer real mental torture. That Strauss found Ochs truly farcical is evident from the music as well as from the composer's correspondence with Hofmannsthal.[2] But, parodoxically, Strauss's genius was greater than his intellect, and some of the musical laughter in the trap-door "fun house" scene contains a note of genuine terror, even of Evil.

Hofmannsthal has characterized the Baron through a special language ("Ochs-ese") as well as through his deeds. (The same is true for Faninal and Sophie, in their comparatively minor roles.) But surely opera is not a medium in which linguistic nuances can, or should, count for very much. To preserve in comparatively dense music the effects of rustic locutions, such as are found in Wycherley or Goldsmith, is a great deal to expect of any composer, though Strauss, who slavishly follows the words,

---

2. Only a fraction of the Strauss-Hofmannsthal letters, and those in fragmentary form, is available in English. In 1927 Knopf issued a translation of the volume, selected, expurgated, and unabashedly published by the authors themselves. Since Strauss's death, three successive "complete" editions have appeared in German, and in 1961 Random House published a translation of the first of these. But it is evident from the contents of the last that all lacunae have not yet been filled. None of the volumes of Strauss's other letters, which date back to his exchanges with Hans von Bülow, has been translated.

achieves an extraordinary degree of success in this. But by the same token, the operagoer must be familiar with the most esoteric allusions of the text and the music. At the same time, the musical characterizations are not always reliable, being belied by stage behavior. In the case of the Baron, for example, while the pomposity of his first theme and the fractured gracefulness of the second could hardly be more fitting, the soft echoes of his dinner-music waltz, which is the opera's most pervasive melody, are unbecomingly sweet.

But the most important question is still that of who is the opera's central character. And if Baron Ochs lacks the necessary qualities, Octavian, who replaces him in the title, is also unsuitable. As a young cavalier, the Marschallin's lover, and someone who behaves both reasonably and naturally, he is the obvious candidate to be the hero of the piece. Yet he is insufficiently developed to carry a pivotal role, and his fate is decided for him by the Marschallin. (It is one of the conventions of *Der Rosenkavalier* that Octavian, the bearer of the silver rose signifying Ochs's betrothal, steps into the shoes of the man for whom he speaks; marriage ambassadors from Tristan to John Alden—the latter by way of acknowledging the Bicentenary—have done the same.)

Of all the characters, only the Marschallin is sympathetic, complex and reflective, and highly developed, and she alone qualifies for that centripetal position which the authors have failed to define. But her role is very imperfectly conceived, and, as aforesaid, she is abandoned after the drama has been focused on her and her feelings, until called upon to resolve the action. And though she is the only protagonist with the intelligence and independence to do this, an inconsistency results, since she is required to condemn Ochs's "debauchery" while at the same time asking him to be discreet about her own liaison. Not that this taints her, for uniquely in her case we have been given the background that explains her actions. At fifteen she was married against her will to a man she still does not love, a fact that enables her to rationalize her affair with Octavian as well as to identify with Sophie, who, at the same age, is threatened by a similar fate.

In the unreal world of *Der Rosenkavalier,* the Marschallin is both realistic and farsighted—at least in what she says, for despite her philosophical attitude toward aging (she is in her early thirties), her chronophobia is so severe that she sometimes turns back the clocks at night. This explains her precipitate termination of the relationship with Octavian and hasty manipulation of his marriage to Sophie. The conflict of the Marschallin's emotions when the loss of Octavian becomes a reality inspires the opera's most human moment, in which the audience feels the truth of Octavian's *"Marie Theres' wie gut Sie ist."* The Marschallin's future matters far more than that of the fairy-tale ending of the Octavian-Sophie story. The libretto invites the suggestion that since others have preceded Octavian in the Marschallin's affections, he will also have successors, but the music persuades us that Octavian means more to her than she will admit to herself, and that she is genuinely in love with the boy. The audience also cannot help believing that Octavian will soon miss her, and that life with Sophie will be much less interesting than it was with the older woman.

The main theme of *Der Rosenkavalier* is the contrast between innocent and experienced love, and the music of both is equally seductive. For the former, Sophie's and Octavian's love at first sight, time itself is held back, the musical elements standing still in a congelation of simple melody, triadic and static harmony, and a glitter of sound evoking the silver rose. The Marschallin's music, at the other extreme and by benefit of contrast, may be interpreted as reflecting her obsession with temporality and the evanescence of earthly passion, partly through the device of a falling major seventh. Of the two musical portraits, that of the Marschallin is capable of greater development, of course, though to choose between her *"Die Zeit, die ist ein sonderbar' Ding"* and Sophie's *"Wie Rosen vom hochheiligen Paradies"* would be difficult indeed.

———

For all of Strauss's and Hofmannsthal's professed intention of composing "a Mozart opera," it seems that only one human being could do that. The "Mozart" in *Der Rosenkavalier*—in Octavian's A-major aria in the first scene, in the chamber-music interlude when the Marschallin is alone—is either superficial, or, like the final Sophie-Octavian duet, sugar-coated. If any other great composer's influence should be acknowledged, it is not Mozart's but Verdi's. This is most obvious in the fugato tarantella of the Prelude and Pantomime in the third act but is found elsewhere in the opera as well—in, for example, a characteristically Verdian octave figuration. Whatever *Der Rosenkavalier*'s extraneous musical sources—and besides Mozart and Verdi they include Johann Strauss and Lehár (the *"Kein Wein"* waltz, which is on the verge of bursting into operetta)—Strauss's comment, on finishing Act One, is incontestable:

> I believe that I have succeeded in capturing the true Viennese spirit and melodic line.

Der Rosenkavalier, that suspension bridge of seventh and ninth chords, and of enharmonic modulations, is a composite of earlier, plushly upholstered melodic, harmonic, and orchestral idioms that, nevertheless, and in every measure, bear the stamp of Richard Strauss.

ELEKTRA AND RICHARD STRAUSS

According to one commentator on Strauss's masterpiece, Hofmannsthal

> drew largely from Sophocles . . . but deliberately chose details from the other two Greek tragedians whenever they strength-

ened his portrayal of the scenes or of the characterizations.[1]

This information is true[2] but fails to mention that the librettist omitted the meaning of the play.

Hofmannsthal followed Sophocles' story in broad outline and, knowing that to make a coherent amalgam of the different versions would be impossible, interpolated a few particulars from Aeschylus and Euripides. But what astonishes is that a writer of Hofmannsthal's stature did not realize that the dramatic validity of any play about Elektra depends on the audience's knowledge of the background, of Agamemnon's sacrificial murder of his and Clytemnestra's daughter Iphigenia. Certainly Hofmannsthal understood that "the past must always be present," as is shown when his Elektra answers Chrysothemis' plea to forget: "I cannot, I am no beast." Yet crucial as is the Iphigenia episode to the Aeschylean and Sophoclean interpretations of the Agamemnon tragedy, no reference is made to her either in Hofmannsthal's play or in the libretto adapted from it. As a result the behavior of his Clytemnestra is without ethical basis or even legal defense. She becomes simply another psychopathic murderess, slaughtering her husband upon his return from war so that she can continue her adulterous relationship with Aegisthus, committing one sin in order to indulge in another.

A still larger error on Hofmannsthal's part is his evident assumption that Greek tragedy can be secularized. But in the theo-

1. Norman Del Mar, *Richard Strauss: A Critical Commentary on His Life and Works*, 3 vols. (Philadelphia, 1962–1973). Readers should be warned of the author's apparent distaste for the opera. "The jangling theme is now transformed into a horrible waltz," he writes, and, "Although naturally vicious, this theme . . . "; "the concentration of women's voices shrieking in almost unrelieved hysteria accentuates to an appalling degree . . . "; "The maidservants revile Elektra with appalling vulgarity . . ."; "There is a ghastly interruption when Elektra realizes . . . "; "Elektra actually performs her awful dance." And so forth. But many of Del Mar's other pronouncements are hardly less peculiar: "Clytemnestra's . . . strength of character was probably unequalled in the whole ancient world." (How could anyone know that?)
2. Except that a characterization cannot be portrayed.

logical drama of Aeschylus—in parts one and two of the trilogy, that is—to avenge, in kind, a crime against a blood relative is a religious obligation. Clytemnestra proclaims this mandate in the very act of killing Agamemnon, and her ethical position is stronger than that of her victim, who, in addition, is held responsible for the loss of Greek lives in his war of conquest— this being the reason for the goddess Artemis' demand that he sacrifice Iphigenia. Obviously Clytemnestra's revenge is part rationalization, since she resents the concubine Cassandra and reveals no feelings for the ill treatment of Elektra or Orestes. Nevertheless, when Clytemnestra confronts her husband, intending to kill him, she is no mere garden-variety homicidal spouse, but, to some degree, a self-proclaimed instrument of divine retribution and an ostensible link in a chain of cosmic events.

Similarly, when Clytemnestra speaks of the murder of Agamemnon in Sophocles' *Elektra*, she says that "Justice slew him and not I alone." Hence it follows that a strictly human perspective not only is incomplete but ignores the philosophical dimension, with its principles of *dikê* and *anankê*, of law and justice. These, being eternal and "universally" understood, are higher than the gods, whose ways, on the contrary, are sometimes incomprehensible to the logical and rational minds of mortals. An immutable law of this kind is set forth in *Agamemnon*: "One act of hubris begets another until the day of reckoning comes."

The deities are less prominent in Sophocles' *Elektra* than they are in Aeschylus, the focus of the author having shifted to character development and dramatic suspense. All the same, the gods oversee human lives, protecting and destroying them, and Elektra herself remarks that Orestes has come "with the favoring hand of Zeus." Nor does Sophocles follow Aeschylus in his singleness of concentration on intellectual concepts, yet the essential theme of the *Elektra* is that the moral order— often, in Greek drama, the natural one as well—has been violently disrupted and must be restored even at the cost of further horror. Otherwise, without the justifying tenet of inexorable forces, Sophocles' play seems excessively brutal and may be misunderstood as a return to the "ethics" of the Homeric Age. Stripped of this theological basis, in fact, the action is reduced to senseless butchery of the kind seen on the ten o'clock Channel 5 news.

To the objection that Hofmannsthal's Orestes and Elektra *do* acknowledge these supernatural agencies—he says, "The gods will be there to help me"; she says, "We are with the gods"— it must be protested that these exclamations are purely perfunctory. This becomes apparent at the end of the opera when Chrysothemis cries, "The gods are good. . . . It is the infinite goodness of the gods that has brought it about." But where did Hofmannsthal find this most inappropriate description of the treacherous, lecherous, jealous, vindictive, and selfish gang from Olympus?

Sophoclean scholars still debate whether Apollo sanctions Orestes' act of vengeance, but it is clear that when Clytemnestra leaves her palace, frightened from a dream, she is on her way to offer prayers to the sun god; and clear that her prayers are blasphemous and offensive to him, since the plan, which can only be his, is immediately placed in motion: to announce the false news of Orestes' death and thus gain entrance for him to accomplish the deed—which could also only be carried out under Apollo's auspices. The impression given by the opera, however, is that human beings are acting independently of divine intervention, nor is Hofmannsthal's Clytemnestra on her way to sacrifice to Apollo when Elektra interrupts her.

Hofmannsthal's reasons for omitting the Chorus may simply have been to avoid this archaic feature and, at the same time, to present the story largely through Elektra's eyes. (Servants appear briefly at the beginning and end, and in attendance on Clytemnestra, but they are merely bit players and no substitute Greek Chorus.) The libretto is virtually a monodrama, in any case, and as such offers no access to Clytemnestra's "true" thoughts, which a Chorus would have revealed. Hofmannsthal's Orestes, too, is a long way from the integral character of the Greek tragedy, in which he appears at the beginning, moreover, and in which the chorus foretells that he will be the one to fulfill destiny. The Orestes of the libretto enters only in the latter part, a reduction of the role that makes the matricide, after a twenty-year interim, seem even more cold-blooded.

———

In the opera, the deceased Agamemnon should almost be listed among the characters, if only because his name is omnipresent in the music: the anapestic motif associated with him (Ă-gă-mēm-nŏn) is hammered out by the orchestra at the beginning, countless times throughout, and at the very end—there in the major mode, inevitably but joltingly: not joy but mourning becomes Elektra.

Of the not-yet-deceased protagonists, Chrysothemis, who does not involve herself in the vengeance, provides little more than contrast, and perhaps too much of that. Her music, perfectly fitting her character, is both the most conventional in the opera and standard Bavarian Strauss. But near the end, when her sister joins in, using the same melodic style, Chrysothemis loses her individuality, especially in the upper range, and even though her high B's occur in the contexts of phrases—"Linear B's," it might be said, if the setting were anywhere but Mycenae. In this duet the composer seems to have discovered his weakness for sopranos singing in the same register; had he known Alessandro Scarlatti's madrigal for five equally high voices, *"Cor mio, deh non languire,"* Strauss surely would have included an all-soprano quintet in one of his operas. But Chrysothemis' most memorable moments are her first and last, in which, characteristically, she calls to her sister, then to her brother.

Elektra is Strauss's Brünnhilde, not only in the sense that the voices should be much alike, but also because the rhythm and some of the melodic intervals of Elektra's *"Totentanz"* are so blatantly reminiscent of *Die Walküre*. Not to notice this would be impossible, and, skillful parodist though Strauss was, he cannot, considering the dramatic situation, have intended any allusion. Furthermore, one of Orestes' motifs is melodically identical—and instrumentally nearly so—to the beginning of the *Todesverkundigung*, Brünnhilde's appearance before Siegmund. *Elektra,* in general less Wagnerian than *Salomé,* is more specifically so in places, and some of these echoes of the forebear are faintly disturbing.

Even in proportion to its greater length, Elektra's music contains more variety than that of any other role, including Clytemnestra's, and the solo flute that "expresses" Elektra's morbid contemplation of her befouled hair—this could have come from Schoenberg's *Pierrot*—is a more novel effect than any in Clytemnestra's "dream" music. So far from limiting Elektra to her obsession, Strauss endows the part with some of his greatest love music, which is expressed through her memories of childhood and through her feelings for her sister and brother. Her intentions toward Chrysothemis have been labeled "quasi-lesbian," but if the libretto supports that view, the music does not. Both sisters are sex-starved, and when the masculine Elektra tempts the feminine Chrysothemis with hints of erotic nights together after the murder of their mother and her lover, Hofmannsthal certainly meant to exploit the "perversity." But the seductive language could be interpreted as purely rhetorical, since Elektra scorns her sister after she refuses to be an accessory to the murder. Judged from the music alone, Elektra's feelings for her brother *would* be considered incestuous, the amorousness of the Recognition Scene being as unmistakable as that of the second act of *Tristan.* But obviously no such thing was intended; Strauss was simply unable to write any other kind of love music.

Although the contrapuntal use of the "wailing" motif in the scene with Elektra is a high point of the score, the musical delineation of Orestes is less successful than that of Aegisthus. Female voices and character-part tenors are still Strauss's forte, and both Orestes himself and his music too directly recall Wotan as The Wanderer. But Aegisthus, with the smallest part of all— he enters the opera only just in time to be murdered—is brilliantly portrayed through a motif that caricatures Agamemnon's and through a neo-classic idiom (an unconscious irony in the case of the latter, in view of the direction of Strauss's own subsequent development).

Clytemnestra is one of Strauss's most original creations, and it is in the evocation of her nightmares, evil premonitions, and lies that he anticipated so much of modern music. Hofmannsthal also seems to have been inspired by the character, and struck by the resemblance between her situation and that of Gertrude of Elsinore, for both queens are taunted by their respective children, Elektra and Hamlet, with hints about adulterous beds and murder; both are shaken by fears of punishment; and the same two children are also mad or feigning to be.

The Clytemnestra scene contains the most "daring" music that Strauss ever wrote, above all in the parallel movement of minor triads from different keys, a device resembling one of Schoenberg's in the *Obbligato Recitative* (composed nine months later), except that Strauss anchors his densest progressions with pedal points or sustaining block harmonies, such as the dozen-measure brass chord played against the chromatic ascent of the remainder of the orchestra as Chrysothemis flees into the palace. But the most extended passage in the score that could be mistaken for Schoenberg himself at the time of *Erwartung* (composed a year later) is the music immediately after the pure triad with which *Elecktra* begins.

When Clytemnestra tells Elektra that Orestes is "weak in the head," the bassoon plays a disjunct, staccato passage that might have come from late Stravinsky. Elektra's *"Dein Auge"* looks forward to *Oedipus Rex*, and the ostinato in the interlude before Clytemnestra's entrance to *Le Sacre du printemps*, while Elektra's dance to death anticipates the *Danse sacrale*, at least dramatically. Scraps of Debussy are also conspicuous in *Elektra*—in the introduction to the Recognition Scene aria, for instance—but whether with the help of that composer's example cannot be ascertained.

Elektra, with its almost mathematical form, its well-calculated changes of pace and hairspring timing, is Strauss's most perfectly made opera. And in spite of the criticisms of the work's dramatic decadence, Strauss's musical architecture enabled him to parallel the most subtle contrivances of the Greek playwrights. Aeschylus, for example, achieved powerful effects of irony by metrical means, prolonging his anacreontics—usually associated with revelry and love-making—into verses that are antithetical in mood; thus his Chorus chants joyfully of the ship bearing Helen ("blown by the breath of Zephyr"), then, with no change of rhythm, of the armies dispatched to hunt for her. Correspondingly, Strauss introduces the false announcement of Orestes' death, at the opera's midpoint intersection, with a tragic motif in three-four meter; then, when Elektra speaks with intentional irony to Aegisthus just before Orestes kills him, the composer recalls the same motif in the same rhythm but transformed into a quietly happy waltz that betrays her true feelings.

———

Anyone seeking to understand *Elektra* should not look to the recent studies any more than to the standard ones. The amount of light generated by Alan Jefferson's new batch of Strauss books,[3] for example, scarcely adds up to one candlepower, and Mr. Jefferson's comments on *Elektra* exemplify the unclear thinking that the reader soon comes to expect from him:

> Hofmannsthal has "modernised" the old story so that it is utterly acceptable and identifiable by every member of the present-day audience.[4]

But surely matricide is a less "acceptable" form of revenge for an audience today than it was for one in an amphitheater in fifth-century Athens. And what does "identifiable" mean? That modern listeners will recognize the story, or find it familiar because of skeletons in their own closets?

Even less illuminating are such comments on the music as

> When one examines the score and listens attentively to *Elektra*, it is only too clear that Strauss worked out every fierce

3. Especially to be avoided is Mr. Jefferson's *A Life of Richard Strauss* (New York, 1973).
4. From his album notes for the Solti-Birgit Nilsson performance on London Records (OSA-1269).

chordal clash with the most dexterous weaving together of his predetermined motifs.[5]

Is this surprising? Did Mr. Jefferson expect to find a notation "Chords to be improvised," and does he usually listen *in*attentively? Surely, too, the motifs were not "predetermined," but, like those in any other opera, designed to suit characters and situations. Another statement, that "the opera is to all intents and purposes atonal," is still more misleading since it seems to imply that the music as a whole resembles the so-called atonal species, or that Strauss intended to compose "atonal" music and failed.

The same author's survey of Strauss's lieder[6] is on a comparable level as well as incomplete. Fischer-Dieskau's recent album[7] of 131 songs, a barometer of the Strauss boom, warrants a guidebook analyzing at least this selection. Yet the recordings are a misapplication of the singer's talents on a vast scale, since most of the songs were conceived for, and should be sung by, a soprano. Only a few, though among them the beautiful *"Im Spätboot,"* are suitable for his baritone, since the ranges are uncomfortable and many of the downward transpositions muddy the harmony and even reverse the sentiment. Strangely, he chose to include the Opus 66 cycle (1913–1918), though it consists of piano pieces, in the main, with little to be sung, and its jokes —the chromatic fugue that switches to a polka, the quotations from Beethoven's Fifth and from Strauss's own works—are embarrassing. What still needs to be emphasized about Strauss's lieder is that many of the orchestral ones contain good, virtually unknown music for orchestra—fewer than a dozen having been recorded, while only the last four are regularly performed.

Mr. Jefferson's picture album[8] gives as many views of opera houses, landscapes, singers, conductors, and Nazis as it does of

5. *Ibid.*
6. *The Lieder of Richard Strauss*, by Alan Jefferson (New York, 1971).
7. *Richard Strauss: Das Liedschaffen*, Dietrich Fischer-Dieskau, baritone, and Gerald Moore, piano (Odeon).
8. *Richard Strauss*, by Alan Jefferson (New York, 1975).

the composer. But this is justifiable, Strauss himself being such an uninteresting photographic subject. Blank of countenance, without animation, eyes inscrutable even on the rare occasions when he is looking toward the camera, Strauss's image nevertheless provides a clue to his personality—his appearance and what is known of his behavior being so disparate. Perhaps vaguely aware that the expressionlessness of this visage requires comment, Mr. Jefferson supplies explanatory captions: "careworn and oppressed," "ill-at-ease," "looking very bored." This last refers to a snapshot showing the composer four seats away from Hitler, and, unlike many others in the room, intently watching the speaker, Joseph Goebbels (to whom Strauss dedicated a song). A remark in the chapter "Strauss and Politics," incidentally, is the most puzzling in the book:

> Strauss's grandsons were half-Jewish. . . . Strauss did save them and at no time were they actually threatened with deportation. Martin Bormann was furious at Strauss's capitulation and wanted to make an example of him.

Does this mean that even Bormann thought that Strauss should have had enough principle to leave the country rather than accommodate to the regime? If Herr Bormann should be found in Paraguay, or elsewhere, it is to be hoped that he can explain Mr. Jefferson's statement.

Michael Kennedy's monograph,[9] an apologia for both the music and the life, goes so far as to extol the *Alpensymphonie*; but rehabilitating former warhorses is a part of his purpose as much as boosting neglected works. Strauss is seen as emerging from the shadows where he had been obliged to tarry during the modernist interregnum, the implication being that a balance has now been restored. The statement "the greatest operas of the 1920s were being written by Janáček" is therefore less a criticism of Strauss than of a narrow avant-garde. Strauss in the twenties and thirties is pictured as an isolated figure, not only oblivious of new music but also incurious about it.

9. *Richard Strauss* (London, 1976).

A court composer in an age of statism, he is cast as an unwittingly compliant servitor of the New Order. But the correspondence with Stefan Zweig reveals that Strauss's reactions were more complex than that as well as duplicitous. When one of his letters to Zweig was intercepted by the Nazis and its contents became a possibly serious threat to Strauss, he wrote a groveling letter to Hitler. Mr. Kennedy forgives this as "the act of a frightened old man," yet other old men, no less frightened, have behaved more courageously. Though it is regrettable that Strauss did not stand up, just this once, it must be remembered that he had never in his life stood up for anything not to his own advantage.

This absence of moral character may be connected with such facts of Strauss's life as the choice of a dominating wife and of a librettist who, so far as subject matter was concerned, led him by the nose; thus he sought external direction to compensate for the lack of internal. Moreover, the meek, impassive-looking figure fantasized himself in music as a conquering hero, Don Juan, proud paterfamilias. For his operas, too, he took some of the most bloodthirsty tales available and, in those with edifying themes, removed the edification.

Still another indication of his personality may be found in the Opus 66 lieder cycle, in which the "split" emotions might be symptomatic of an actual breakdown. Finally, lacking an integrated philosophy, he placed so much importance on money that he authorized a film, which even he knew to be a mistake, of his most popular opera. Nor was he above composing to please the public—or to shock it, which comes to the same thing. Otto Klemperer was close to the truth when he explained that Strauss cooperated with the Nazis because "Germany had fifty opera houses, America two."

Richard Strauss could live *Ein Heldenleben* only in his music and in his daydreams. But not many dreamers are so hard-working, or possess gifts of such magnitude. The combination enabled him to create three of the few enduring operas of this century.

SOME OTHER COMPOSERS

MUSICAL R̡
FOR A POLITICAL SEASON

The musical repertory of Western Europe, so far as the general public and the concert establishment are concerned, consists of the popular masterpieces of the eighteenth, nineteenth, and early twentieth centuries. Rich as this heritage is, it should be expanded by at least five hundred years to include the treasures of the age of Guillaume de Machaut (ca. 1300–1377) and Francesco Landini (1325–1397). Because of a few examples of "old music" that did slip across the time barrier, such as Wagner's arrangement of Palestrina's *Stabat Mater,* music lovers have at least been aware that the distant epochs before Bach must have more to offer. Yet by still-prevailing late-nineteenth-century standards, if a composer as ancient as Machaut were to receive much attention, it would be as a "primitive."

Despite the growing historical consciousness in the century of Burckhardt and Schliemann, of the great musicians, Brahms alone knew the works of Bach's immediate German, French, and Italian predecessors. As late as 1910, the one composer of vision directly involved with fifteenth-century polyphony was Webern, through his edition of Heinrich Isaac (court composer to Lorenzo de' Medici). Schoenberg, who was soon to employ technical devices resembling those of the Flemish masters, disdained such revivals as "antiquarian."

Practical as well as cultural reasons account for the long neglect of early music. Until recently, reliable transcriptions, let alone performing editions, were extremely rare; and so, too, were the instruments for which such music was originally written. As a further deterrent, many of the pioneering performers appeared to be forbidding eccentrics, glorying in the dull and archaic—perhaps an ungenerous statement in view of the superficial comprehension of the music even two generations ago and of the indifference of musicology to performance. Quite naturally, music lovers have been slower than museum-goers to recognize that the "primitive" can be profound, and that, so far from deserving our condescension, Machaut's rondeaux, for example, both demand our respect and are, in truth, too sophisticated for us.

One bias against "old music," even among those disposed to give it a fair hearing, arises from a question about its emotional remoteness. Understandably, a person whose ear has been attuned to composers from Mozart to Debussy is skeptical about the power of music six hundred years old to inspire sentiments comparable in *degree* to that of the familiar masters. Not that one would expect the emotion engendered by a piece of Machaut's to be of the same *kind*, of course, even in the case of such universal themes as "romantic love," whose conceptions and conventions differ in every period. But emotions, like concepts, move in and out of fashion, and some of those of the trecento have all but ceased to exist. Religious feelings cultivated in the theological world of Aquinas, such as the exaltation of God in the Doxology, play no part in the lives of most of today's "intelligentsia," one purpose of whose education was to immunize them against these irrationalities. When listening to Machaut's motet *O livoris feritas*, therefore, this contemporary audience can perceive the intensity, purity, and strength of the music but can neither understand nor experience its emotion, a real and ferocious hatred of the Devil. The composition is bound to have an impact on anyone who hears it, but how much more powerful this must have been for those who shared its creed!

It may be that historians will date the widespread acquaintance with "old music" from the recording industry's discovery of a new market to be exploited. Certainly the reasons for the current boom seem to be more pragmatic than artistic: the overcrowding of the catalogue of standard favorites; the advantage of not having to pay royalties to long-dead composers; the modest salaries for performers who are few in number, lack stellar rank, and carry no union cards—unless zink and krummhorn players have lately been organized.

Compared to recordings, live performances have had only a minor influence. But prior to the eighteenth century little music was composed for presentation in concerts. Until the late 1500s, it was written for the liturgy, for ceremonies sacred and secular, and for the recreation of a ruling class that sang and played it —passive listening having been only a small part of musical life then, though now increasing to what threatens to become the eventual exclusion of active amateur participation. Moreover, up to the time of the prima donnas of the later Italian madrigal, the virtuosi who entertained wealthy patrons were, first of all, composers. Yet while the polyphonic Masses of the fifteenth and sixteenth centuries should become a normal part of today's concert repertory, the greatest music of the fourteenth century is less suited for live performance, successions of complex short pieces being difficult to digest except when related in cycles such as those by Machaut.

Two new types of "old music" recordings have now become endemic—the anthology mixing the creations of several cultures and centuries, and the album featuring quaint and creaky instruments. The confusingly large span of the anthologies could be a result of the popular comparison between science and art: since the rate of scientific change in the past thirty years supposedly has been greater than in all previous time, the arts (and especially music) in so distant an era as that of Machaut are assumed practically to have stood still. However this may be, many of the performances on these *omnium gatherum* recordings do not even vaguely delineate the chosen earlier period, whose music they inadequately represent and often badly distort, as when huge choruses are employed to sing the most intimate of madrigals.

The reconstruction of old instruments did not begin until the realization that modern ones could not produce the right diction, and that this was more important than the right timbre. But "orchestral" music as such was almost wholly undeveloped before the Gabrielis and the composers of pavanes, gailliards, and other court dances; instruments in the fourteenth century were used mainly to accompany singers. Thus many of the ensemble pieces on these records are actually modern arrangements, some of them as cute, no doubt, as Haydn's *Toy* Symphony, but of little interest as music. The solo-instrument literature, especially for lute and organ, is older and larger, and devotees of Leonardo will recall that the purpose of his first visit to the Duke of Milan was to deliver a stringed instrument for Lorenzo de' Medici.

———

Three excellent records have lately been issued of music by the two greatest composers of the fourteenth century, Machaut and Landini,[1] an event which has renewed this reviewer's belief that the future of music lies as much in the cultivation of works written in the centuries before Bach as in the development of increasingly versatile electronic means with which to convey messages of ever-diminishing value—or so it often appears. These records can be recommended to listeners who have had no exposure to the music of the period, and little enough to its literature and art. The performances can hardly be improved upon, the voices having the right quality for the music, the singing intelligence and imagination.

The choice of the composers is easily explained: Machaut and Landini dominate their century and its respective French and Italian "Ars Nova" movements. Incidentally, not all readers may be aware that Machaut the composer was also Machaut the poet, since in the five centuries after his death he was better known for his literary skills than for his musical ones. The radical reversal of his reputations in the two arts is recent, his recognition as one of the great composers being not much more than fifty years old. His poetry, though not highly regarded at present, nevertheless continues to appear in new editions, and the latest of these, *La Louange des Dames*,[2] should be mentioned

1. *Guillaume de Machaut: Chansons I* and *Chansons II* (2 records). Thomas Binkley, director and lutenist; Andrea von Ramm, soprano; Richard Levitt, countertenor; Sterling Jones, stringed instruments. Studio for Early Music, Cologne (EMI Records, C 063-30 106 and C 063-30 109).
   Francesco Landini. Same (EMI Records, C 063-30 113C).
2. Edited by Nigel Wilkins (Edinburgh, 1972). The text is based on the Vogüé manuscript, now in New York. Professor Wilkins does not translate the 282 poems, and the music is transcribed by a far-from-calligraphic hand.

if only for the reason that it includes twenty-two of his musical settings.

The practical reasons for choosing Machaut and Landini above any other composers of the era are hardly less important. First, the works of both survive in sufficient number that the listener can become accustomed to the attributes of the individual composers as well as to those of the period. (Machaut collected his works, but the existence of 153 pieces by Landini—out of a total of some 600 for the whole "Ars Nova" period[3]—is truly remarkable, since he was blind from childhood; moreover, all but a few of his compositions are found in at least two copies, which testifies to his stature and popularity.) Second, modern transcriptions of the extant works of both musicians are available, hence the listener can "follow the score." And, finally, since all of Landini's and nearly all of Machaut's music is secular, some audiences will be more comfortable with its subject matter. Though it is true that Machaut's so-called magnum opus is a Mass, this work is not typical of its composer. No doubt some readers will have heard it, and, as a result, have formed prejudices against his other music—the marvelous ballads, virelais, and motets; these have been overshadowed for far too long.

The Landini album must be faulted for failing to provide not only English translations of the verse, which is in the trecento Florentine vernacular, but any vital information whatever. Sources are given for two instrumental arrangements of vocal pieces but not for the *ballate*, *cacce*, and *madrialle*—Landini's only forms—which comprise the other twelve selections on the record. Furthermore, editors and versions are not identified, no notice is given of transpositions, and so little is said about the music itself that the listener who might want a closer acquaintance with its structural features would be obliged to consult a dozen histories, and even such specialized works as Marrocco's *The Music of Jacopo da Bologna*[4] (Landini's master) and *Fourteenth-Century Italian Cacce*.[5] The latter explains the tradition of the

3. See *Italian Ars Nova Music*, by Viola L. Hagopian (Berkeley, 1972).
4. Berkeley and Los Angeles, 1954.
5. Second, revised edition (Cambridge, Mass., 1961).

yelps and cries in *"Così pensoso,"* Landini's vivid *peschia,* and draws attention to the unusual form of the canonic imitation— not only at the fifth but also between the tenor and the counter-tenor—in *"De' dimmi tu,"* his no less masterful *caccia.* The album does cite a few biographical facts and quotes some of the well-known references by contemporaries, but for a period as little known as this one, a musico-historical-sociological analysis is required—on the order of Max Weber's long superseded but in some ways still unsurpassed *The Rational and Social Foundations of Music.*

The principal source for Landini's works, containing no fewer than 145 of his pieces, is the Squarcialupi Codex, one of the most beautiful and valuable of music manuscripts. Its illuminated portrait of Landini and a folio of his music are reproduced on the record cover, though the accompanying notes do not identify either the manuscript or the piece, a famous madrigal, *"Musica son' che . . . ,"* in which the composer disparages the craze for new types of popular music; Landini himself, of course, composed for an exclusive, aristocratic circle.

Antonio Squarcialupi (d. 1475) was Lorenzo de' Medici's organist, and a singer and lutenist highly praised in one of Galeazzo Sforza's letters, but it is not known whether the compilation of the works of the twelve "Ars Nova" composers that bears this musician's name was commissioned by him or obtained later. Completed ca. 1420, which is remarkable because of the change in musical styles in the quarter of a century after Landini's death, the manuscript, now in the Biblioteca Laurenziana, was acquired by Lorenzo's son Giuliano from a nephew of Squarcialupi. The second largest source for Landini's works, this one containing seven of the eight pieces not found in the Codex, is also in Florence, in the Biblioteca Nazionale, while the other most important manuscripts are in Paris and London.

The advantages of being able to compare copies of any manuscript are obvious, but the value is far greater in the case of music that must originally have been dictated, verbally or by being performed in slow motion, by a blind man. Luckily, Landini's transcribers possess a kind of synoptic gospel, especially useful for collating different distributions of syllables and melismata (and different lengths of ligatures), as well as accidentals, which may vary from one manuscript to another, and in the choice of which the performer's role in Landini's time remains for us largely unclear.

More important still, notations of rhythm sometimes conflict, and even a listener with no knowledge of Landini's style will soon realize that in one place the recorded performance of *"Ma' non s'andra"* cannot be correct. By the laws of Landini's mensural notation, the duration of one note is equal to the durations of either two or three notes of the next smaller species, the three-to-one ratio being called—after the Trinity—*tempus perfectus,* the two-to-one *tempus imperfectus.* (Machaut was primarily a three-meter composer, Landini a two-meter one.) The meter may change within a piece from duple to triple, or vice versa, but in strict accordance with these proportional relationships. In addition, since the time values of notes are not only relative but absolute, it is obvious that the "free" and very uncertain change of tempo occurring in the performance of the first section violates Landini's rhythmic system.

This error may be attributable to Johannes Wolf's transcription of the Squarcialupi Codex (published in 1904), for Wolf does not follow the change of meter in the manuscript from duple compound to duple simple; groundbreaking musicologist though he was, Wolf possibly concluded that the change must be a mistake because of the extreme rarity of such instances in Landini's work.[6] But the singers do not adhere to the tempo even of Wolf's one-meter version, nor do they include an attractive cross-rhythm found in the Biblioteca Nazionale manuscript. Yet if the listener is not too bewildered by the rhythmic side of the performance, what will most impress him about the piece is its tonal structure, the G-minor first part and D-minor second, and the progressions

6. *Cf.* Leonard Ellinwood's transcription in *The Works of Francesco Landini,* Medieval Academy of America (New York, 1970). Furthermore, where Wolf adds regular bar lines, which imply false emphases on words and syllables, Ellinwood inserts broken lines, reserving the solid ones for the actual *punctus divisionis* of the manuscript. Ellinwood also reduces the note values of the originals, or of their modern equivalents, by only one half (vs. Wolf's basic quarter-note unit) and substitutes the G clef for the C—all improvements, in this reviewer's opinion.

to the subdominant, dominant, and tonic, just as if the music had been composed in the eighteenth century.

Recordings of such music should probably not be played non-stop and, in the case of this Landini album, it might be wise to begin by hearing a single composition over and over. Perhaps the most appealing is the *ballata* "Eyes that are full of sadness and a heart that is heavy." Here the blind composer seems to be singing about himself, and the music has such extraordinary power to move that the three stanzas will seem too few. The smallest devices are remarkably effective: the countermotion, the stepwise ascent of a fifth in the upper voice at the start, the triad (a dissonance according to the theory of the time) at the high point, and the suspenseful syncopation at the beginning of Part Two. In the recording, the countertenor part is played by the lute alone, which, since this line crosses the superius, gives the latter extra relief as well as the pre-eminence it should always have in Landini's music. This upper part is so idiomatically "Italian" that certain passages might have been interpolated by Monteverdi or even Puccini:

In the Squarcialupi Codex the composer is identified on each folio of his music as *"Magister Franciscus Cecus Horghanista De Florentia."* (*Cecus, il cieco,* "the blind one.") His epitaph, in San Lorenzo, reads, in part:

> Deprived of the light Francesco . . . whom Music extols above all others for his great intellect[7] and his organ music, rests here, his soul above the stars.

———

Machaut composed in a greater variety of forms than Landini, and is much the larger figure historically, but his polyphonic

———

7. Landini was also renowned as a disciple of William of Ockham.

music is far more difficult to listen to than that of the Florentine, as well as more difficult to "hear," especially in the dense textures and intricate counterpoint of the four- and five-voice ballads and rondeaux. Like Schoenberg, however, whom in a few complex passages he sometimes resembles, Machaut indicates the principal voice; this is usually not the uppermost but the next lower one, which is not naturally focal for today's listening habits. In the ballad *"De toutes flours,"* the vocal line is never "covered," and, by itself (insofar as it can be heard that way), will sound to some like Gounod. But contrapuntal variation, not "melody," is the essence of Machaut's art, and the listener should try to digest not only the voice part but also its full instrumental context.

The song cycle *Le lay de la fonteinne* is especially suitable as an introductory work, since it alternates monody and three-voice canons (superbly sung on the EMI record by a girls' chorus from Marseilles). Canonic art does not contain finer examples than these five pieces, for while Bach and Mozart, with the scope of the tonal system, created grander works, Machaut's canons are rhythmically more absorbing. In fact, musicians tend to think of rhythm as Machaut's forte, but when listening to these canons who can doubt that all of the elements are indivisible aspects of the same perfection of the form?

"Harmony," properly speaking, is not an element in Machaut's linear world, and his harmonic intervals, theoretically at least, are extremely limited. Tonality, with its modulations and key relationships, is of course a long way in the future, yet Machaut may seem to approximate "tonal" functions, demarcating phrases and segments of forms, for example, simply by switching to new "harmonic" positions, or anticipating the cadence formula of a later time by sustaining the "leading tone," "harmonized," like the "tonic," a fourth below. This anachronistic listening is rightly deplored by pedagogues, but can today's audience hear *"De toutes flours"* and *not* notice the emphasis on the "dominant," the "key-related" sequences, and even the "sevenths"?

The ballads are regarded as representing a later stage than the motets in the evolution of Machaut's music. But this writer stands in even greater awe of the motets, above all of the French and profane *Quant en moy* and of the aforementioned Latin and ecclesiastical *O livoris feritas*. A second recording of the latter is available for comparison in the Archiv Production *Alte Werk* series, along with three other, no less astonishing motets; and this other interpretation, less spectacularly performed but sung at the notated pitch, doubles the instrumental *cantus firmus,* thus giving it more prominence than it receives in the EMI record, where it is almost overwhelmed by the brilliant singing of the upper two parts.

———

These recordings are suggested as an antidote to the cacophony emanating from the arenas of politics, and as a reminder that voices from long ago can be more soothing.

LISZTOMANIA

I saw Liszt face to face. Great men are like mountains, they are best seen to their advantage from a distance, when there is still a ring of air around them. He looked as if he had been treated at the orthopaedic hospital, where he had been straightened out; there was something spidery, something demoniac about him, and as he was sitting there in front of the piano, pale and with a face full of strong passions, he seemed to me like a devil who was trying to liberate his soul by playing.

—H. C. Andersen, Diaries, *Vol. II, 1836–1844*

Liszt: The Artist as Romantic Hero[1] can be enjoyed as a historical novel, if the reader is able to overlook the book's commen-

1. By Eleanor Perényi (Boston, 1974).

taries on the music. The characters are as large, and some of them are as loathsome, as any in Balzac. Also, the biography has none of the faults of the semifictional genre, the concocted scenes and embellishments of actual ones.

A knowledgeable study of Liszt's music, however, has yet to appear. This is not to say that the accounts of his life are notably higher in quality, but only that the music, elusive in essence and still far from a discriminating appreciation, is the more neglected and difficult subject. Mrs. Perényi's title excuses her from the obligation to discuss it. Furthermore, her monograph stops short at the point when Liszt took holy orders and ceased to be a "romantic hero" though continuing to compose. But the meaning of the life is in the music, if not in Mrs. Perényi's sense that it

> was confessional . . . the autobiography he didn't write . . . landscapes observed, arias overheard, erotic and religious experience, poetry and history. . . . It wouldn't be difficult to draw a picture of his life from the music alone.

In fact, it would be quite impossible to draw any picture containing more objectivity than a Rorschach test. The author's assertion exposes a musical naïveté[2] which is the book's principal weakness.

Another defect is the curious mixture of grandiloquence and slang which makes up Mrs. Perényi's style. On the one hand, for example, she describes the B-Minor Sonata as a "cosmic self-portrait," and, on the other, reports that people were "bowled

2. Not many of Mrs. Perényi's observations about music, whether Liszt's or in general, bear repetition. Nor is her music history reliable. Thus she writes that "Schumann made a special trip to Leipzig to meet Liszt in 1840," when in fact Schumann lived in Leipzig and made the trip to Dresden; and that "To Liszt, *Carnaval* scarcely qualified as music," whereas Liszt actually lauded *Carnaval* above Beethoven's *Diabelli* Variations. Worse still, Mrs. Perényi states that "Liszt reached the twelve-tone scale half a century before Schoenberg," apparently unaware that Schoenberg's scale was the same as Mozart's, and that European music had "reached" it centuries earlier. But how can a Liszt scholar speculate that "a passage like the second subject of the *Dante Symphony* is possibly the first to be written in 7/4 time"? The meter occurs in Berlioz's *Cellini*, which greatly influenced Liszt, and which he conducted before composing the *Symphony*. And how can anyone who has heard *Don Giovanni* say that "the brasses, the woodwinds, the timpani are nineteenth-century products"?

over" ("[George] Sand was indeed bowled over"), driven "up the wall," and asked to "cough up" five thousand thalers. More important than this, since it creates an impediment to communication, is Mrs. Perényi's addiction to floating pronouns. Thus she writes of another publication on Liszt that

> Paganini gets eight pages. More unaccountably, since he is an infinitely more careful and discriminating scholar and critic than Walker, the best probably that we have, Humphrey Searle,[3] passes over detailed discussions. . . .

And the following excerpt starts the reader on a labyrinthine expedition, the masculine pronoun referring to a still-living biographer of Wagner and the nearest proper noun after that to "Liszt":

> . . . Lilli Lehmann, singing *Mignons Lied* one day at Wahnfried, provoked the remark that he hadn't realized Liszt composed "such pretty songs." . . .

It is regrettable that Mrs. Perényi did not amend her title, reduce the space allotted to such background figures as Victor Hugo, and provide a biography that included Liszt's later years.[4] In many ways these are the most absorbing, as well as the most in need of thorough exploration. Existing accounts are paralyzingly banal, and either disingenuous or grossly distorted— that of Ernest Newman, for instance, establishing a kind of

3. If Searle is indeed the "best scholar and critic that we have," some of his verbal explanations concerning his work (in *The Music of Liszt* [London, 1954]) would do little to confirm this stature. He writes, and Mrs. Perényi enthusiastically quotes him: "The serial technique of Schoenberg . . . uses precisely the methods of Liszt's thematic transformation within the framework of an entirely different language." Even metaphorically this is both untrue and impossible.
4. For a study of the final period of Liszt's life (1871–1886), see *Twilight of Ferencz Liszt*, by Bence Szabolcsi (London, 1959). Neither of the two most valuable Liszt books has yet been translated into English, Peter Raabe's *Franz Liszt: Leben und Schaffen* (revised edition published in 1968) and *Correspondence de Liszt et de Madame d'Agoult* (published by Liszt's grandson in 1934).

world's record in antihagiography. Since Mrs. Perényi's view of Liszt's life as a layman is balanced and by no means uncritical, it would seem reasonable to expect the same qualities in a continuation of the biography after the composer became a cleric. Her forte is his love life—though her most memorable line in this regard could have been inspired by Swann and Odette rather than by the bachelor Liszt:

> Every love affair reaches a point that in retrospect ought to have been the finish, and it is at this point that many lovers decide to marry.

Mrs. Perényi is adroit, too, in reducing the euphuistic epistolary manners of the period to plain sexual facts. She observes of a tender message from Liszt to Marie d'Agoult, "He isn't just describing post-coital detumescence," and of a letter from Sand denying her liaison with Charles Didier, "Didier, by the way, *was* her lover."

Thus it is to be hoped that Mrs. Perényi may one day be persuaded to give her answers to, or informed guesses about, similar questions in Liszt's later years. Among the more tantalizing would be the rumors that the date of Liszt's ordination was advanced to ensure him against having to marry Princess Carolyne; the mystery as to which of the Abbé's passions, besides those for the Baroness Myendorff and the young Countesses Janina and Schmalhausen,[5] were actually consummated; the full story of Agnes Klindworth, who was the most attractive, if only because the most discreet, of his long-term mistresses; the evidence for Newman's[6] assumption that Franz Servais was Liszt's son; and the facts, if any, in Claude Rostand's[7] statement that women made

5. To please this young lady Liszt added cadenzas to his Second Hungarian Rhapsody. These are marked by the symbol SCH in Volume III of the New Liszt Edition (Budapest, 1972), which also identifies some of the features that Liszt imitated from indigenous models in both music and dance, such as, in the Third Hungarian Rhapsody, cimbalom articulation and heel-clicking cadences.
6. *The Man Liszt: A Study of the Tragi-Comedy of a Soul Divided Against Itself,* by Ernest Newman (New York, reprint, 1970).
7. *Liszt,* by Claude Rostand, translated by John Victor (New York, 1972).

"outrageous propositions" to Liszt, despite his seventy-four years and purple sash of a Canon of Albano. Finally, what was his secret?—apart from Marie d'Agoult's incomplete revelation that "even when he is most passionate, most altered by desire, one feels nothing gross in these desires." All of which sounds like afternoon television. But the Liszt scandals *did* attract an audience of comparable size, one far larger than did the astonishing music that he was producing at the same time of life.

Mrs. Perényi believes that "male resentment of Liszt"—which in Sainte-Beuve's case she ascribes to envy of his "beauty and virility"—focuses on

> two aspects of his amorous career: the number of his conquests and their quality.

Social quality, presumably. But surely the two outstanding "aspects" of his later career in this sense were the youth of the conquered and the durability of the performer. Skepticism on either score ought to be allayed by the story of young Olga Janina, who invaded the septuagenarian composer's monastic hide-out disguised as a boy, and apparently found her experience there so gratifying that when Liszt left Rome shortly before a later rendezvous, she followed him with pistols halfway across Europe.

"Heine was one of the first to notice the sexual side of Lisztomania," Mrs. Perényi says. But the composer's father seems to have predicted it: "You belong to art," he told young Franz, "but women make me frightened for you." Mrs. Perényi helps to date the beginning of the rock-audience reaction:

> Women did not show the symptoms of orgasm at Paganini's concerts, and at Liszt's they did.

But Paganini looked like Dracula in an etiolated phase; and it *was* a question of physical attractiveness, Liszt's facial expression—"simply grand," George Eliot wrote—apparently hypnotizing the female contingent. Distraction of the audience away from the content of the music and toward the countenance of the performer, and reading this as a guide to the meaning of the music, seems to have started with Liszt.

Testimony concerning the in-person behavior of Liszt the seducer is naturally meager, but if he appears to have been more fatuous in the flesh than in writing, no doubt that depends on the addressee, in this instance George Sand:

> Can I allow myself to hope that . . . you would . . . be willing to count me among the five or six people whom you receive more or less willingly on rainy days?

Compare this with his egotism when basking in the adulation, and cultivating the puppy love, of a pupil:

> Little by little . . . Liszt recounted his success and pleasures in Society . . . pursuing a fascinating woman who . . . had been married . . . to an elderly man. . . . He had gazed on her eyes from midnight until three o'clock. . . .[8]

After this display of vanity, it is tempting to say that Liszt deserved his scribbling mistresses—and a punishment of having to read all twenty-four volumes of Princess Carolyne's *Internal Causes of the External Weakness of the Church*, as well as the stultifying novels of Countess Marie (alias Daniel Stern). But the story of these pretentious women is less germane than the explanations for Liszt's having tied himself to them. Apart from escaping Lisztomania and the ravages he suffered as a performer, he recognized and feared the absence of inner direction:

> I feel no vocation. . . . I do not have a calm and sustained conviction. . . .

Well aware of the flaws in his life and work, he realized that in his struggle to achieve his goals as a creative artist he could not do without the goading, as well as the security and solicitude, of his aristocratic protectresses. His later escape into the Church

8. From the Diary of Valerie Boissier, 1832.

was obviously motivated by the same needs—protection and an order externally imposed.

Yet however despicable these parasitical personal relationships, any judgment of Liszt's ethics must take into consideration his immense strength of will in renouncing his career as a touring virtuoso in order to dedicate himself to composition. And whatever his deficiencies, his redeeming qualities were of a rare kind. He was prodigally generous with his colleagues, tirelessly transcribing and performing their music, putting his own work as a composer second to the promotion of that of Berlioz and Wagner. And he has had neither precursor nor successor to rival his openness toward music of differing tendencies, championing, as he did, Verdi as well as Wagner, Tchaikovsky as well as the Russian "Five," giving unstintingly of himself to all. Nor did he "react" against younger composers, as most others after a certain age have done.

Liszt believed that Balakirev and Rimsky-Korsakov were

> ploughing more fertile ground than the backward imitators of Mendelssohn and Schumann.

Referring to Anton Rubinstein, who represented the opposite point of view, the composer of *Liebestraum* amplified his own:

> Rubinstein may . . . fish deeper in the Mendelssohn waters, and even swim away if he likes. But sooner or later I am certain he will give up the apparent and the formalistic for the organically real.

The philosophy is unchallengeable, at least verbally, and Liszt's side is clearly the right one to be on—particularly with Rubinstein on the other. If in practice the "organically real" sometimes seemed amorphous and even improvisatory, the *Tristan* Prelude would refute criticism. The nemesis was Brahms, who took the Mendelssohn-Schumann route and nevertheless managed to compose "organically real" music—most of which is still alive, moreover, unlike all but a fraction of Liszt's.

Liszt was always in the van of progress, ready—too ready, Heine wrote—to take up with anything new, including such experimental notions as that of showing colored slides during performances of his *Dante* Symphony. On another level he was a major innovator in musical philosophy, as well as in form, harmony, "thematic transformation," keyboard technique; and his influence has been diffused through composers as different as Debussy and Saint-Saëns, Scriabin and Ravel, Mahler and Stravinsky. The association of the last two names with Liszt may be surprising, but Mahler's exploitation of voices in symphonies —in one instance with the same Goethe text—his subject matter, and his alternate use of Latin and German owe much to Liszt's example. In Stravinsky's case, certain echoings, such as that of the first cadenza in *Totentanz* in the second tableau of *Petrushka,* are unmistakable. More important, the idea of *Pulcinella* came from Liszt[9]—probably from the *Réminiscences de Don Juan,* an original composition in something of the same sense as Stravinsky's, and one that must be included among Liszt's most successful *opera* (though apparently neither Mrs. Perényi nor Searle considers it worthy of mention).

The progressives of today have taken up Liszt more as a cause than a composer in his own right, what matters to them being less the music itself than whether Liszt was "ahead of his period" in it, or used unrelated chords and avoided perfect cadences "for the first time." The new attitude is that Liszt's "unknown" music, together with that of the final two decades—the *Années de pèlerinage* III and other contemporaneous piano pieces—is the superior one. But the "unknown" Liszt consists mainly of religious music and songs, and in score,[10] at least, discloses nothing that will substantially enhance his reputation. True, the sacred

9. "I . . . am guilty of having borrowed from Pergolesi for my *Pulcinella.* What is more, Liszt supplied the example" (*Comoedia,* January 21, 1924).
10. In addition to the Gregg reprint of the Breitkopf and Härtel "complete" works, several volumes have recently appeared in a Soviet edition, while most of the late piano pieces have been issued by the Liszt Society in London. An Eulenberg miniature score of the *Requiem* is now available, too, as well as a good recording, and, finally, a complete recording of *The Legend of St. Elizabeth.*

works employ unusual instrumental combinations—bass trombone and organ in one instance, two horns in another, harmonium, harp, and piano in a third—but these do not modify this opinion.

The religious compositions, in any case, must be approached by way of their stylistic features. Liszt knew his church's music, the best as well as the worst of it, and perhaps for this reason he is more traditionalist than innovator in his own contributions. It is worth remembering, too, that taking the tonsure had little effect on either the caliber or the quantity of the work. Unlike Fra Angelico, the *Abate diàvolo* did not consecrate his art to his religion but dashed off a variation on *Chopsticks* and wrote a second *Mephisto Waltz* in the same year that he produced music for the Pope. It should be enough to say on the subject that the *Magnificat* in the *Dante* Symphony is as fine an example in the sacred category as any in the "unknown" Liszt.

Songwriting might have become a more significant mode of expression for Liszt if he had been possessed of a nationality. Strangely, he was without a native language, knowing no Hungarian at all, nor even anything about the land of his birth, his study of Magyar music and history dating from comparatively late in life; thus he could not have escaped the charge of shamming when he sent for a Hungarian redingote to wear in London. But neither was he French or German, the languages of his songs except for a few in Italian and one in English (by Tennyson). Yet despite this anomalous cultural and linguistic situation, a few of the lieder are among the better pieces of their kind.

As for the cultists of the late works, this group ignores what is most widely recognized as Lisztian, esteeming the music chiefly for its similarities to that of more modern composers, Debussy above all. But in saying "like Debussy"—of the *Eglogue*, for instance, or the *Angelus*—is the listener not also declaring a preference *for* Debussy? Some late Liszt, including *Nuages gris*, *Les Jeux d'eaux à la Villa d'Este*, and *Von der Wiege bis zum Grabe* (despite this Attlee era title), is extraordinary music, a manifestation of one of those breathtaking developments in an artist's old age that seem to betoken a change of personality but that give testimony to continuing discovery and refinement. Even so, the later works are not without shortcomings, one of them being the measured but interminable silences during which a piece like the *Sunt lacrymae rerum* loses volition.

It is convenient to divide the music into works for orchestra and for piano solo. The former category is comparatively small in quantity and, with one important and some minor exceptions, belongs to the period 1848–1861; the latter is vast and represents the entire life. The exception, *Von der Wiege bis zum Grabe*, is the most unlikely creation ever to come from Liszt's pen, at any rate from the perspective of his established characteristics. The first and last sections are naturally the most appealing, and their orchestral sound is of an extreme delicacy. Anyone hearing the score for the first time would mistake it for a newly unearthed one by Debussy, or, in the middle section, for one by Bartók. Its critics maintain that it falls off at the end, but are they not forgetting that Liszt was always a programmatic composer, and that hence the withering away is perfectly appropriate?

The formal aspects of the earlier symphonic poems are of more moment than their instrumental ones. At the outset, in fact, Liszt knew so little about the orchestra that he sought help from others and revised the first few poems as many as two and three times. These single-movement "symphonies" so successfully challenged the traditional species that Liszt's example was followed by most younger composers (always excepting Brahms) until Mahler synthesized the two forms. Yet the forms were not new, both in the sense that five of them were actually overtures, and that the vogue of program music had been launched twenty years earlier by Berlioz's *Symphonie Fantastique*. Liszt's, however, were destined to be the most popular models.

Their unpopularity today is justified, the worst of them being presentable only as prankish examples of bad taste. But even their best moments—the "Apotheosis" in *Die Ideale*, the episode in *Les Préludes* that seems to have attracted the composer of the "Forest Murmurs" in *Siegfried*—do not exactly transport the listener. *Les Préludes* merits its status as the only active survivor, for it alone contains memorable melody and pleasant barbershop harmony. But in spite of these features, the music's unimaginative rhythms have consigned it to the park band.

Searle acclaims another of the poems, *Hamlet,* as

> one of Liszt's masterpieces. . . . It consists of a slow introduc-tion, a dramatic and violent Allegro, and an ending [in] the manner of a funeral march. . . . A remarkable psychological portrait emerges.

The listener might conceivably wonder how this portrait is achieved, or even how the music relates to the play at all. If, by error, the title were changed to *Macbeth,* or *Everyman,* or the *Transmigration of Souls,* would anyone complain that the music was less apt? The timpani part is marked *"vacillando,"* it is true, but, without consulting the score, who could tell whether the player was actually vacillating or simply playing the written rhythm? Musically speaking, *Hamlet* is marked by an absence of tension and invention, and by a too conspicuous presence of Liszt's vice of exact repetition. If a "psychological portrait" had been his aim—which is by no means evident from his verbal in-terpretation of the play—then the discrepancy between intent and realization is close to one hundred percent.

Hamlet is far from the worst of the poems, however, the rivals for that distinction being *Ce qu'on entend sur la Montagne* (the answer to which is, "Very little") and *Tasso,* although *Festklänge* should not be denied the right to compete. *Ce qu'on entend* is one of the much-revised early pieces, but it should have been worked over until totally deleted, being so barren of ideas that the score reader sometimes wonders if he might have forgotten to turn the page. When the hero has finally climbed his Alp, his feelings of piety are expressed in a hymn, at the beginning of which Liszt writes *"Andante religioso,"* as if the character of the music could not be determined without verbal help.

For all that has been written about the way Liszt's music looks forward to *Tristan* (actually his most *Tristan*-esque piece is the second of the Villa d'Este group, composed fifteen years after the opera), it must be remarked that he looks backward far more often, and in despair, to Chopin. The composer who owes most to the poems, however, the Tchaikovsky of *Francesca da Rimini,* is seldom mentioned in connection with them. Both Liszt and Tchaikovsky repeat mindlessly and rely on dynamics as a substitute for inner musical tension. But where the Russian is maudlin (and orchestrally skillful), the Hungarian is empty of any feeling (and orchestrally clumsy). The bombastic ending of *Tasso* is beneath even bad Tchaikovsky.

Surprisingly, for they belong to the same period, the *Faust* and *Dante* symphonies are greatly superior to the symphonic poems. One of the reasons for this is that the symphonies are elevated and transformed by their choral endings. Another is that by this time (the mid-1850s) Liszt's instrumental imagination had begun to show itself in such small combinations as the quartet of violins and the oboe and viola duet in *Faust*. But the orchestrations of the entire *Gretchen* movement (in *Faust*) and some of the *Purgatorio* movement (in *Dante*) contain novel and delectable blends of color. Finally, it should be mentioned that if any piece by Liszt is the source of a work by another composer, then *Parsifal* is indebted to the ending of the *Dante* Symphony. Here the triadic theme, the instrumentation, the meter and rhythm might almost be mistaken for an early draft of the final Grail scene.

Nevertheless, the listener automatically imagines a piano playing such orchestral accompaniment figures as the string arpeggios in *Les Préludes*, and Liszt's orchestra does in fact seem incomplete without the piano. It is odd that the composer so rarely brought piano and orchestra together, and that neither of his concertos fulfills the high promise that might have been expected of a virtuoso-composer. But is Mrs. Perényi not misguided in choosing the Second Concerto over the First, which she ranks with "the rhapsodies and the operatic paraphrases" as being "from the second or third drawer down"? The beginning of the First Concerto is as stunningly original as any in the repertory, and the remainder of the work is at least tolerable, while the Second contains more exciting materials, but they are disappointingly developed.

One reason for the superiority of the third "concerto," *Toten-tanz*, is that the variation form, which provided a path as well as stimulated Liszt's powers of invention, was more suited to his talents than that of the free-roving quasi-sonata. Two other sets of variations, the *Paganini* and the *Weinen, Klagen,* are among his incontestable successes. But the *Totentanz* variations are exceptional in range of mood, wit (the glissandos in the piano part), rhythmic vitality, and control—no effect is exaggerated. In the opening measures, and perhaps for the first time in modern music, the piano is treated as a percussion instrument, and in fact is doubled by one, the timpani, producing a result similar to that of Bartók's tone clusters.[11]

As a composer for the piano, Liszt made enormous contributions to its technique, but in the expression of emotion he is peculiarly limited. He strives for exaltation but attains it only rarely (as in the ending of the *Sursum corda, pèlerinage* III), his strongest sentiments being nostalgias (*Valse Oubliée* is his title *par excellence*) and musings about death (*La lugubre gondola*). Instead of passion he provides mere excitement, in the grandiose, in keyboard acrobatics, in speed and volume. In *D'Après une lecture de Dante, fantasia quasi sonata,* for instance, he offers not one moment for meditation before unleashing a barrage of chromatic octaves, pounding crescendos, reiterated rhythms. These and other vulgarities were unknown to music before Liszt, at least on anything like the same scale, yet his vulgarity weighs less heavily against him than his emotional hollowness.

"My mission will be to have introduced poetry into piano music with some brilliance," Liszt wrote. He was mistaken. His mission was to introduce new forms, harmonies, colors, and pianistic fireworks. In these he is an original, as well as a lesser composer than his devotees protest, a larger one than his detractors concede.

11. Strangely, Bartók described the *Totentanz* as "startlingly harsh from beginning to end." See his "Liszt as Composer," an address to the Hungarian Academy of Science, 1934, included in *The Essays of Bela Bartók* (London, 1976).

POSTSCRIPT: In a letter published in *The New York Review of Books*, March 6, 1975, Mrs. Perényi took issue with some points of this notice of her book. The same column published this reviewer's answer, which is appended here since it amplifies the article. Mrs. Perényi's arguments are easily inferable from the replies they provoked:

TO THE EDITORS OF *The New York Review*:

I criticized Mrs. Perényi's biography for musical unsoundness and slapdash writing but neglected to mention the book's Olympian condescension ("[Liszt and Berlioz] are essentially aristocratic composers, Wagner a pleb") and deficiency in elementary logic. Her letter now exposes these faults too glaringly to be overlooked. She asks how a statement can be both "untrue" and "impossible," admitting that, to her, the sentence in which I employed this distinction is impenetrable. Quite simply, a statement is untrue when it is incorrect in fact, impossible when what it says could not occur in any case; the two words are by no means preclusive. Thus Mr. Searle's statement—

The serial technique of Schoenberg . . . uses precisely the methods of Liszt's thematic transformation within the framework of an entirely different language

—is factually untrue. And the same statement is also impossible, since the serial technique of Schoenberg *could* not "use precisely" the putative "method" of Liszt.

But to begin at the beginning:

1. Mrs. Perényi is under the impression that my article, "Lisztomania," "was, or ought to have been," confined to a review of her book. But my purpose was to discuss Liszt's music as a whole, and it is the reviewer's prerogative, as well as accepted practice, to consider only those parts of a publication that are relevant to his topic. All the same, I did summarize Mrs. Perényi's volume, while giving only passing notice to two others sharing with hers the review portion of the article, a fact she

ignores. Mrs. Perényi's carelessness with words is exemplified in the way in which she changes my suggestion about "reducing the space allotted to Victor Hugo" to "sinking" that worthy.

2. Mrs. Perényi writes that "Craft is fussy about phrasing (I am scolded for 'floating pronouns' " [sic]). Actually my review fussed about elementary grammatical errors, especially the large number of indefinite antecedents, not about "phrasing." I gave up on the latter but can recommend the book to anthologists of peculiar usages:

> No doubt it amused Liszt to live like a feudal lord . . . in afterlife he was fond of visiting his magnate friends in Hungary.

(As a ghost?)

3. "There is no special reason for thinking [that Berlioz's *Cellini*] had a great influence on [Liszt]," Mrs. Perényi writes. But this influence is real and deeper than she seems to recognize. The extent to which Liszt involved himself in the opera—and it was he who persuaded Berlioz to revise it—would alone bear out David Cairns's observation: "For Liszt, *Cellini* was one of the foremost works of his time." The evidence of the influence becomes apparent from a comparison of the two scores. And the dates *do* matter. *Cellini* was performed a decade before Liszt "sketched out" his *Dante* Symphony, and he must have known the opera long before his decision to present it. Seven-four meters, or alternating fours and threes, are at least as old as Monteverdi, but why does Mrs. Perényi appeal to an authority whose testimony is simply a repetition of the question?

4. Mrs. Perényi refutes a point that I never raised. I did not deny that instruments differ greatly, though called by the same names, in the eighteenth, nineteenth, and other centuries. But I do continue to contradict her claim that "the brasses, the wood-winds, the timpani are nineteenth-century products." The eighteenth century had them too, and Mozart's flute would be recognized as a flute, and not some other instrument, in the nineteenth century as well as today. All of this is explained in

countless histories of musical instruments published in the forty-five years since the obsolete edition of Grove which Mrs. Perényi chose "at random." As to the relevance of *Don Giovanni*, it is in Shaw's well-known remark:

> The [brass] statue music [is] still as impressive as it was before Wagner and Berlioz were born.

5. To answer Mrs. Perényi's question, the scale used by Mozart and Schoenberg had been employed for centuries before *both* composers. If the point only "seems to be" a misuse of the word "scale," however, Mrs. Perényi has not grasped the importance of the matter, which is not simply the misuse of a word but the failure to differentiate between categories of musical material and methods of organizing it.

6. Mrs. Perényi took too seriously my reference to three bits of biographical trivia, yet my question about the date of the ordination is not answered in the four pages she cites. Regarding the Franz Servais affair, it is accepted that Carolyne could not have been Servais's mother, but this is hardly proof that Liszt, whom he resembled, was not his father. Finally, if Mrs. Perényi has told all that is known about Agnes Klindworth, why does the book fail to mention her more familiar name, Mrs. Street? Similarly, one wonders why Mrs. Perényi's letter confines the liaison to Weimar, while her book says that

> after 1855 Agnes moved to Brussels—where Liszt contrived to see her quite often.

I am sorry to have distressed Mrs. Perényi, but the correction of erroneous and misleading pronouncements is one of the requirements of criticism.

R. C.

THE NOSTALGIC KINGDOM
OF MAURICE RAVEL

In the century since the birth of Maurice Ravel, two or three Promethean composers have transformed the identifying features of Western music. Ravel's influence was of a different and lesser order. Unlike Schoenberg, the creator of *Ma Mère l'Oye* and the *Trois poèmes de Stéphane Mallarmé* was not only of his time but wholly circumscribed by it, playing only a minor role in shaping the future. This is not an adverse judgment of him, especially in view of what that future has become, but it provides a perspective on his achievements, unnecessary as that may seem in the case of music at once so unproblematic and so enduringly popular. Yet the core of Ravel's personality is an enigma, reflected throughout his work in certain limitations of development, in the narrowness as well as the perfection of his expression, and in the disparity between the most and least successful in the comparatively small body of his music.

The centenary observances in New York have consisted of a concert of little-known or unknown minor pieces (at Queens College), a rash of orchestral and recital performances much like those of last year or next, and an exhibition, by the Dance Collection of the Library of Performing Arts, of several important manuscripts, as well as letters, programs, photographs, and set and costume designs. In mid-May,[1] the New York City Ballet lavishly presented three programs (four times each) containing a total of fourteen works by Ravel and two by Debussy-Ravel. Only *Daphnis et Chloé*, *La Valse*, and *Boléro* were composed as ballets, but with Ravel's collaboration three more were made of *Ma Mère l'Oye*, *Valses nobles et sentimentales*, and *Le Tombeau de Couperin*.

1. 1975.

Since the ballet company also performed *L'Enfant et les sorti-lèges*, here classified as a choreographic work, the observation must be made that the rhythms and forms of the bulk of Ravel's music are those of the dance. This in itself should justify a dance festival devoted to a composer whose work is rarely experienced outside of the concert hall. Furthermore, an attempt to demonstrate the choreographic viability of Ravel's music was an homage that New York was uniquely able to render him. It is only regrettable that his most successful theatrical work, *L'Heure espagnole*, was not given concurrently on one of the city's other stages.

As for publications, the failure of the centenary to elicit a volume of letters is disappointing, since Ravel's reclusive personality might be penetrated only through his and his family's intimate communications. Surely personal considerations cannot have been an issue in withholding the 1,500 letters that have been counted in private collections, for the most recent contribution to the correspondence is forty years old.

Some compensations will be found in Arbie Orenstein's *Ravel: Man and Musician.*[2] In addition to essays on the composer's aesthetics and creative processes, Mr. Orenstein provides a biography, a bibliography, a discography, and exhaustive program notes for each work. His book, in fact, is the first on the subject to combine a complete survey of the music with a substantial store of information about the man. Owing to Ravel's hermetic privacy, the biography will be read for clues; thus the mention that he was fond of "Tea for Two" becomes significant, perhaps because of some similarity to Ravel's harmonic style, and so does a note about the importance that he attached to Condillac's *Traité des sensations*, that book's discussion of phenomenological exteriority presenting a metaphysical parallel to Ravel's illness.

Mr. Orenstein does not direct his attention to the two most troubling questions in Ravel's life, his sexuality and his terminal disease, but the book contains material for answers to both, as

2. New York, 1975.

well as for treating them as aspects of one and the same problem.[3] Concerning the first, Mr. Orenstein limits himself to the statement:

Although not insensitive to feminine charm and beauty, there was apparently no romantic attachment at any point in [Ravel's] career.

About the second, no more is said than:

Because of medical ethics, the exact nature of Ravel's malady has remained obscure. It is clear that no tumor was found, and that Dr. Vincent succeeded in equalizing the level of the cerebral hemispheres, one of which had become depressed.

Medical ethics or medical ignorance? In either case, these same non-explanations have been repeated since Ravel's death, though the medical facts could hardly have been suppressed, since it is unlikely that an organic basis for the illness was ever found. (According to rumor Ravel had hereditary syphilis, and Dr. Vincent is supposed to have told his confidants that the composer's brain cells were in an advanced state of decay.) In 1932 the composer was involved in a minor automobile accident, apparently sustaining no injuries. But less than a year later he was incapacitated by what seemed to be aphasia, and by 1934 he was able to write a letter only with the aid of a dictionary from which he copied each word. The "tumor" operation was performed three years after that, and Ravel died.

A functional diagnosis never seems to have been considered, though as early as 1912 Ravel was subject to attacks of "incipient neurasthenia" that obliged him to live for extended periods in semi-retreat. Furthermore, the "aphasic" failures of communica-

---

3. Neither does Mr. Orenstein pursue the question of Ravel's possible Jewish ancestry. That his paternal great-grandfather was a Sephardic rabbi was generally assumed to be fact—by Stravinsky, for one, who had the story from Ravel's biographer, Roland-Manuel. But surely some records must exist.

tion began after the death of the composer's mother, or approximately fifteen years before the accident and terminal illness. Mr. Orenstein describes Ravel's attachment to her as

the deepest emotional tie of his entire life [and] her death [as] a blow from which the composer never fully recovered.

Although rejected for military service at the age of twenty, at forty Ravel was driving a truck somewhere near the front. Yet his only complaint was about the separation from his mother. In June 1916, he wrote to a friend: "I suffer from one thing, not being able to embrace my poor mother." The composer's breakdown and aphasia, or middle-age autism, began soon after his mother's death, in January 1917. "Intense need to work," he writes to his publisher, but "am absolutely incapable of obeying the impulse," and although possessed by musical ideas, Ravel was unable to compose or even to write. At the age of forty-five he confessed:

I think of those former times when I was so happy. . . . It will soon be three years since [mother] died, and my despair increases from day to day. . . . I no longer have this dear silent presence enveloping me with her tenderness, which was, I see it more clearly now than ever, my only reason for living.

Ravel never outgrew the world of his childhood, which he continued to furnish with toys, mechanical birds, music boxes, figurines—his first opera includes a scene for marionettes—bibelots. At thirty he composed a *Noël des jouets* and at fifty the doll's-house opera *L'Enfant et les sortilèges*, which, though a miniature in every sense, is also the largest work of his later life. Nor is it farfetched to associate the fanfares in the backgrounds of such pieces as *L'Enfant* and *Ma Mère l'Oye* with the world of toy soldiers. And when Ravel composed mourning music for a death in his fairyland, naturally the object of his imagined grief was a child, and of course a noble one, a princess whose obsequies could be observed only in the most formal of dances from a remote and romanticized past. Whatever else may be said about this combination of Velázquez tableau and sentimental nursery drama, manifestly the undevelopable form, the repeated melody, and the preciosity of the instrumentation—the petite horn-in-G instead of some prosaic instrument—are the essence of Ravel.

Fairy tales, in fact, are at the heart of Ravel's imaginative world, inspiring his most affecting music. The childlike poignancy and ingenuousness of *"Petit Poucet"* and *"Le Jardin féerique"* from *Ma Mère l'Oye*, and of the Princess's *"Hélas! petit ami"* from *L'Enfant* are unique in the art. Whereas Schumann evokes childhood from without, Ravel's creations are of the child spirit itself. He feels and expresses an intensity of emotion in his world of make-believe that he apparently is unable to do in the outer world of maturity. The tenderness in his adult songs (in the *"Trois Beaux Oiseaux du Paradis,"* for example) is not that of one person for another but rather of a nostalgia for a distant and exotic time and place, found either in literature—Ronsard, *Don Quixote*—or in painting, for Ravel once identified the landscape of *Daphnis and Chloé* as

the Greece of my dreams . . . which is the same as that depicted by late-eighteenth-century French artists.

One effect on Ravel's music of his inability to emerge from the emotional world of his childhood is that he became a sophisticated innocent, cultivating worldly tastes as protective disguises; the spirit whose home was close to the child's playroom lived beneath the apparel of the dandy, behind the show of the connoisseur and *bon vivant*. The musical translation of this is "orchestration," which in Ravel's case may appear to be more important than substance, a distinction he categorically denied: "There is no such thing as a well-orchestrated piece but only a well-written one." Yet he contradicted this in a remark about Debussy, who was "angry that he orchestrates so badly." Ravel went so far as to express the desire to re-orchestrate *La Mer*. What this would have been like can be imagined to some extent from the admirable clarity of his instrumentation of Debussy's *Danse*. That Ravel did not bequeath this lesson in the textural decongestion of *La Mer*[4] is a pity. How much more interesting it would have been than his transcription of Mussorgsky's *Pictures*, which not only fails to enhance the original but actually dissipates the "impressionistic" blur in *"Cum mortuis in lingua mortua"* that had had such a profound effect on French music two generations earlier.

Ravel's deep attachment to the past may also be attributed to his arrested emotional growth. He was a neo-classicist from the start, his first published work being the *Menuet antique*, which he was to follow with three further examples in that form, a curious one for a young composer in the early years of the twentieth century. But archaicism pervades not only the music— in the use of modes, for example (the Aeolian *"Pavane de la Belle au bois dormant"*)—but also the subject matter (*D'Anne jouant de l'espinette* and *Le Tombeau de Couperin*). This is one of the reasons that chronology in Ravel's work can be difficult to determine; others are that the characteristics of his style were formed at an early date, and that his technical mastery could have been expanded, after about 1908, only with different directions in which to move and new territory to conquer.

Still another effect of the life on the work, or parallel between them, is in Ravel's predilection, also from the beginning, for small forms (the *Epigrammes de Clément Marot*). Even the operas are brief, their single acts being comprised, in the case of *L'Heure espagnole* (which lasts less than an hour), of twenty-one scenes, and of *L'Enfant* (which is approximately the same length), of a series of short adventures, each complete in itself.

But the operas are miniatures quite apart from their musical dimensions. The age of the elementary-school hero of *L'Enfant* determines the limits of the work's dramatic appeal, which creates

---

4. But the orchestration of his own *Une Barque sur l'océan* is muddier than Dubussy's of his *La Mer*. Also, the music is much more ominous in the orchestra than it is in the piano original, but apart from that, the transcription is technically below Ravel's par, the repetition of the first phrase in the flutes, for example, being especially dull.

an obstacle to performance on opera stages. (No doubt the ideal "performance" will one day be installed among the electronic entertainments of Disney World.) The dramatic level of *L'Heure espagnole* is that of a Feydeau farce, but the joke on which the opera is based is a schoolboy's. As for *Daphnis et Chloé*, the one large-scale work, it is both episodic in the wrong sense, stopping and starting according to the dictates of the choreography, and far too long; the Suite No. II, which Ravel extracted from the last part, proves Mies's law that less can be more. The ballet does not justify Ravel's description of it as a "Choreographic Symphony in Three Movements," nor does it bear out his claim that "the development of a small number of motifs assures the symphonic homogeneity of the work."

One further parallel between Ravel's childhood and his art is that he is essentially a musical storyteller, more inspired by poetry, and more stimulated by words, syllables, literary programs than by the problems of traditional musical form. To some of his scores he even affixed epigraphs—from Baudelaire, Perrault, the Comtesse d'Aulnoy, Mme Leprince de Beaumont, and Henri de Régnier. In the case of the last there are two, one of which, in the *Rapsodie espagnole*, has little discernible relationship to the music. *Gaspard de la nuit* is subtitled "*Poèmes pour piano*" and in *Daphnis*, words are used to supplement the music: "*Emotion douce à la vue du couple*," Ravel writes over a particularly cloying progression. In fact only a comparatively small part of his work is without programmatic content, while in the realm of "pure" music only his Trio and perhaps the Sonata for Violin and Cello are wholly successful.

Ravel was at his best in setting words. His first entirely original work, as well as one that reveals a new, ironic side, is the *Histoires naturelles* (1906), while the *Trois poèmes de Stéphane Mallarmé* (1913) stands at the peak of the development of his musical language and style. In the *poèmes*, influenced by Stravinsky's *Japanese Lyrics*, nostalgia is a lesser element than innovation and discovery. But Mallarmé is an equally potent force, and the primary element in Ravel's music is poetry, above melody, harmony, instrumentation. He crystallizes each syllable and gives

each line and word musical rhythms that preserve Mallarmé's—
at the same time sparing him any vulgar melisma or false agogic.
And in at least one line, *"Princesse, nommez-nous berger de vos
sourires"* (from *"Placet futile"*), Ravel surpasses himself in an
ingenious syncopation.

———

Perhaps the most curious aspect of Ravel's failure to evolve concerns his orchestral music and work as an orchestrator. Since
instrumentation was the greatest of his musical skills, how could
he have failed to recognize his extraordinary talent for it until the
advanced age of thirty-two? The explanation would seem to be
in the hostile reception of the first piece that he attempted to
orchestrate, the *Ouverture de Shéhérazade* (which he subtitled
"Introduction to a Fairy Tale"). But would even the most sensitive composer have been discouraged for five years from trying
again, and returning to the wreck of the first attempt to salvage
a second? The new piece eventually was modified into the popular
Shéhérazade song cycle, which, Mr. Orenstein reveals, was considered the first clear demarcation between "Ravel" and "Debussy," though if the cycle were being heard for the first time
today, and attributed to Debussy, surely not many people would
identify the orchestrator as Ravel.

The *Rapsodie espagnole* was a *coup de foudre*, orchestrally
speaking,[5] and the instrumental mastery and imagination that
distinguish every measure of *L'Heure espagnole* (both composed
in 1907) are even more astonishing. Ravel pretends that the
orchestra of the opera is simply an accompanist and commentator,
but it actually takes the principal part. Unusual registers are
exploited; novel effects, such as string glissandos on harmonics,
are introduced; and even the tuba is called from the depths
to sing an aria in its mellow upper voice. Ravel also employs the

———

5. Stravinsky, in Morges, to Diaghilev in Rome, November 21, 1916: "I have
just come from Paris. . . . I saw both Ravel and Debussy at a rehearsal of the
Concerts Colonnes for the *Rapsodie espagnole* and *Saint-Sébastien*. . . . Except
for one or two pieces, I do not care for *Saint-Sébastien*, but I greatly admire
Ravel's *Rapsodie*."

sarrusophone (as well as its mouthpiece alone, in 1960s avant-gardist style), and in a way that determines the character of the whole work, just as saxophones determine the character of *Boléro*. But Ravel was always enlarging the orchestral palette, even, in his very last opus, introducing the vibraphone. His one failure, in this sense, was the addition of a wordless humming chorus to enrich the colors of *Daphnis et Chloé*, an unfortunate anticipation of Hellenic travelogues.

Ravel's least dated orchestrations are his simplest; that of *Ma Mère l'Oye*, for example, which has few doublings, emphasizes pure timbres, and confines each piece to its own instrumental combinations and featured soloists—as in the contrabassoon for the amorous roaring of "the Beast." And while Ravel generally paints backgrounds and establishes moods before unveiling his principal subjects (*cf. La Valse*), in "*Petit Poucet*" and "*Le Jardin féerique*" he begins directly with the melody. (The same is true of the *Pavane pour une infante défunte* and of the second movement of the Concerto in G, but the former repeats too literally and the latter does not stay on course.) Finally, the mediums of the piano (four-hands) and orchestra are so master-fully employed in the two versions of the piece that the listener cannot tell for which one the music was originally conceived. As clothing goes out of fashion, however, so do orchestrations, and today some of Ravel's seem overdressed with percussion and harp arpeggiation. Later in life, too, he mistakenly tried to reproduce rather than to represent, as in the caterwauling and other voices of nature in *L'Enfant*.

———

Ravel's musical nostalgia can be analyzed in terms of melody, instrumental color, harmony, rhythm. The first of these is charac-terized by modalities and by patterns that emphasize rising fourths and fifths and falling minor thirds. As for the second, sufficient to say that it makes all the difference that a flute (and not a clarinet) plays the theme in the second of the *Valses nobles et sentimentales*. And harmonically, Ravel uses (and sometimes abuses) pedal points, parallel fourths and fifths, unresolved ninths and elevenths, the lowered ("blue") seventh, and the seductive effects of the minor triad on the dominant moving to the first inversion on the subdominant; but his harmonic gifts were greater than his demands on them, as the *Trois poèmes de Stéphane Mallarmé* indicates.

Ravel's rhythmic sense, on the other hand, is of a different caliber, and, as one of the first champions of *Le Sacre du printemps*, he might have been expected to engage in further rhythmic exploration himself. If his giddier finales, such as the *Bacchanal* in *Daphnis*, contain his poorest music, the principal fault is the banality of the rhythm. Correspondingly, most of his superior pieces, including his favorite *valse* forms, are in slow tempi.

While part of the continuing appeal of Ravel's music is attributable to its nostalgia, sensuousness, and—when the composer enters the imaginative world of childhood—purity of emotion, another reason for the popularity of both the man and his music is that they are quintessentially "French." This is evinced in the pursuit of clarity and precision, the dedication to craftsmanship, the fastidiousness and formality, the sensitivity to musical color and perfume, the love of finery and the awareness of fashion. French, too, is Ravel's wit—in his impersonations of birds in the *Histoires naturelles*, for example. But Ravel never crossed the borders of his Gallic heritage and sensibilities, fond as he was of journeys in fantasy to exotic places such as Madagascar and the Near East. And though he was attracted to the music of many peoples, his settings of their songs are more "French" than "African," "Hebrew," "Greek," or even "Spanish." Iberia naturally had a special importance in the work of a composer born of a Basque mother within sight of the Cantabrian coast, yet even here the local idioms and colors, jota and guajira, habanera and malagueña, are secondary to his own.

Ravel never regained his path after the War, when he became the influenced rather than the influencer. To compose at all, in fact, seemed to be increasingly difficult for him,[6] and he never

6. Ravel, in St. Cloud, to Stravinsky, in Morges, September 16, 1919: *"Je continue à ne rien f . . .* [the ellipsis is Ravel's] ; *je suis probablement vidé."*

again found either the fecundity or the musical quality of the decade that culminated in the Mallarmé *Poèmes* and the Trio. Moreover, much of *La Valse*, his first post-War piece, had been written long before.[7] The two sonatas that followed took several years to complete, and the hard labor in them is more audible than the charm, which had theretofore been synonymous with "Ravel." Neither of the concertos is satisfying, Gershwin in the G Major not having been assimilated, while the other is at a disadvantage because of the restrictions of the solo performer. But the materials are less refined at every level than those in the pre-War pieces.

—

Ravel must have suffered great mental anguish not only in his final years but also in the 1920s when he was condescended to by his youngers (and inferiors). "Naturally most of the young composers of the day believed in a necessary reaction against the Debussy-Ravel influence," one of them, Arthur Honegger, later explained. At the same time, Ravel's fame increased, and he conducted the Piano Concerto in G and the *Boléro* internationally with enormous success—although the latter piece would itself seem to be either a portent of mental breakdown or, at the unlikely opposite extreme, evidence of a high psychotic breaking point.

Those who saw Ravel when he was stricken with his disease testify that his outstanding quality was courage. An obituarist who had known him as an artist more intimately than anyone else mentions this courage as a quality of his whole life as well:

> The death of Ravel did not come as a surprise to me. I had known for some time that the seriousness of his illness was causing the gravest concern to those closest to him. I also knew that the type of illness would put an abrupt end to his musical productivity.

7. Ravel, in Saint-Jean-de-Luz, to Stravinsky, in Clarens, September 26, 1914: "I have just been obliged to abandon [the opera] *La Cloche engloutie* and a symphonic poem, *Wien*, that I was expecting to finish this winter."

He was my friend for a long time. I knew him when I made my debut in Paris with *The Firebird*, and it was then that he played some fragments for me from his wonderful *Daphnis*, which he was composing at the time.

France loses one of her greatest musicians, one whose value is recognized throughout the world. He now belongs to history, assured of a place of glory in the domain of music, a place that he conquered with courage and unfaltering conviction. [Igor Stravinsky, in *L'Intransigeant*, Paris, December 29, 1937.]

Towards Schoenberg

The best of Arnold Schoenberg's occasional writings on music[1] are as richly instructive as his theoretical and didactic ones. Like them, too, many of the essays depend on examples printed in music type, which sets Schoenberg apart from other composer-writers, such as Berlioz, whose many verbal talents the creator of *Pierrot Lunaire* lacks, or Schumann or Debussy, who are simply more enjoyable to read. But the substance of the musical journalism of these three is less profound than that of *Style and Idea*, and the rewards of Schoenberg's book warrant the greater effort it requires, especially in the chapters "Twelve-Tone Composition" and "Theory and Composition." Yet even these are not difficult for anyone conversant with the general principles of musical forms and of such basic devices of harmony and counterpoint as chord inversion and canon. Finally, Schoenberg's own chronological and autobiographical account of the evolution

1. *Style and Idea: Selected Writings of Arnold Schoenberg*, edited by Leonard Stein, with translations by Leo Black (New York, 1975).

of atonality and twelve-tone composition is still the most accessible.

———

By contrast, the reader who will profit most from Charles Rosen's *Arnold Schoenberg*[2] is one with prior knowledge of the composer, which may raise a question about the market for the Modern Masters series. Laymen have apparently not complained of obstacles of a specialist nature in the monographs on poets, philosophers, psychologists, sociologists, political activists—with which the collection has thus far been overbalanced at the expense of those on artists and cinematographers (the latter now possessing the widest of all powers to influence). But who except musicians will be able to follow Mr. Rosen's exposition of Schoenberg's serial system, though this is admirably lucid as well as free from the diagrammatic and numerical sigla that limit to initiates the readership of most new publications on the subject?[3]

The reasons why the Modern Masters volume is sometimes more difficult to digest than that of Schoenberg on Schoenberg are that the composer did not understand his work in the same way ("I see things that at the time of composing [were] still unknown to me"), that he did not write about his later and more complex developments, and that because of the recent exponential increase in the quantity and sophistication of Schoenberg studies, a musicologist of Mr. Rosen's caliber must contend with a multitude of new material. In short, the contemporary scholar is obliged to keep in perspective a greatly expanded view of his subject, as well as, in Mr. Rosen's case, to concentrate it into the abbreviated format prescribed for Modern Masters. Owing to this last circumstance, too, Mr. Rosen could not afford to spell out any step that might be taken for granted. Having said this, however, one must add that a characteristic of all of Charles Rosen's criticism is his directness in identifying and confronting central issues.

2. New York, 1975.
3. See, for example, Allen Forte's *The Structure of Atonal Music* (New Haven, 1973).

The editorial decisions in publishing an enlarged edition of *Style and Idea*[4] involved questions of selection, of sequence, and of language—the last in problems of translation as well as in the possible correction of the author's grammar and vocabulary (for instance, by putting within brackets an obviously intended word after the one Schoenberg actually used). The book's solutions to all three problems are disappointing. Too many of the additions do not enhance the picture of Schoenberg, while some of them, such as the causeries on national music, which expose his chauvinism and egomania, are damaging:

> Wagner's music was not only the best and most significant of its age . . . but it was also the music of 1870 Germany, who conquered the world of her friends and enemies through all her achievements. . . .

> [In the 1914–1918 war] the battle against German music . . . was primarily a battle against my own music. . . .

Not against that of Richard Strauss? Was Schoenberg already in 1914 regarded as a threat of European proportions? Of Italian national music in the 1920s, he remarks that it was

> written on higher orders (whereas I, in my reactionary way, [stuck] to writing [my music] on orders from The Most High) . . .

which illustrates how his wit in his writing sometimes comes through as arrogance.

The new volume also makes available some of Schoenberg's criticism of his contemporaries, but none of it redounds to his credit. In particular, the article on an early opera by Křenek could have awaited a future "Complete Writings." Nor does a

4. The original appeared in 1950.

piece that accuses Webern of brainpicking, written two months before Schoenberg's death, increase the author's stature, though it does reveal that he withheld his discovery of the twelve-tone concept (early 1920s) from his pupil. Elsewhere in the book Schoenberg mentions that he confided in Webern about the use of a twelve-tone *theme* in *Jacob's Ladder* (1917), which is not the same thing, of course; but the editor should have referred the reader to the other article in both cases, and should have partially balanced Schoenberg's late view of Webern by including the 1947 preface to the latter's Concerto for Nine Instruments—a brief statement, yet one that emphasizes the solidarity between the two men.

——

On the other hand, the essays on Bach, Brahms, Liszt, and Mahler, containing Schoenberg's most valuable criticism, might have been more effectively placed nearer the beginning of the book. It was in the masters of the past that Schoenberg found his own principles, and his illustrations of transcendent musical laws in Bach and Brahms provide an excellent introduction to the continuation of them in his own art. Furthermore, his hubris is less obtrusive while he is observing, for example, that the first three movements of the *Pastorale* Symphony employ almost no minor chords, and that one of Beethoven's means of avoiding the minor was

> by leaving many sections in unison unaccompanied, where the melody is understood without the harmony[;]

or when he is ferreting out the psychological weakness in Liszt that partly explains the failure of his music:

> He, for whom the poet stood foremost, suppressed the poet in himself by letting other poets talk him into too much. He, who felt form as formalism, created a far worse formalism—one which is uninhabitable, because in his forms invented by the intellect no living being has ever dwelt . . . ;

or when he is absorbed in the notion that Karl Philipp Emanuel Bach, and not Johann Sebastian, must have devised the "Royal Theme" of the *Musical Offering*—as a joke to prevent the elder Bach from displaying his contrapuntal versatility:

> In the *Art of the Fugue* a minor triad offered many contrapuntal openings, [but] the Royal Theme, also a minor triad, did not admit one single canonic imitation. All the miracles that the *Musical Offering* presents are achieved by countersubjects, countermelodies, and other external additions.

The editor of *Style and Idea* might in some cases have sacrificed literalism for exactness of meaning. Thus "pitch" could have been substituted for Schoenberg's ambiguous "tone," when the more clearly defining word is what he means. But in a construction such as "By avoiding the establishment of a key modulation is excluded," not to have inserted a bracketed comma after "key" is inexcusable. Finally, whatever Schoenberg's shortcomings as a writer, the only truly mystifying verbiage in the book is contributed by its editor, who nevertheless maligns the composer's English:

> Despite the advice of some of his American pupils, the present writer included, [Schoenberg] doggedly pursued his own path.

The reader will appreciate this doggedness when he tries to penetrate the editor's statement that

> Although the present volume contains most of Schoenberg's longer articles in both German and English, no more than a small portion of his other writings appear [*sic*] herein.

But the present volume does not contain *any* article in German. And what can possibly be meant by the claim:

> Published articles . . . have been used as the basic material in Schoenberg's own English wherever possible, supplemented

by manuscripts, in various stages of completion, which often serve to illuminate certain points which do not exist elsewhere.

If a point does not exist elsewhere, how can it be illuminated anywhere? And does "wherever possible" refer to the intelligibility of the composer's English or to the fact that some of the originals were in German? Passages such as these arouse the reader's suspicion that in the comment,

[Schoenberg] had little use for a grammatically correct, so-called polished style of writing that would not [sic] clearly present his ideas,

the editor is speaking not for Schoenberg but for himself.

———

The most personal of the pieces appearing in English for the first time[5] is Schoenberg's circular letter to friends in Europe after nearly a year (the winter of 1933–34) as a refugee in the United States. His grumblings about the musical and other miseries of America are surprisingly good-humored—compared, that is, to most of his other references to the struggles of his life. Undoubtedly Schoenberg did provoke more relentless opposition than any other major composer, and his belief in and assertion of his genius not only are excusable but were indispensable. Yet to be constantly reminded of his heroic persistence and matchless achievements ("One of the greatest virtues of my music is that . . .") eventually dampens the sympathy of the reader, who begins to feel that Schoenberg should have found consolation in the certainty of having determined the course of music in his time, as well as realized that the hostility he aroused was commensurate to his importance. "It was as if he saw that the controversial nature of his work was central to its significance," Mr. Rosen remarks, but though the composer unquestionably did see this, he seems to have been unable to accept it.

5. Schoenberg's diary at the time of *Pierrot Lunaire*, the *Berliner Tagebuch*, should have been translated and included in this edition of *Style and Idea*.

In fact the resistance to Schoenberg's music is perfectly understandable, and his own wishful explanation—that bad performances were to blame and that, if heard as intended, the music would win acceptance—indicates only one of the causes. Good readings of at least some of his music are no longer uncommon, after all, yet its audience appeal has not grown proportionately. As Mr. Rosen says, "Better performances do not make difficult music popular"; and Schoenberg's creations *are* more complex, densely packed, faster moving for their contents than those of any of his contemporaries.

Some listeners would add that Schoenberg's expression is more intense and disturbing, and that his art lacks emotional diversity, its domain being that of the macabre and of the more ingrown manifestations of middle-European expressionism—to which those who are most familiar with the music might rejoin that it is also euphoric (the Orchestra Variations), sweet (the Serenade), and not without an "Apollonian" side (the composer's own adjective for his Septet). But in his first chapter, Mr. Rosen examines such attempts at affective attributing and justly concludes that they are based on incomprehension:

did [Schoenberg] go so far in the destruction of the tonal system that had ruled Western music for centuries in the interest of giving form to an anxiety that was part of his public as well as his private universe?

The misunderstanding inherent in these questions—the reason why they ought not to be answered—is that they suggest that a style is a simple vehicle for expressing a meaning or an emotion; they turn the style into a pure form and the emotion into a pure significance. But a form and its meaning cannot be divided so simply, above all in a work of music.

At last it seems generally to be accepted that Schoenberg's compositions of the years 1909–1913, together with some of his serial pieces of the 1920s and later, are the fulcrum of twentieth-century music. This is not an aesthetic judgment, of course, yet Mr. Rosen leaves no doubt that, of contemporary composers, Schoenberg alone satisfies the condition of true originality, which requires the exploration of a self-created universe coherent and rich enough to offer possibilities beyond the development of an individual manner.

As for the Schoenberg influence, Mr. Rosen is too conservative in estimating that it has now "surpassed that of Bartók and even perhaps of Stravinsky," since, soon after Schoenberg's death, his influence already included Stravinsky. But does Schoenberg (or Bartók, or Stravinsky) still exert any direct influence on most new music being composed today, except in the sense that this music could not have existed without his (and their) innovations? Not insofar as resemblances are concerned, at any rate, or the extension of traditions, the Schoenberg "school," except as a subject of academic study, now appearing to be defunct, by-passed by others arising from different directions.

—

Anyone who knows or has read Charles Rosen recognizes the awesomeness of his intellect. For those who may not be aware of his prodigal gifts, it should be said that Mr. Rosen is a polymath who could contribute to at least three other categories of the Modern Masters series—linguistics, painting, literature. Furthermore, he always treats the most highly developed aspects of his subjects, and in language of such precision and elegance as virtually to defy both paraphrasing (which explains why no summary of his *Arnold Schoenberg* is attempted here) and quotation (most of his arguments being too tightly embedded in contexts to be successfully extracted). When an aperçu can be detached, however, it promises to stand by itself for as long as any writing on the second Viennese school:

[The] miniatures of Webern, Berg, and Schoenberg do not diminish the emotions they express but enlarge them, as if fragments of feeling were blown up by a powerful microscope.

Mr. Rosen's *Arnold Schoenberg* is one of the most brilliant monographs ever to be published on any composer, let alone on the most difficult master of the present age. It is also the first essay on Schoenberg that is beyond partisanship, as well as the first to place him in the perspective of four centuries of European music. Being concerned primarily with the exposition of musical ideas and artistic logic, Mr. Rosen provides only incidental bits of biography. Nor is his book essentially a work of criticism, though it contains critical insights of a very high order—on style, above all, which will not surprise anyone who has read Mr. Rosen's *The Classical Style.*

Still less is *Arnold Schoenberg* a "survey" of the music. Mr. Rosen concentrates on a few works, mainly of the period immediately before World War I—more on these, in any case, than on the serial pieces of the two decades following it. This focus is now widely shared, yet some of the comments on the serial music could provoke controversy, such as the claim for the Third Quartet as a more "ambitious and in some ways [more] fully achieved" creation than the Orchestra Variations (which is given only two paragraphs). The other most controversial matter is not new but a seemingly permanent part of all discussion of Schoenberg: the assumptions that "harmony is conveyed" as powerfully along a musical line as it is by "a simultaneous chord," that "harmonic tension" can be "displaced" to "the melodic line," and that "harmonic dissonance [can] be reconstructed by shape and texture." These are now accepted *ex hypothesi* by perhaps a majority of listeners, though some continue to regard them as incapable of proof.

———

Having said this much, the reviewer can do little more than add a few footnotes of his own, and perhaps help in some trivial tidying up for future editions—since, as if in compensation for the elevation of the discourse, the text does contain a number of minor errors. Thus the chronology of the Paris and Vienna concerts mentioned on page 5 should be reversed. And surely *Histoire du Soldat* has been mistakenly included in a list of works exemplifying "the evocation of the elegant surface of the past." Also, it is not true that *Erwartung* requires "numerous rapid and expensive changes of scene." Actually there are four, staged on a single set, taking place in or around a forest at night, and requiring only a few props—moon, bench, pasteboard house, corpse (optional).

Mr. Rosen is somewhat careless, too, in defining octave transposition as "the shifting of one or more notes of a melody to a higher or lower register" (only of a melody?), and canon as "a form in which every voice sings the same line but enters at a different moment" (and never at different pitches?). And his description of the *Sprechstimme* part in *Pierrot Lunaire* as having "a certain improvised freedom of pitch" is insufficient, since it neglects to mention that Schoenberg insisted that the performer follow at least the direction of the notated interval.

Occasionally, too, Mr. Rosen overstates, not in his theses but in the illustration of them. This is hardly of any consequence when, apropos the deployment of the orchestra in *Erwartung,* he writes that

> sixteen first violins and fourteen seconds are called for but used all at once only at a very few points.

(Actually all thirty of them play together in 127 out of 426 measures, or for nearly a third of the time.) Nor is the exaggeration serious when, in the demonstration of his argument that "pitch is . . . not by any means always the most important [element]," Mr. Rosen asserts that in the third piece of *Pierrot Lunaire*

> the clarinet part could be transposed a half-step up or down while the other instruments remain at the correct pitch, and (although some effect would be lost) the music would still make sense; but if the dynamics are not respected, the music becomes totally absurd and makes no sense at all.

Not *much* sense, but certainly *some*, as old recordings with practically no range of highs and lows tend to prove. If a clarinet in B flat were substituted for the one in A, however, "some effect would be lost" only on a listener who had not heard the music before, since anyone even slightly acquainted with it would experience acute discomfort, at least in measures 6–9, where, debatably, the pitches are more important than the dynamics.

———

But a similar magnification of fact also occurs in connection with one of the book's principal subjects, the "saturation of [the chromatic] musical space" in *Erwartung*. "Tonality contained within itself the element of its own destruction," Mr. Rosen writes. One part of this element is modulation, the transition from one key to another, or

> the setting up of a second triad as a sort of polarized force or anti-tonic against the tonic; the second triad functions as a subsidiary tonic in that part of the piece where it holds sway, and acts as a means of creating tension. Since dissonance is the essential expressive element of music, and modulation is dissonance on a large scale, it makes expression *for the first time an element of the total structure*. The concept of modulation was eventually to prove the powerful force that corrupted tonality.

Another part, or aspect, of the same thing is chromaticism, the use of the subdivisions, or semitone intervals, of the diatonic scale. Chromaticism, Mr. Rosen observes,

> contains a kind of magnetic impulse to fill out the space. . . .

> Most composers must have been aware of the tendency to fill out the chromatic space as a kind of gravitational force. . . .

> The tendency to fill out the chromatic space becomes naturally more marked by the middle of the nineteenth century. . . .

> It was Schoenberg's genius to have recognized almost unconsciously the dispossession of the principal means of musical expression by the new force of what had been a subordinate and contributing element.

This is true, but the illustration that follows overlooks a detail which spoils the perfection of the case. "The last page of *Erwartung*," Mr. Rosen says, consists of

> massed chromatic movement at different speeds, both up and down. . . . [The] low woodwinds begin, triple *pianissimo*, a rising chromatic series of six-note chords. The other instruments enter with similar chords moving up or down the chromatic scale . . . with the dynamics remaining between triple and quadruple *pianissimo*.

In fact, however, the basses begin at a louder dynamic level than that, and they are clearly intended to stand out. ("Schoenberg never abandoned [the] hierarchy of principal and subordinate voices," Mr. Rosen remarks, in connection with another work, and the distinction is "rigidly enforced by the dynamics.") Moreover, the basses descend not chromatically, but in whole-tone scales (in thirds with the contrabassoon), which are in contrast to chromatic movement. Finally, by rounding out two full octaves, these scales provide a residual sense of a traditional species of cadence.

———

The core of *Arnold Schoenberg* is a discussion of *Erwartung*, perhaps the most radical of all musical creations, as well as, in the opinion of many, the composer's highest achievement.[6] "This

---

6. Mr. Rosen's belief that "concert performances have become relatively frequent" seems overly optimistic. Composed in 1909 (in seventeen days!), *Erwartung* was first performed only fifteen years later, by which time its expressionism was regarded as embarrassingly "passé." In fact the music had so little effect then that Schoenberg's pupil and biographer, Egon Wellesz, actually characterized it as "standing on a traditional foundation." In view of *Erwartung*'s musical superiority and historical importance, however, performances are rare indeed, a fact that is reflected in its representation in the record catalogue by only one fifteen-year-old and inadequate album. *Erwartung* will receive the attention it deserves only when a superstar soprano "discovers" that it can be a sensational concert vehicle.

quintessential expressionist work," as Mr. Rosen writes, is a "well-attested miracle, inexplicable and incontrovertible." Few would demur, while, concerning the intractability of the piece to traditional analysis, no one could. Schoenberg himself described one of the chief difficulties:

> A great number of more-than-five-tone [-pitch] chords . . . have not [sic] yet been systematically investigated. It can be maintained neither that they belong to a tonality, nor that they point toward one. And conversely . . . no proof has yet been brought that these properties are entirely lacking.[7]

And Mr. Rosen observes:

> Almost all of the chords in *Erwartung* have six notes.[8] . . . [The] six-note chord is generally made up of two three-note chords outlining the seventh, e.g., a fourth above an augmented fourth. . . .

But to give any more of this analysis would require the quotation of Mr. Rosen's musical examples, so it must suffice to say that his exegesis of the chordal structure of the work is the most convincing that has so far been made.

The listener with no experience of *Erwartung*'s harmonic language nevertheless senses its consistency. But he apprehends the form of the piece at a different level from that of chordal relationships. Mr. Rosen states that

> It is in the field of rhythm that the large form of *Erwartung* is most immediately perceptible . . . [the] contrast between passages with a marked *ostinato* effect and those with no repeating figures of any kind [being] the chief instrument in the definition of the dramatic action of the mono-drama.

---

7. *Style and Idea*, p. 281.
8. That is, at least six different pitches; most of the chords have many more than six notes, and some have more than thirty.

This is indisputable, but it overlooks still another rhythmic factor, and one that must be counted among the score's most innovatory features: the unprecedented fluidity of tempo. In fact the tempo changes every three to four measures (on an average), when not actually in flux (accelerating or decelerating; also—a novelty far ahead of its time—individual sections or groups of instruments sometimes play "out of tempo," faster than the orchestra as a whole).

Erwartung also has "a shape related to the libretto," as Mr. Rosen acknowledges, but apart from rhythmic delineation, he does not say what this is. Perhaps a layman might describe it as a progression from sudden changes of direction and mood, new starts and resolutions—conveyed, to some extent, by a fragmentary, recitative style—to longer lines and more songlike passages in the later portions of the work. And, in correspondence to this, the same listener would probably retain an impression of an over-all increase in orchestral density and volume from a single instrument at the beginning to that "saturation of musical space" at the end, this being parallel to the greater intimacy of the musical dimensions in the first scenes as compared to the broader, more "open" final one. And the hypothetical listener would very likely have had a sense of increasing movement from the more static earlier scenes to the last one, in which the majority of fast-tempo passages occur. But all of this is only to say that Schoenberg's music drama, like numerous operas by other composers, intensifies as it develops.

—

"There is no fully developed sense of key anywhere in *Erwartung*," Mr. Rosen remarks, and it might be added that whatever *un*developed sense of key it may contain is at best ambiguous, ephemeral, and probably illusory, affirmable only during some of the *ostinati* and in melodic phrases, for although melody and harmony are never completely detachable, spacing (as at 418) can make them more so. But other elements than the harmonic must be considered, especially since one of them, as Mr. Rosen rightly maintains, is even more important. "Form was as basically thematic for Schoenberg as it was for most nineteenth-century composers," he writes.

> The really revolutionary art was less the destruction of the tonal frame with the *George-Lieder* of 1909 than the renunciation of thematic form as well with *Erwartung* in the same year. In this work Schoenberg did away with all the traditional means in which music was supposed to make itself intelligible: repetition of themes, integrity and discursive transformation of clearly recognizable motifs, harmonic structure based on a framework of tonality.

The statement is unchallengeable, except, possibly, that it does not allow for elasticity among other arbiters of the "clearly recognizable," and that the "traditional means" to intelligibility, not completely itemized in this quotation, should also include such small features as the use of sequences. But in spite of Schoenberg's renunciation of "thematic form," does not comprehension increase with the recognition of recurring thematic figures? Here Mr. Rosen has not completely overcome the long-standing predicament that the lack of well-defined terms has created for all musicians. Thus his definition of a motif as "a succession, generally short, with a latent power of development, of creating a larger continuity" is more precise than his description of a melody as "a definable shape, an arabesque"—only that?—"with a quasi-dramatic structure of tension and resolution." As Mr. Rosen says:

> Both motif and melody are *tonal* forms. The power of development and variation that lies in a motif is given by the context of tonality. . . . The structure of melody is equally tonal: a melody is intended above all to be memorable, and its mnemonic powers comes [*sic*] from the adherence of its line to tonal functions. . . . Motif generates melody: that is the traditional relation between them. . . .

But since motifs and melodies are also found in atonal music, the statement reveals one reason why they are more difficult to remember in Schoenberg than in Beethoven—namely, that the contexts of atonal harmony are infinitely more complex and difficult to perceive than tonal ones.

This explains why the historical significance of *Erwartung* can be regarded as greater than that of Schoenberg's twelve-tone compositions, which "required a mimesis of tonal melody." For *Erwartung* is

> "athematic" or "nonmotivic" in the sense that understanding and appreciating it does not require recognizing the motifs from one part of the work to another as all music from Bach to Stravinsky demands. . . .

This statement, too, is unexceptionable: *Erwartung* can be appreciated independently of the recognition of motifs. Yet the musical experience is deepened by an awareness of the motivic relationships—which will differ from one listener to another because of the "developing variation" (Schoenberg's term for a principle of all of his music), the transformation, and even the mergers to which the motifs are subjected. An interval is inverted, or replaced by a slightly larger one—on the grounds that contour is more important than exact distance (as in the case of the *Sprechstimme* part in *Pierrot Lunaire*). Also, at least one motif in *Erwartung* is as short as a single interval, the minor third that occurs three times in the first melodic passage (bassoon to oboe) and obsessively after that, especially in the vocal part.

These comments are merely a part of one reader's marginalia. Now it must be said that with this book Charles Rosen not only has created impossibly high standards for the Modern Masters series but also has notched the profession of writing about music to a level that no colleague can readily approach. His *Arnold Schoenberg* is indispensable to anyone seeking to understand the crucial musical ideas of the first three decades of the twentieth century.

Ives's World

The lack of intelligent literary society is not responsible for the shortcomings [of Hawthorne, Poe, and Whitman]; it is much more certainly responsible for some of their merits. The originality, if not the full mental capability, of these men was brought out, forced out, by the starved environment.

—*T. S. Eliot, in* The Athenaeum, *April 25, 1919*

Like other biographers of Charles Ives, Frank R. Rossiter[1] celebrates the most astonishing composer of his time as a purely American phenomenon, the offspring of the same New England culture that was to provide the *materia prima* of his music. Mr. Rossiter believes that

> most of Ives's major compositions had their inspiration in either the music or the life of his boyhood town.

Undoubtedly Ives's musical imagination was still ignited in later years by early experience, but the reader should not conclude that a causal relationship existed between the life and the work of art, or that background structures and influences can account for development beyond the point at which formulas are replaced by originality.

The statement also fails to consider the unique degree of independence which Ives's creative mind had attained during the decade of his principal achievements (1906–1916), and how much of his greatest music is in no way connected with his "boyhood town." One example is the masterpiece of his Second Orchestral Set, an impression of the noise and movement of a New York crowd responding to the news of the *Lusitania* tragedy

1. *Charles Ives and His America* (New York, 1976).

(though the "program" is inconsequential). Others are the ending of the Second Quartet, and the even-numbered movements of the Fourth Symphony, these being conceived in adult experience of a philosophical and mystical kind remote from the composer's early days in Danbury.

Mr. Rossiter excels as a historian of the social castes of the Connecticut of Ives's youth and years at Yale, as well as of the New York business world of the composer–insurance broker's middle age. These explications are helpful to an understanding of such paradoxes as those of the commoner proud of his gentility and of the Thoreauvian who made himself into a wealthy man. Valuable, too, are the chapters devoted to the long struggle for recognition, with reference material here (which includes some from the Ives Oral Archives) as absorbing as the text itself.

The discussions of the music and of the psychology of the composer are less fully illuminating. "Ives was the only one who did not work in the shadow of Europe," Mr. Rossiter writes. But a neophyte listener who begins with the Tchaikovsky-over-shadowed First Symphony might feel that "Charles Ives and His Russia" would have been a more suitable title for at least some of the book. And the Second Symphony, despite its use of popular American tunes, represents a significant advance on the First only in that Ives must have realized, while finishing it, that his talents would never flower in secondhand traditional forms.

Yet even these early academic exercises exhibit qualities of sensuousness that, puzzlingly, Mr. Rossiter does not hear in any of Ives's music. (Not even in *The Housatonic at Stockbridge?*) And it must also be said that at least one contemporary trans-atlantic composer, Claude Debussy, did influence Ives—in, for example, the comparatively late Third Violin Sonata.

One of the book's theses is that the cultivated tradition in American musical life was dominated by women, and consequently that a boy aspiring to a career in music was regarded as a "sissy." Ives apparently felt tainted to the extent that he

needed to excel at sports as an offset to his public identification with serious music.

In fact, Mr. Rossiter's *Ives* is a case history of a deeply suffering victim of "the music of the ladies," as the composer calls it. That the subject became a paranoid obsession with him seems clear, to judge by quotations from his conversations, letters, and even scores (*"andante emasculata"*), and by some of his behavior. Thus when Henry Cowell, his closest associate in the early 1930s, was imprisoned for homosexually molesting a minor, Ives not only failed to offer financial and other aid to his friend but brutally disavowed him. Could Ives have been unaware of Cowell's sexual proclivities? (This must seem doubtful to anyone who knew Cowell, a kind and gentle person capable of spending an evening cutting out paper dolls, as he did with this reviewer's niece.) Mr. Rossiter does not explore such questions, but his readers can hardly escape the conclusion that Ives's hatred of effeminacy protests too much, and that fears for his own masculinity might be considered among the reasons for his reclusiveness.

What Mr. Rossiter does argue is that Ives opposed a cultured, imported "female" music with a vernacular, indigenous "male" one, and that he

erected . . . a dichotomy between manly dissonant music and effeminate easy-on-the-ears music.

The latter contention is supported with a statement by the laureate Ivesian, John Kirkpatrick:

As Ives grew older, he felt an ever greater need to express his rebellion through ever greater dissonance. . . .

But these equations are too simple. The composer was increasingly preoccupied not with "dissonance" but with richer and more complex textures. And though he was hardly a conformist, the "rebellion" theory, on such a scale, is in conflict with the man's religious nature and affirmative genius.

Ives's music is in need of corrected editions, better performances (especially recorded ones), and discriminating criticism. Overdue for retirement, on the other hand, are such received

214 — CURRENT CONVICTIONS

notions as that his importance is primarily as an "innovator," and that his artistic isolation had a deleterious effect on his work. Actually, Ives was not "ahead" of anybody, for the reason that no one followed him, and though the rhythmic and intervallic vocabularies of those stunning pieces, *Tone Roads No. 3* and *Over the Pavements*, do indeed "anticipate" the linguistic modes of European composers, the origins and expressive purposes are so different on each side as to be unrelated. Not until today can Ives's heritage be understood. In his own time his greatest music was recognized as such only by its intensity, since the language was then generally unintelligible.

Ives was "cut off from meaningful dialogue with other musicians," Mr. Rossiter writes, lapsing into Kissinger-ese. But *which* musicians, may one ask, especially during the period of the still scarcely believable Fourth Symphony? And to what end these encounters? "To be made better and spoiled," as Ives himself said? In fact, it is unthinkable for the composer of the "Browning" Overture to have an audience or to be a member of a circle of musicians. Ives could not have begotten this music under other conditions, and we should rejoice that he had the courage to persevere on his lonely path.

Books

TELLING TIME

From Stonehenge to Monte Alto, solar observatories are among the most enduring monuments of prehistoric cultures. Other timekeeping tools used by these megalithic builders, whose very existence depended on accurate predictions of changes of season, include the sundial, clepsydra, and gnomon, as well as two-symbol numerals, the concept of zero, and spherical trigonometry. Whether or not time was conceptualized in any culture that survives only through ruins and artifacts, the peoples themselves were highly skilled in chronometry. On the other hand, in that summit of civilization, fifth-century Athens, the measurement of time was haphazard, calendars differing from city to city, and even the years beginning on different days, a chaotic state of affairs satirized by Aristophanes in *Clouds*. And Greek tragedy, which was to discover and exploit philosophical concepts of time, itself developed in a society that was far from time-conscious.[1]

—

Again today, as in the Mexico of the Mayans, but not as in Aristotle's Greece, philosophies of time are regarded as less important than the instruments of its measurement. This can be attributed partly to the negative reason that ontological arguments, such as Kant's idea of time as a mental form, have been around for some time, while the measuring techniques are largely new. Among the positive reasons, the most important are the unrelenting challenge to discover the time structure of the

1. "The Greeks' involvement in the present . . . blinds them to the . . . age and permanence of Egypt's human institutions. . . . The Egyptians distinguished more sharply than the Greeks do between the time when the gods ruled Egypt and the rule of men. . . ." (*Herodotean Inquiries*, by Seth Bernardete [The Hague, 1969], p. 61.)

218 — CURRENT CONVICTIONS

universe and the impact of space exploration. Both have been sensationally publicized, the former because signals from particles of electromagnetic force traveling faster than light in superdense stars have raised questions even about time-reversal invariancy, subatomically speaking. And as for walks on the moon, surely part of their fascination has been due to a vicarious global escapism involving the illusion of crossing the boundaries of terrestrial time.

The newer clocks include the hydrogen, the radiocarbon, the potassium-argon, and the atomic or caesium, this last, coordinated with pulsars, now having replaced sidereal timekeeping as the standard measurement. But in addition to these and other technological devices are the many natural clocks only lately understood, for time is recorded by both organic and inorganic matter. The best-known are tree rings, varve-counts, and the dating of coral from its remains at the bottom of the sea up to the living polyp. More recently, the discovery of a correspondence between ridges on the fossils of tidewater marine animals and the number of days in the lunar month enabled paleontologists to determine the rate of decrease in velocity of the earth's rotation from the twenty-one-hour Cambrian day to our ever-lengthening one. But glaciers, too, are now used as calendars, the date of freezing being ascertainable from the ratio of oxygen isotopes in water molecules.

Still another gauge is the tooth. Thus the recent discovery in Queensland of the skeleton of a labyrinthodont among fossils associated with a much later period has changed most estimates of the extinction date of the amphibian by a hundred million years. Dentistry, in fact, has become increasingly important to anthropology, and in the Siwalik Hills excavations the dental distinction between hominid and anthropoid primates appears to be the crucial one—evenly worn molars being a sign of the rapid maturation of the ape, unevenly worn ones of the longer stages of growth in creatures already on the path to *Homo sapiens*. (The apprehensive reader should see his odontologist at least twice a year!)

Time is not yet conceptualized in Homer, and sequence, continuity, and perpetuity do not obtain. "In the *Iliad* there is virtually no interest in chronology, absolute or relative," Hermann Fraenkel wrote, and Professor De Romilly[2] adds that "time is never the subject of a verb in Homer and the idea of time does not appear to have been an important one before Greek tragedy." Hence the discovery of the many aspects of time and the development of the tragic form are simultaneous.

To borrow Gordon Kirkwood's well-known comparison of the Homeric and Sophoclean treatment of the scene of Ajax's farewell to his son, that of the dramatist has "immeasurably greater tension . . . compression and urgency."[3] But this is natural since the epic is without time limit, while the tragedy must run its course during a single revolution of the sun.

Furthermore, the tragedy is constructed around a crisis, and, accordingly, urgency is a necessary element. Finally, the involvement of past and future is essential to tragedy. The "weight of the past" must participate in the decision of justice—*krinein*, to judge or to decide, also being the source for "crisis"—though at the same time the narration of past events is in the historical present, Professor De Romilly's "tense of everlasting reality."

The action begins at a particular time, but the origins of the problem that will precipitate the crisis are in the past. Thus tragedy and time-philosophy, the examination of relationships among past, present, and future, are inseparable. The tragedies of Aeschylus, Sophocles, and Euripides bring into usage such modern expressions as "the time has come," "now is the time," "this is the decisive time," "just in time." But whereas the elements of suspense, expectation, and chronological chance—the encounter of Oedipus and Laius at the crossroads—are still contemporary, ancient concepts of time remain in the structure of tragedy, such as the Greek idea of a permanent, unchanging cosmos, in contrast to our notions of evolution and perpetual transformation.

2. *Time in Greek Tragedy*, by Jacqueline De Romilly (Ithaca, 1968).
3. In *Classical Drama and Its Influence* (London, 1965).

Stepping outside the province of drama, Professor De Romilly discusses the personification of time and quotes Thales, for whom time is the "cleverest of all" (*sophotaton*); Heraclitus, who says that "time is a child playing dice"; and Pindar, who remarks that "the old part of age is moving about me" (as distinguished from "*in* me"). She goes on to characterize this personifying as "natural" but offers no explanation for this word beyond the general observation that the Greeks did in fact attribute personal qualities to abstractions. Her book, otherwise, contains handy comparisons of time in Aeschylus, for whom it teaches a lesson; time in Sophocles, who emphasizes its power of alteration; and time in Euripides, for whom it is irrational and elusive, evading man's predictions. But she does not say that it is Euripides who stresses time's destructive aspects and the recognition of oneself as its plaything and dupe, and who therefore provides so many parallels with the images, visual and verbal, of Renaissance and Baroque art:

Thy Glass Will Show Thee How Thy Beauties Wear.

Since no translator is credited, the English is presumably that of the Sorbonne scholar herself. But the writing is not good enough. "This is clear and precise," she explains at one point. "Or isn't it? I must be honest"—we naturally supposed that she was—"and confess that there remains a doubt." It should be mentioned that her statistical comparisons among the three playwrights neglect to include a percentage calculation. Thus she reveals that the adjective *chronius* occurs twenty-nine times in Euripides as against twice and four times respectively in Aeschylus and Sophocles, but she fails to consider that the extant plays of Euripides greatly outnumber the still-existing ones of the others.

———

The awareness of time is said to be biological, the result of a metabolizing, oxidative process in the brain cells. But the question of what constitutes this awareness, and the modes in which

it functions, does not appear to have an answer. Is it a part of—
the end product—or a step beyond that brain-cell biochemistry?
If, moreover, the state of being "aware" involves a degree of
perception, then time awareness would seem to be not truly biological, since that word implies the universal, while perception
is subjective.

In a well-known music-school demonstration, an illustration of
normal perception, two students, standing back to back and beat-
ing time with a metronome, drift from the fixed tempo and from
each other as soon as the mechanism is stopped. Examples of
abnormal perception are provided by the study of learning dis-
abilities. Some children who evidence no organic defects in
ophthalmological, otological, neurological, and psychometric
tests are nevertheless unable to perceive, or distinguish, words
on a page, or to register them in the ear. Yet, and fortunately,
these dyslexiacs[4] can be taught to perceive through a third learning modality, the kinesthetic, and to apprehend a letter by
touching it on a typewriter key, or, in the manner of Braille, by
shaping it in three-dimensional materials such as blocks and clay.
In this way one mode of perception is substituted for another.
And therefore, if perception is a biological gift, its amount,
quality, and application are highly variable.

———

This much is certain: the biological time clock is conditioned by
the individual metabolic one, which seems not to remain either
wound up or coordinated with others for very long—as experiments with spelunkers show, these subterranean explorers soon
losing their sense of the circadian cycle when actual contact with
it is severed. As far as the temporal dimension is concerned, then,
instinct, or inborn propensity, would appear to be mere conditioning. For another instance, some infants raised on demand-
feeding methods later reject the ritual of morning, noon, and
evening meals, continuing to respond to hunger drives that assert

4. See *Developmental Medicine and Child Neurology*, published from the
Montefiore Hospital, New York, April 1975.

themselves at irregular hours. Yet the daily cycle, once incorporated in the nervous system, is difficult to eradicate, especially in compulsive degrees (as in the case of W. H. Auden, who contended that he ate only because the clock said that it was time to do so). But even here individuals differ, as illustrated by studies in reactions to flight dysrhythmia. History's many professional torturers long ago discovered that the most effective way of "breaking" a victim was by constantly disrupting his routine. If not already underway, a valuable psychophysiological research project might be the investigation of the duration of the human organism's ability to survive without some kind of time structure.

Acknowledgment must be made of other agents and states of being by which and in which the time sense is distorted or suspended. These include alcohol, narcotic drugs, dreams, mystic transcendences, psychic phenomena (especially precognition), all forms of illusion,[5] and especially the arts. In music, the perception of time ranges from simple succession—Hume's "Five notes played on a flute give us the impression and idea of time" —to the complex integration of melody, harmony, and rhythm that constitutes the *Eroica* Symphony, in which the changing psychological reality of each listener reflects his individual experience of temporal modes.

But arts, philosophies, and religions are escape hatches of another order, leading to their own realities. In a dualistic system (a structure of reality and a structure of mind), man, the alien in a pre-existing temporal-spatial continuum, was forced to invent phenomenological time, and to measure it in the reality of his own nature—until the escape into "change-independent" subjective time becomes the escape from "temporal existence" into "eternity," when, as the Angel says in the Revelation of Saint John the Divine, "There shall be time no longer."

5. That some illusions diminish with the lengthening of perception time, while others become stronger, is well known. See Jean Piaget's *The Mechanisms of Perception* (New York, 1969) and Ernst H. Gombrich's "The Evidence of Images" (in *Interpretation: Theory and Practice*, edited by Charles S. Singleton [Baltimore, 1969]).

A PROPOS ELIOT'S PROSE

TO THE EDITORS OF *The New York Review of Books*:

Having recently read the same books that Michael Wood reviews so expertly in "The Struggles of T. S. Eliot" (*NYR*, May 13), may I report one of my conclusions that differs markedly from one of his—and, incidentally, express my astonishment at his statement

> Of the uncollected criticism, I have seen only Eliot's reviews in *The Athenaeum* ... [?]

Can a professor of English really have escaped *The Criterion*, let alone all of those famous prefaces—to *Huckleberry Finn* and Valéry's *Art of Poetry*, and, to name only a few of the women who come and go, to *Bubu of Montparnasse* and Simone Weil, Djuna Barnes and Marianne Moore?

But first, while Mr. Wood is mildly skeptical of the policy of selection in one of the books he reviews, Frank Kermode's *Selected Prose of T. S. Eliot*,[1] I completely disagree with it. "There is a large body of criticism by Eliot that has never been collected," Mr. Kermode writes.

> Some of it is of great interest. . . . But . . . an editor ought, I think, to respect the initial act of selection made by the critic.

Mr. Wood's comment is that

> the rightness of following Eliot's lead [is] perhaps not as self-evident as Kermode seems to think.

---

1. This title can be misleading in that some readers might suppose that the basis for selection was quality of style rather than content, and that Eliot's critical works are now read for the delectation of the writing.

But hasn't Mr. Kermode actually stated the exact opposite of what "an editor ought" to do? It is my understanding, at any rate, that his first function is to pick and to choose rather than to follow or even to respect the judgment of the author. Surely Mr. Kermode's assessment of Eliot, not Eliot's of himself, is what the reader anticipates and deserves, and it is unlikely that the two views should coincide. And why, more than a decade after the poet's death, should his tailored image of himself be treated with this deference?

As for my differing conclusion, this concerns Mr. Wood's remark that

> we can admire . . . the "deliberate clarity" of Eliot's thought, as long as we understand that it is a clarity of articulation, a matter, usually, of scrupulous syntax rather than rigorous vocabulary. What Eliot *says* is sometimes foggy; what he means is perfectly clear.

When Eliot's writing is foggy, so is his meaning, at least sometimes, and his syntax can be confusing indeed. In the introduction to *Nightwood*, for instance, he discourses on prose style in prose that, if submitted by a student, would result in his or her transfer to a course in remedial English—unless what would seem to be a recent emigration from Germany were a mitigating factor:

> He ceased to be like the brilliant actor in an otherwise unpersuasively performed play for whose re-entrance one impatiently waits.

But, in fairness, Eliot questions whether his introduction, which is foggy both in what it says and in what it means, is not "perhaps too pretentious for a preface" (to be merely pretentious presumably being acceptable).

Eliot's vocabulary, on the other hand, is usually rigorous—so far as can be determined, which is not at all in such cases as "narthekophoroi"[2] (not found, in this form at least, even in Liddell and Scott) and "reperpend."[3] And certainly Eliot's sharp-

2. *The Athenaeum,* July 25, 1919.
3. "Literature, Science and Dogma," *The Dial,* March 1927.

est criticism, and some of his most valuable, is of the word-by-word kind. The recent publication (1975) of Alexander Sackton's *The T. S. Eliot Collection of the University of Texas at Austin* indicates what may be expected when Eliot's letters to younger contemporary poets are finally made available. To quote only one instance, he responds to Henry Treece's line, "His fiery breath fried all besieging knights," with the question, "How can you fry without fat and a pan?" But Eliot's war on the misuse and corruption of words was lifelong, and passages such as the following, on the substitution in the liturgy of "infinite" and "eternal" for "incomprehensible" and "everlasting," are among the highlights of his critical work:

> The word "infinite" (besides being less comprehensible than "incomprehensible") has gained a shoddy prestige from the reputable uses of the word in mathematics. . . . the word "eternal" evades all difficulties of time. Whether the words were supposed to clarify theology or not, they make the English language vaguer.[4]

Yet in his own prose Eliot often seems to be oblivious of even the most elementary uses of punctuation, adding commas where they intrude:

> It is to be observed, that a society, and a literature, like an individual human being,[5]

but omitting them where they are essential:

> The exposure, the dissociation of human feeling is a great part of the superiority of Beyle and Flaubert to Balzac[6]

and using them to enclose restrictive clauses:

> When the unexpectedness, due to the unfamiliarity of the *metres* to English ears, wears off and is understood, one ceases to look for what one does not find in Swinburne; the inexplic-

4. *The Criterion*, May 1927.
5. *What is a Classic?* (London, 1945).
6. *The Athenaeum*, May 30, 1919.

able line with the music which can never be recaptured in other words.[7]

Nor does Eliot seem to have any idea of the functions of semicolons (see the last quotation) and colons, evidently turning to them simply when at a loss to know what to do:

> The renovation of the versification of Racine has been mentioned often enough; quite genuine, but might be overemphasized, as it sometimes comes near to being a trick. . . .[8]

As for the variety of errors in Eliot's grammar, this ranges from such blunders as using "between" for "among"

> The classical qualities are scattered between various authors and several periods[9]

to misrelating participial phrases

> Being a period of rapid assimilation the end may not know the beginning, so different may the taste become. . . .[10]

He introduces superfluous words:

> Whether these are memories of six or seven years ago, or out of a more remote past, it makes no difference. . . .[11]

He confuses adverbs and adjectives:

> It is this intensity . . . and consequent discontent with the inevitable inadequacy of actual living to the passionate capacity . . .[12]

7. "Reflections on 'Vers Libre,' " *New Statesman*, March 3, 1917.

8. *Baudelaire* (London, 1930).

9. *Religion and Literature* (London, 1935).

10. *The Use of Poetry and the Use of Criticism* (text as in first edition, London, 1933).

11. Introduction to *France Remembered* (Chesham, 1944).

12. *The Athenaeum*, May 30, 1919.

He mixes tenses:

> But to have been otherwise, his books would have had to be
> conceived on a much larger scale;[13]

He fails to complete parallel constructions:

> . . . I have more sympathy with Dante the man, than Goethe
> the man. . . .[14]

He does not conform first-person possessive plural pronouns:

> Like the first period of childhood, it is one beyond which I
> dare say many people never advance; so that such taste for
> poetry as they retain in later life is only a sentimental memory
> of the pleasures of youth, and is probably entwined with all
> our . . .[15]

Two features of Eliot's prose are clumsiness of word order

> Mr. Yeats sometimes appears, as a philosopher, incoherent[16]

and the wrong placement of modifiers

> the people do not know enough of English literature to be even
> insular.[17]

Yet the full awkwardness of the writing is exemplified only in
such mazes as the following, the first of which lacks the grammatically essential words that would lead to an exit:

> Not only have the words "organized" and "activity," occurring
> together in this phrase, that familiar vague suggestion of the
> scientific vocabulary which is characteristic of modern writing,

13. Foreword, *Contemporary French Poetry* by Joseph Chiari (New York 1952).
14. *Dante* (London, 1929).
15. *The Use of Poetry and the Use of Criticism.*
16. *The Athenaeum*, July 25, 1919.
17. *The Athenaeum*, June 13, 1919.

but one asked questions which Coleridge and Arnold would not have permitted one to ask.[18]

The second example is a nonprobative remark, but an exceedingly peculiar one:

Finally, when Valéry died, in 1945, his death seemed to mark the end of an age, with greater definitiveness and solemnity than that of any other European author of his generation could have done.[19]

Only "seemed to," yet "with greater definitiveness" and even "solemnity"? And how can Eliot compare the effect of deaths that did not occur? Surely if Mann had died in 1945 or Claudel (or Eliot himself), these events would have competed with Valéry's demise in marking "the end of an age," at least in "solemnity."

The third example displays no clear notion of what constitutes a subject and a predicate, not to mention the nonrelated pronouns, suspensions, run-on sentences, improper capitalization, purely decorative colons, and even malapropisms:

We do not proceed, from Liberalism to its apparent end of authoritarian democracy, at a uniform pace in every respect. There are so many centres of it . . . that the development of western society must proceed more slowly than that of a compact body like Germany, and its tendencies are less apparent. Furthermore, those who are the most convinced of the necessity of *étatisme* as a control of some activities of life, can be the loudest professors of libertarianism in others, and insist on the preserves of "private life" in which each man may obey his own convictions or follow his own whim; while imperceptibly this domain of "private life" becomes smaller and smaller, and may eventually disappear altogether. . . .

18. *The Perfect Critic* (London, 1920).
19. Foreword, *Contemporary French Poetry* by Joseph Chiari (New York, 1952).

We are in danger of finding ourselves with nothing to stand for except a *dislike* of everything maintained by Germany and/or Russia; a dislike which, being a compost of newspaper sensations and prejudice, can have two results, at the same time, which appear at first incompatible. It may lead us . . .

If we have got so far as accepting the belief that the only alternative to a progressive and insidious adaptation to totalitarian worldliness for which the pace is already set, is to aim at a Christian society, we need . . .

Those who, either complacently or despairingly, suppose that the aim of Christianization is chimerical, I am not here attempting to convert.[20]

Perhaps it is time for Eliot scholars to examine his syntax as well as his symbols.

Yours, etc.

R. C.

(Published, in shortened form, in *The New York Review of Books*, June 10, 1976.)

The above letter provoked two replies, my answers to which (in *The New York Review of Books*, July 15) are printed below. Meanwhile, I had reread the whole of Eliot's early criticism— that preceding *For Lancelot Andrewes* (1928) and Eliot's announcement in this book of his conversion to classicism in literature, royalism in politics, anglo-catholicism in religion. After that date, when Eliot turns his attention to sociology and religion, his prose is generally flabbier. Rereading this later criticism, too, I found it to be even more parochial than memory had led me to expect. At times in *The Idea of a Christian Society* (1939) and *Notes Toward the Definition of Culture* (1948) he

---

20. *The Idea of a Christian Society.*

seems unable even to consider ideas with which he is not in sympathy. And in practice this leads him to exclude almost everything that does not proceed from his co-religionists (as well as from much that does, for he is obsessed by the fear of heresy even among the duly baptized and confirmed). Some of these limitations are exposed in a review of Freud's *The Future of an Illusion* that Eliot wrote in 1928 at the crisis of his development. This is a head-on collision with the founder of psychoanalysis, whom Eliot dismisses not because his arguments might be unscientific or irresponsible but because of his failure clearly to define "illusion." And thereafter Eliot does not see, or cannot admit, that Freud's enormous and profound influence, whether beneficial or pernicious, is a more significant subject for social criticism than is a Lambeth Conference. The poet's sociology was quickly made obsolete by more comprehensive attitudes resulting from developments in newer sciences, but after this date his criticism generally becomes peripheral.

In contrast, Eliot as a young literary critic is at the very center of his world, and some of the gifts that he displays, especially of eye and ear in singling out truly original lines in the poetry of others, are phenomenal. And in the ability to illuminate an essential difference between, for example, Shakespeare and Marlowe, by comparing short extracts from each, this Eliot seems to be without peer. Yet most of these early writings are marred by an insufferable omnicompetence and condescension:

> Of all modern critics perhaps Rémy de Gourmont had most of the general intelligence of Aristotle.[21]

Consider the much-quoted remark about Henry James's

> mastery over, his baffling escape from, Ideas; a mastery and an escape which are perhaps the last test of a superior intelligence. He had a mind so fine that no idea could violate it. . . . He is the most intelligent man of his generation. . . .[22]

21. *The Perfect Critic.*
22. *The Egoist*, January 1918.

It takes one to recognize one, no doubt. But the reader who is puzzled by how the almighty arbiter can be so well informed about the intellectual ratings of the artists, philosophers, scientists, and writers among James's coevals is forgetting that minds ravaged by ideas are disqualified. Furthermore, Eliot actually does succeed in demonstrating something of his meaning of the "fineness" of James's mind by comparing his and Henry Adams's accounts of approximately the same experience. Eliot observes that

> Henry James was not, by Adams's standards, "educated," but particularly limited; it is the sensuous contributor to the intelligence that makes the difference.[23]

Sometimes the assumption of superiority is merely laughable, as when this younger compatriot of James refers to the advantages

> in coming from a large flat country which no one wants to visit. . . . [Really? No one?] . . . Europeans have preferred to take their notions . . . of the American from, let us say, Frank Norris if not O. Henry. [And not Mark Twain?][24]

On the other hand, almost every one of Eliot's reviews contains a brilliant formulation:

> This grasp of the uniformity of human nature and this interest in its variations made Turgenev cosmopolitan and made him a critic. He did not acquire these two qualities; he brought them with him. . . .[25]

And even his rhetoric is of a high order:

> The majority of people live below the level of belief or doubt. It takes application, and a kind of genius, to believe anything,

23. A review of *The Education of Henry Adams: An Autobiography*, in *The Athenaeum*, May 23, 1919.
24. *The Egoist*, January 1918.
25. *The Egoist*, December 1917.

and to believe *anything* (I do *not* mean merely to believe in some "religion") will probably become more and more difficult as time goes on. . . . We await . . . the great genius who shall triumphantly succeed in believing something. For those of us who are higher than the mob, and lower than the man of inspiration, there is always *doubt*; and in doubt we are living parasitically (which is better than not living at all) on the minds of the men of genius of the past who have believed in something.[26]

Occasionally he attains wisdom:

Great simplicity . . . represents . . . the triumph of feeling and thought over the original sin of language.[27]

———

Here are the two subsequent letters to *The New York Review of Books*:

Michael Wood's reply to my letter (in the *NYR*, June 10) demands a further response. He writes:

I don't think of Eliot's *Criterion* pieces as criticism, and I don't think of the prefaces as uncollected. They are in books, after all. . . .

Whether "collected" means scattered in many books or gathered into one, most of those with prefaces by Eliot were published in such limited editions that these volumes are unavailable even in libraries. Since only five hundred copies were printed of *Le Serpent* with Eliot's preface—the basis of a recent attack on his "French connection"—few readers can have referred to the text. And, more important, Eliot's only essay on Donne was never reprinted from the long-unobtainable *Garland for John Donne*.[28]

26. *The Enemy*, January 1927.
27. *The Athenaeum*, April 11, 1919.
28. Cambridge, Mass., 1931; 769 copies printed.

But why does Mr. Wood think that Eliot's reviews in *The Athenaeum* qualify as criticism, while the remarkably similar ones in *The Criterion* do not? Certainly the articles that Mr. Wood commends on Kipling, Yeats, and Pound in the former publication hardly differ in approach and method of exposition from those on Housman and D. H. Lawrence in the latter. In the *Criterion* reviews, too, Eliot confronts his contemporaries more directly than perhaps anywhere else, as in the essay on Lawrence,

> He did not understand . . . that of any two human beings, each has privacies which the other cannot penetrate. . . .

which is much less vague than the analysis of him and of other heretics in *After Strange Gods*. But isn't *The Criterion* itself criticism, even if Eliot's book reviews are not that but some other category of literary scrutiny?

"Now should I have lain still and been quiet" (Job 3:13).

R. C.

TO THE EDITORS OF *The New York Review of Books*:

Mr. [Christopher] Ricks betrays his lack of a sense of the ridiculous in contributing his research about two commas[29] while failing to see that this only draws attention to the overwhelming number and weight of my remaining "strictures." More serious is his unjustifiable substitution of "needless"—meaning "unnecessary"—for my very different word "obtrude." Being a teacher of English, Mr. Ricks might also have mentioned that the second comma occurs in another of those grammatical tangles as exemplified in my June 10 *NYR* letter:

> Consequently, we must believe that "emotion recollected in tranquillity" is an inexact formula. For it is neither emotion, nor recollection, nor, without distortion of meaning, tranquillity.

29. These, proving to be misprints, have been deleted here, and two other examples substituted.

The realization continues to grow that Eliot's prose was often shockingly bad, and that this seems not to be admitted because of adulation for his poetry.

I erred in assuming that the last edition of the writings of an author of Eliot's stature would be the most reliable, Mr. Ricks in believing the first to be the authoritative one. Yet with just a little more nit-picking, he would have discovered that a later edition of *The Use of Poetry and the Use of Criticism* corrects the grammar and even alters the substance of a passage that I quoted in its first form.

My conviction that "among" is indeed preferable to "between" in the cited example has survived a study not only of the *Oxford English Dictionary* but also of contemporary grammars. Finally, grateful as I am for the quotation from Dr. Johnson, whose dictum so emphatically supports me, I have never been contemporaneous with him; Mr. Ricks's statement "Dr. Johnson was less peremptory than Mr. Craft" lacks an essential present-tense verb.

R. C.

IN SEARCH OF ALDOUS HUXLEY

The British reception of Sybille Bedford's biography[1] reveals that late-1930s attitudes toward Aldous Huxley have scarcely changed: he is still the clever novelist gone preachy and dull, the scion of England's best-bred intellectual family run off to live on

1. *Aldous Huxley: A Biography* (New York, 1974).

the wrong side of the cultural tracks, one of the brightest minds of the Realm defected from respectable agnosticism to bizarre religions and pseudo-sciences. For one old-friend critic, Raymond Mortimer, the mere mention of Huxley's residence in Southern California is enough to explain his downfall. The new account of his life might at least have been expected to change that perspective. Yet in spite of her intentions of fairmindedness, Mrs. Bedford does not wholly succeed in escaping the same insularity.

For better or worse, how differently a less traditional biography might have treated the same material! Apart from concentrating on the "psychodynamics" of the life rather than on its external events, this hypothetical history would address an audience possessing values the very opposite of Mrs. Bedford's, one revering the prophet Huxley rather than the littérateur, the moral and sociological visionary rather than the paragon of the classical education, the explorer of unorthodox approaches to the understanding of cosmic laws instead of the high priest of "hard" science. As for Huxley the pacifist, still not forgiven by older critics, a new generation acclaims him as one of the first non-conquering heroes in its braver new world. His formerly suspect interests, moreover—ESP, acupuncture, yoga, and so many others—are no longer cultist pursuits on California's wilder shores of experiment but accredited studies on reputable campuses. In later years, of course, Huxley left his Litt.D. critics far behind, yet few of his true disciples have been prepared to follow him the whole way.

Huxley's development as a writer is generally regarded as a decline from the 1920s *romans à clef* about ego-eccentrics of the British intelligentsia to the homilies of the forties and fifties on the evils of overpopulation and assorted disasters of the modern world. And it is widely agreed that, after the early period, his fiction includes nothing to compare with *Antic Hay* and a few of the stories—"Young Archimedes," for one, in which he manages to construct an absorbing tale around a demonstration that the square of the hypotenuse of a right triangle is equal to the sum of the squares of the other two sides. Yet of all his books, *Brave New World* (1932) is the most assured of a place in history, if not literature. And, arguably, in some of the later nonfiction, such as *Gray Eminence* and the essay on Maine de Biran, Huxley's narrative skills increased.

At the same time, the development of the person can be looked upon as an ascent from mere brilliance into wisdom, from "superiority" into humility, from the satirist of individuals to the philosophical activist for the human condition. The question, then, is whether literary criteria are applicable to the later books. After all, the best of them are admittedly didactic, and while some, including *Ape and Essence* and *Island*, employ fictional forms, these neglect even the minimal requirements of the novel. Huxley himself rejected literary criticism as "pharisaical" and useless as a paradigm for the criticism of life.

The new biography contains the first full account of the latter half of Huxley's productive years, and if only for this reason the corresponding portions of the book are the most interesting. By access to family records Mrs. Bedford was also able to cover the pre-California period more thoroughly than did her predecessors, devoting more space to the young novelist's amorous encounters, for example, as well as to that symptom of personal crisis, the prolonged attack of "writer's cramp" at the time of *Eyeless in Gaza*. Unfortunately she does not offer convincing explanations for either the "understanding" complicity of Huxley's wife in the love affairs or for the impending emotional collapse.

Surely Mrs. Bedford attaches too much significance to an episode in an inn somewhere beyond the Mexique Bay when a berserk drunkard threatened Huxley with a gun. At any rate, it is hard to accept her suggestion that he was more ashamed of his "cowardice" in concealing himself from the would-be assailant than proud of his simple good sense in doing so. But even if her interpretation were true, this ridiculous incident can be no more than superficially related to Huxley's subsequent fits of depression and self-doubt. Mrs. Bedford rarely speculates about underlying emotional causes, however, and she may well have sacrificed a private theory to her high standards of good taste.

———

The documentation of Huxley's thirty-five-year marriage is so compendious and contains so much about his wife that the book might have been titled "Maria Huxley and Her Husband Aldous." Surprisingly, this material leads to some inescapable conclusions about the relationship. In fact it becomes more, rather than less, difficult to understand why he chose to marry Maria Nys, the Belgian girl he had met at Garsington. A priggish letter written in May 1918 reveals his disapproval of her as she was and his condescending wish that she be made over. The letter also exposes his utter incapability of feeling:

> I have tried to persuade Maria to . . . centre her life on thought rather than sensation, to adopt some fixed intellectual occupation . . . and not merely to live on the aesthetic sensations of the moment. She is educating herself . . . and the process gives her a solid foundation for her existence. . . .

The mystery of the decision to marry is compounded since it was not precipitate and not the result of external pressure on either side. Furthermore, since the two were living in different countries, Huxley could have withdrawn from the engagement without causing embarrassment. The reasons why he proceeded with it, therefore, must be related to the traumas of his youth: his mother's death by cancer, the suicide of a brother, the *keratitis punctata* which left him almost totally blind.[2] These agonizing and disabling experiences of his adolescence must have numbed him to such an extent that he could no longer trust any love relationship. Less important, but also to be considered, is the

2. Concerning Huxley's eyesight, the testimony of witnesses differs, some reporting that he was unable to see at all, others that his powers of vision were subject to considerable change according to his emotional state. But whatever the truth, the reader should have been more frequently reminded of the affliction; Mrs. Bedford, who knew Huxley, is inclined to take it for granted, and she seems to assume that others are able to do the same. Some readers, perhaps remembering Henry Green's *Blindness*, will regret that so accomplished a novelist as Mrs. Bedford did not offer at least one view of the world through Huxley's reduced vision, and, so to speak, *ab intra*. Mrs. Bedford does not mention the celluloid goggles, with pinholes to prevent staring and to force the eyes to exercise, that Huxley used for much of his reading and writing in the early 1950s.

likelihood that he may have felt physically inferior and self-conscious because of his semi-blindness and his abnormal height. And, though as remote from reality as such a conception assuredly is, he may well have had a sense of intellectual inferiority, for all his life he suffered from doubts about his abilities, as evidenced in his unremitting deprecation of his own work. Finally, he regarded himself as something of a misfit in society, as a letter written years later acknowledges:

> I am distressed to hear that I can be so paralyzing to people, a defect attributable to a certain shyness and difficulty in personal communication.

On Maria's side of the ledger was an apprehension about the compatibility between her friend and herself, a sense of alienation in his world, and a realization that she would have to repudiate her Catholicism and suppress her essentially intuitive nature. What might have overcome her misgivings was the challenge of helping Aldous to lead a comparatively normal life, caring for him physically, supporting his self-esteem, and exercising her genius for friendship. She was to select many of his associates for him and to sustain his relations with them. Without her, in fact, he might have disappeared into the library stacks, and, in a kind of Gregor Samsa metamorphosis, turned into a species of talking bookworm. In any case, and in lieu of evidence of all-consuming passions, these are at least possible explanations for the alliance of such a temperamentally and educationally unsuited pair.

Wise as Maria could be about people, she was not at ease with her husband's intellectuality. And although immersed in the worlds of science, literature, and the arts, she enjoyed them only in relation to him—except for music, so important to her husband, where her dislike was too strong to be concealed. Yet in spite of these limitations, Huxley increasingly relied on her judgment of his work. He may have been clutching at straws, for he needed approval and was hypersensitive to criticism—of which, to borrow a word that helped to make his second wife famous, he was more and more the "target."

The very abundance of Maria's letters—the main substance of the biography's more than seven hundred pages—as well as the extent to which she reveals herself in them, indicates that all was not well at home. She writes about her loneliness, her fatigue and chronic ill-health, her nostalgias for Europe and family. These last were not shared to anything like the same degree by her husband, for whom life in Southern California seemed to renew its fascination. But the recurring theme of her correspondence is that of protectiveness toward him, a protectiveness that suggests the possibility of underlying hostility. Certainly Maria had reason to feel hostile about her husband's affairs early in their marriage. Then, too, he was more demanding than he probably realized, restless in body as well as in mind, forever traveling and changing residences, even moving about the room while he talked. In making plans, he rarely seems to have considered his wife's health or feelings, as when he callously disregarded them while on a mule-back safari in a remote region of Mexico. (Mrs. Bedford sees the conduct with which this unnecessary expedition was carried out as exemplary of Huxleyan pluck and determination.)

But Maria also drove herself, like her automobiles, in an almost demonic way, in her last years even chauffeuring her husband through the wilderness areas of the Western states so that, Goethe-like, he could contemplate a rare weed, an unusual rock formation, the mating habits of Gila monsters. She resented having to do this and sometimes expressed her anguish to friends. All of this, of course, is the reverse of the usual reports, which pity Huxley in his blindness and admire him for persisting in his insatiable quests for knowledge of obscure places and things. Yet even in Mrs. Bedford's very different interpretation, it would appear that another of his visual handicaps may have been his inability to see the person closest to him.

Maria's protectiveness and self-sacrifice toward her husband were also shown by the way she spared him her worries and complaints and never added her burdens to his. This forbearance seems to have been carried to pathological extremes. Incredibly, less than a month before her death he was still referring to her illness as "lumbago"—and seeming to believe it. But can it be possible that Huxley, with his encyclopedic knowledge of medicine, did not understand his wife's true condition? Did no physical contact exist between them? Is it conceivable that the usual block against recognizing and accepting manifestations of cancer spread to so perceptive a diagnostician? And, finally, even if he were afraid to admit the truth, why could he not see it?[3]

That he did not, this reviewer can testify, having been present when, less than a week before Maria's death, Huxley, in a state of shock and despair, telephoned to Gerald Heard to relay the news of her condition. (Heard, who already knew it, later reacted with ecstatic exclamations to the prospect of still another mortal being able, as he said, to "tear off the mask.") With respect to all of this, Mrs. Bedford regards Maria's behavior as exhibiting saintly devotion and courage. But is it not something less romantic? And, in truth, are not the circumstances of her death really a final subconscious act of rejection and punishment? And does this not place the entire marriage in a much-altered light?

———

"The two great formative friendships of [Huxley's] maturer years [were] D. H. Lawrence and Gerald Heard," Mrs. Bedford writes (omitting some grammatically necessary words). It was Maria who fostered the connection with Lawrence, sharing a natural affinity with the man who possessed so many of the qualities that her husband lacked. With Lawrence's death Huxley lost a friend, a writer whom he admired, and a critical voice which he esteemed. Although shortly afterward Huxley debunked the philosophy of *The Plumed Serpent,* he continued to respect the humanity of its author, whom he portrayed as a symbolic figure of his time in a horrendous utopia. Lawrence's death had a profound effect on Maria; until the end of her life she continued to recall his final hours, which moved her with the force of a religious or mystical experience.

3. "The outcome of Maria's illness had been certain since the summer of 1952, but emotionally Aldous had rejected the prognosis. Maria, several times, had said to the Kiskaddens: 'Aldous doesn't know; he doesn't want to know.'" (*Letters of Aldous Huxley,* edited by Grover Smith [New York, 1970], p. 731.)

Considering Mrs. Bedford's acknowledgment of Gerald Heard's pre-eminence in Huxley's life, her skimpy treatment of this extraordinary figure is perplexing. And she has almost completely ignored the main sources. It is true that when she began the biography, Heard himself was partially paralyzed and unable to communicate. But Michael Barry, his constant companion and a long-time observer of Heard's relationship with Huxley, is mentioned only once, while Christopher Wood, who toured with Heard during his initial joint lectures with Huxley in America in 1937, is not even directly quoted. As for the third witness, Christopher Isherwood, the impressions of this subtle "camera" are doubtless awaiting development in his own darkroom. But the fact of Huxley's deference to Heard in their early years is a conundrum that Mrs. Bedford has not solved.

Could it be that Heard's "charisma" had captivated even Aldous Huxley? To watch the two of them in conversation, at any rate, was to be convinced that Huxley enjoyed the companionship of this scintillating crackpot more than that of anyone else. And in California, at least, Heard was the only man with whom Huxley could match wits, verbal dexterity and parure, information and mad-scientist ideas. And when the two of them were together, everyone, including Maria, was relegated to the foot of the table. She displayed no annoyance at this, though by the early 1950s her husband's partnership with Heard was over and the latter's schedule of mortifications had begun to exacerbate her. So had Heard's homosexuality, and, unusual as it is to encounter the prejudice in an intellectual circle such as this one, antipathy to homosexuals was strongly pronounced in Huxley himself. But, whatever the causes, the two men saw each other less frequently in the later years, and this in spite of their many mutual friends among the swamis, hypnotists, mediums, chiromancers, scientologists, organic nutritionists, and drug experimenters.

———

Huxley's second marriage contrasts with his first in almost every respect. For one thing, the cast of characters has changed, with not only a different woman but also a different man. The blow of Maria's death catapulted *him* into a radical awareness of his emotional deficiencies and of the emptiness of an existence in which intellectual values overshadow all others. For instance, the letters he now addresses to his son expose a belated realization of his former remoteness as a parent, while those to friends, with expressions of sympathy and insights into their problems, are scarcely recognizable as having been written by the author of *Point Counter Point*. Lawrence had described the emotion of that novel to Huxley as no more than "an attempt at intellectual sympathy," and, whatever his reaction to this criticism at the time, it is hard to believe that thirty years later he would have disagreed with it. Near the end of his life Huxley wrote:

> I keep asking myself what I ought to do . . . in the probably not very long future that is left to me. How to be more loving, more aware . . .

And, to a question about his ultimate philosophy, the reply was: "Try to be a little kinder."

Obviously Laura Huxley further inspired her husband's fundamental alteration of values, at least at the beginning of the marriage. Moreover, she was a psychologist who believed in promoting his independence, insisting that he *could* see, *was* able to do things by himself, did *not* require a system of defenses from the world. She was as "under"-solicitous, in short, as Maria had been "over," thereby predictably appalling many friends of the first marriage. But Laura's approach proved to be beneficial; Huxley soon began to lead a less sheltered life than ever before. Part of this came about because Laura was a career woman for whom the marriage involved other goals besides that of her husband's self-sufficiency. She had been a concert violinist, then became a psychotherapist, and was later to expand into a best-selling "Self-Help," "How To" author. Both she and her husband understood that, inevitably, the marriage must be regarded as simply another phase of her vocational life. But for Huxley it meant more than that. He was in love with her, as the tenderness and affection in his letters reveal:

In spite of this stupid little 'flu, I love you. . . . Goodbye, my darling. *Ti voglio bene.* . . . Be well, my sweetheart, and let us try to be happy and peaceful . . . because of one another.

This, for a while, they seemed to be, and his interest in her profession led him to suggest that they might work as a team:

I believe we can do quite a lot, you complementing me, I complementing you.

For her part, she borrowed ideas from him, pursuing them further and more zealously than he did, since he never lost his congenital skepticism and sense of balance. But slowly recognition must have come that they were seeking different satisfactions from the marriage, a large part of whose purpose seems to have been fulfilled for Laura when she proved her skill as his therapist. Then the exigencies of her career began to separate them and to leave Aldous both alone and lonely.

This much is an almost unavoidable deduction from his letters. In one of them, written from Berkeley a year and a half before his death from the cancer that they both knew about, the reader learns that Laura had accompanied him there but stayed only long enough to help him find an apartment. Then, little more than a year before his death, he was informed that a new operation was necessary. He wrote to Laura, who happened to be in Italy:

[B]ecause death seems to have taken a step nearer, everything seems more and more beautiful.

Finally, a mere three months before the end,

Aldous set out for Belgium on his own. (Laura was too busy trying to meet the deadlines of *her* book. . . .) [Italics added.]

Yet it must be said that by this time Huxley was almost constantly traveling to lectures and conferences, as if trying to run away from the cancer, and that Laura may have found this exhausting. But beyond that, who could criticize her, the practitioner of a psychology whose tenet is that everyone should "do his own thing"?

———

The totally documented biography, reconstructed from all the recorded trivia of the daily life, has become one of the most effective means of obliterating its subject's personality. Shortcuts result in slanted views, but the latter still may be preferable to unselective and less biased ones, for which, in any case, the future will have room. Mrs. Bedford never exceeds the point beyond which detail begins to obscure rather than to illuminate.

But neither does she attempt to assess Huxley's proper place in the Pantheon. To some extent this may be because of her own involvement with the Huxley family, the considerable role that she plays in the book, and the imprimatur implied by its dedication to the widow and son. Perhaps, too, Mrs. Bedford considered that her task, and it must have been a formidable one, was simply to present a comprehensive selection of the material. But above all, she may well feel, along with almost everyone else who knew Aldous Huxley, that the man, Aldous *ipsissimus*, rather than the shelves of his too-quickly-begotten books, will prove to be the subject of more lasting interest.

A NEW INTERPRETATION OF HEGEL?

The avalanche of more than 1,500 books and studies of Hegel in the past five years is submerging even the most dedicated scholars, who cannot keep abreast of more than a fraction of these publications. And if the experts are unable to "cope," imagine the bewilderment of the laity! The first choice from among the most recent batch of books might well be Charles Taylor's *Hegel*[1] if only because it seems to promise a general, comprehensive treatment. Yet some readers might be more attracted to Professor Gadamer's *Hermeneutical Studies*,[2] for the opposite reason of its smaller scope, concentration on particular features, and perhaps novel exegesis, as suggested by the title.

What is the result of reading both volumes? Perplexity and confusion, to a degree. Thus Gadamer postulates that Hegel was the first modern philosopher to have realized the primary importance of the "speculative" dialogues, the *Parmenides, Philebus*, and *Sophist*, while the ostensibly compendious Taylor work not only makes no mention of these but also seems to relegate Plato to an indirect role in the formation of Hegel's thought. For instance, Taylor writes that

the term which irresistibly springs to mind is Plato's Idea. Kant borrowed the term. Now Hegel follows suit.

Not that divergences in emphasis among critics are unusual, or of much consequence to non-specialists, but a disparity of this dimension would confound anyone.

Similarly, those seeking an explanation for the suddenness and magnitude of the Hegel boom will find many contradictory answers. In one opinion,

Hegel continues to matter because his philosophy impinged upon the central theme of political thought, the relation of theory to practice.[3]

But the chief concern of the author here is with

1. Cambridge, 1975.
2. *Hegel's Dialectic: Five Hermeneutical Studies*, by Hans-Georg Gadamer, translated and with an introduction by P. Christopher Smith (New Haven, 1975).
3. *From Marx to Hegel*, by George Lichtheim (London, 1971).

Lukács, Adorno, and Marcuse, who hold in common the notion that Marxism is to be understood as the legitimate heir of German Idealism.[4]

Taylor's text, on the other hand, does not even refer to Adorno and Marcuse, and it confines comment on Lukács's landmark studies[5] to three footnotes. Moreover, the disregard of the Hegelian viewpoints of Adorno and others of the Frankfurt School is a serious omission, since these socio-political thinkers helped to catalyze the new German interest responsible for the majority of those 1,500 dissertations. Still another reason for saying this is Taylor's belief that the new interest in Hegel is partly a reaction to the positivism of "Anglo-Saxon philosophy," which is to ignore the failure of the firm of Ayer and Austin, Ryle and Strawson to make any inroad on the extensive territory of the late Martin Heidegger.

Professor Taylor's *Hegel* has been so widely and exhaustively discussed that some of the criticisms must themselves be included in future commentaries on the book. Two reviews in particular cannot be ignored, a long, favorable one by Professor Ernest Gellner,[6] and a slightly briefer, almost completely dismissive one by Professor Walter Kaufmann.[7] Gellner's article, unfortunately, would hardly qualify him as a responsible writer. Thus he announces near the beginning of his exposition that

When modern man speaks nonsense, the chances are more than even that he borrows his idiom either from Hegel or from Freud.

But surely vast quantities of nonsense derive from people whose idiom owes nothing to Hegel. And how did Professor Gellner determine that "the chances are more than even"?

4. *Ibid.*
5. *The Young Hegel: Studies in the Relations Between Dialectics and Economics*, by Georg Lukács, translated by Rodney Livingstone (London, 1975).
6. "Hegel's Last Secrets," *Encounter*, April 1976.
7. *Times Literary Supplement*, January 2, 1976.

The following passages are no-less-typical specimens of Gellner's style:

> What exactly did Hegel achieve . . . ? He re-humanised the world, and as if this weren't quite a big enough job on its own, he did a few further things on the side.

> Though Taylor ["Chuck," to Gellner] gives a very thorough and exhaustive account of all aspects of Hegelianism, it is the culture-romanticism—which he calls expressivism—which really turns him on. . . .

While Gellner's jargon will "turn off" some readers, his syntax will confound all of them:

> Hegelianism was an important move [movement?] in the re-humanisation of the world. It [?] opposed its [?] disenchantment. . . .

> Kierkegaard, Hegel's second most important disciple, had a similar reaction though he envisaged the contrasted reality in a different manner. The capacity to generate such extremities [extremes?] of reaction seems to be of the essence of his [?] thought.

Taylor, who currently holds a chair at Oxford, must feel uneasy with the compliments— "the admirably correct Taylor," "Taylor succeeds brilliantly"—of such a champion. In conclusion Gellner writes:

> "Expressivism" is not an option which need tempt us. Thanks to Taylor, I understand it, and Hegel, better than I did before. I doubt whether they [?] could find a better exposition or [?] advocate.

With Professor Kaufmann, on the other hand, the present writer finds himself in general agreement, taking issue only with some of the presentation, such as Kaufmann's remark that Taylor's "frequent solecisms are pointless." (Just which solecisms might *have* point?) And when Kaufmann takes Taylor to task for employing "such words as . . . 'revendicated,'" the objection may be made that the term is valid but that Taylor misuses it. The real roadblocks in Taylor's vocabulary are not so much his rare and strange forms ("historial," "vehicled," "diremption") as his obsolete usages:

> the image of the leap dispensed Marx from having to think about the organization of freedom.

It is more common to hear of Marx being "dispensed" from a place—Union Square, for instance—than from an obligation.

But Kaufmann's judgment on Taylor's grammar as "often faulty" is a serious understatement, since the professor frequently seems not to have heard of agreement between subject and verb:

> both Aristotelian hylomorphism and the theory of expression makes us look on them as totalities. . . .

The book's non-sentences, too, must number in the hundreds, many of them leaving the reader to wait in vain for predicates:

> So that we might look at *Capital* as one of those great works of mature science, like Darwin's evolution theory, or later Freud's psychoanalysis, which incorporate the insights of the earlier Romantic period. But that this involved Marx's view . . .

To what might "this" refer? And where did Taylor acquire the notion that "later Freud's psychoanalysis" (meaning the work of the final years?) has been accorded the universal status of a "mature science"? Obviously any interpretation of the already dense and convoluted Hegel requires the exact opposite of this kind of writing, which, furthermore, undermines the reader's confidence in Taylor's own thinking. And positively unnerving is Taylor's projection of Hegel's terminology into the minds of ancient Athenians:

> Socrates himself . . . accepts the idea of *Sittlichkeit*. . . .

Kaufmann condemns Taylor as "tediously prolix" (which is also *un mot de trop*), observing that

> if everything said a great many times were said twice only, the book would be less than half as long as it is. . . .

As a matter of fact, the book would be only half as long as *that* if so much of it did not have to be read twice. Yet if the repetitions were eliminated, this *Hegel* would be not more concise but only more evidently incomplete. Then, too, while Taylor exasperatingly reiterates fairly simple precepts, some that are crucial to the whole subsequent development of philosophy are allowed to slip by surreptitiously, as in the following uncut excerpt purporting to explain the origin of Hegelian dialectic. The passage is representative: instead of an original, reasoned explication of Hegel, Taylor offers no more than a muddled paraphrase. The "basic dichotomies" to which he refers are those "between individual and society, between finite and infinite spirit, or [sic] between free man and his fate":

> Hegel's answer is that each term in these basic dichotomies when thoroughly understood shows itself to be not only opposed but identical with its opposite. And when we examine things more deeply we shall see that this is so because at base the very relations of oppositions and identity are inseparably linked to each other. [But *why* are they linked, and *how*?]
>   They cannot be utterly distinguished because neither can exist on its own, that is, maintain itself as the sole relation holding between a given pair of terms. Rather they are in a kind of circular relation. [*Why* "circular"?]

An opposition arises out of an earlier identity; and this of necessity: the identity could not sustain itself on its own but had to breed opposition. [But what is meant by "an earlier identity," where did it come from, and how did an opposition "arise" out of it?]

And from this it follows that the opposition is not simply opposition, the relation of each term to its opposite is a peculiarly intimate one. It is not just related to *an* other but to *its* other, and this hidden identity will necessarily reassert itself in a recovery of unity. [But to what do "it" and "its" refer? And why "necessarily"?]

That is why Hegel holds that the ordinary viewpoint of identity has to be abandoned in philosophy in favor of a way of thinking which can be called dialectical in that it presents us with something which cannot be grasped in a single proposition or a series of propositions, which does not violate the principle of non-contradiction. . . .

And so on. Much of Professor Taylor's book is as lacking in definition of terms, imprecisely formulated, and loosely connected as is this excerpt. Professor Gellner to the contrary, the reader, for all his pains, will not attain a deeper understanding of Hegel, though books such as this *do* help to explain why students drop out of philosophy courses and even blame themselves for their inability to comprehend what is plainly incomprehensible.

The broad readership, attracted by the title *Hegel*, might reasonably expect some biographical information—unfashionable as it has become to suggest that the "lives" of thinkers and artists could have any real bearing on their "work," a view which represents the triumph of Eliot's separation between "the man who suffers and the mind which creates." Yet one tenet of Hegel's *Phenomenology* is that all products of mental activity must be seen in relation to their embodying minds, or, as Taylor says:

It was a basic principle of Hegel's thought that the subject and all his [*sic*] functions . . . were inescapably embodied. . . .

A two-page "Biographical Note" is buried near the end of the book, but this says no more than would a perfunctory encyclopedia entry, being remarkable only for the statement

> Hegel was fortunate to die in the middle and not at the end of this apogee. [But an apogee is a point in an orbit, farthest or highest, and cannot have a middle or an end.]

In fact, Hegel's life was exceptionally enriched by personal influences, above all by his friendship with Friedrich Hölderlin in their seminary years, and by associations with Rahel Varnhagen's salon[8] and with the Mendelssohn family. Goethe himself apparently received his first account of Hegel's lectures on aesthetics from the young Felix Mendelssohn, who had been acquainted with both men since childhood and had attended Hegel's classes at Berlin University. (One wonders whether Mendelssohn expressed to Goethe the reservations about the "aesthetics" that are found in the composer's correspondence.) As for Hölderlin, a footnote on the last page of Taylor's text suddenly confronts the reader with what may well be even this book's most cryptic remark:

> Hölderlin's position . . . may be inaccessible to philosophical statement . . . but to those who want to resume the task of Hegel's generation, Hölderlin may point a surer way.

!!! What??? After struggling through nearly six hundred pages about the philosopher, are we now being advised that this time would have been better spent on the poet (whom Heidegger, for one, did not find wholly "inaccessible to philosophical statement")? And in view of the industrial and every other kind of revolution of the last century and a half, how, pray tell, would anyone go about resuming "the task of Hegel's generation"?

Taylor's main contribution to a new perspective on his subject is his grafting of Herder's "expressionism" onto Hegel. In Gellner's words,

8. *Rahel Varnhagen*, by Hannah Arendt (New York, 1974).

The key notion in Taylor's critique of the modern world *and* of his exegesis both of Hegel and of Marx, is *expressionism*.

But Gellner does not mention Herder. Isaiah Berlin defines the term as

> the doctrine that human activity in general, and art in particular, express [*sic*] the entire personality of the individual or the group, and are [*sic*] intelligible only to the degree to which they [*sic*] do so. Still more specifically, expressionism claims that all the works of men . . . are not objects detached from their makers, [but] are part of a living process of communication between persons and not independently existing entities. . . .[9]

Taylor, however, places Herder's "expressionism" at the center of Hegel's philosophy and goes sailing under this wrong flag throughout the book, even though Hegel's indebtedness to Herder on this question has never been established. Berlin notes that

> the idea that great poets expressed the mind and experience of their societies and were their truest spokesmen, was widespread during Herder's formative years,[10]

while Kaufmann contends that

> Hegel was monumentally uninterested in Herder and hardly ever referred to him. But when he did speak of him, it was to disparage him.

In sum, Hegel cannot be pushed into the role of Herder's disciple, at least in this matter, nor does Taylor make a convincing

9. *Vico and Herder*, by Isaiah Berlin (London, 1976).
10. *Ibid.*, p. 147. Berlin does say that Hegel's definition of freedom seems to "owe much to Herder's teaching," and that Hegel's "concepts of becoming, and of the growth and personality of impersonal institutions, begin their lives in Herder's pages." A phrase in Berlin's *Karl Marx*, too, "the Germans put forward the metaphysical historicism of Herder and Hegel," may have misled Taylor into believing that the philosophers collaborated.

case for doing so when he says that "Hegel agreed with Herder" on certain concepts, both men surely having agreed with many other philosophers on many other concepts.

Yet what disturbs is not so much Taylor's mistaking the source of Hegel's "expressionism," or failing to demonstrate an understanding of it, as his inflation of its importance in Hegel's philosophy, and, to the same measure, in that of Marx as well. At one point Taylor goes so far as to characterize Marx's work as "Promethean expressivism," though acknowledging in a concluding chapter that

> Many . . . would object to an interpretation of Marxism which places it in what I have called the expressionist tradition. Of course, Marxism is more than this. . . . [But] certainly few would want to deny that the young Marx is the heir, through Hegel, of the expressionist aspiration, which, in the early 1840s . . . is married with the thrust of the radical Enlightenment to produce the peculiarly powerful Marxist synthesis.

But, on the contrary, many would deny this association of Marx with the "expressionist aspiration," and in spite of these belated qualifying remarks, the Professor has misidentified the two parties in wedlock, Hegel's philosophy of history and his dialectics being more essential to the Marxist synthesis than what, in effect, is a largely subjective element. Nor is this to confuse Marx with Marxism, which was ultimately to suppress subjectivism in every form.

Taylor gives a creditable account of the influence on Marx of Hegel's description of the self-alienating process and of the idea of self-creation in work, as well as of Hegel's recognition that these phenomena were collective rather than individual. But here, precisely when the reader most wants them, Taylor does not cite chapter and verse, simply claiming that the debt to Hegel

> comes through Marx's text, even when he is not engaged in acknowledging it. [Why "engaged in"?]

Taylor sums up that while

Hegel's conclusions are dead, yet the course of his philosophical reflection is very much to the point. . . .

The most valuable of these still-pertinent "reflections" appears to be Hegel's perception of the emptiness of the "ultimate dilemma of absolute freedom." But has this condition ever existed in human societies, and is it an imminent threat? Actually, Taylor's arguments for a return to such "reflections" are weaker than one of his arguments against it:

> If Hegel had been right, men would have recognized themselves in the structures of the rational state, and industrial society would not have taken the path it has.

No doubt the general reader continues to think that the current interest in Hegel is still due to his political writings, and to his reputation as the founder of historical determinism—the gravitation toward a perfected society that somehow turned into the Soviet dictatorship. But even without reading those 1,500 studies, it seems safe to attribute the philosopher's vogue among academicians to his reinvestment of man with qualities and potentialities that the "rational-animal" *philosophes* had taken away, to his opposition to dualisms, reductionisms, and behaviorist psychologies, and to his understanding of the organic nature of the development of institutions, ideas, and events, which are parts of larger wholes. Despite its devastating heritage, his dialectic nonetheless could have been an instrument uniquely potent for enlightenment and growth. Yet the profoundest reason for the Hegel revival may be no more than a nostalgia for Romantic Idealism, a response to the bankruptcy of our private and public, individual and collective, morality, and of power and money values as a way of life.

———

Kant and Hegel were the last . . . who could write on aesthetics without understanding anything about art.
—T. W. Adorno

Since the *Aesthetics*[11] contains Hegel's principal philosophical ideas, these lengthy lectures can provide an orientation to the whole of his work for anyone who prefers to read about Greek sculpture rather than, for example, the logic of ontology. But the obstacles are formidable, and at times it is difficult to believe that this branch of the philosopher's system could have exercised the influence it once did.[12] For one thing, Hegel's "aesthetic" categories—"symbolic," "classical," and "romantic"— accommodate his theory of historical progression more conveniently than they do artistic criteria. For another, he considered works of art to be embodied "ideas," "truths," "forms of knowledge," even though he recognized the untranslatability of the medium.

Largely irrelevant, at least for most readers today, are Hegel's discussions of his concept of beauty, and of such of its qualities (and virtues) as symmetry, balance, harmony, and proportion. Nor does the obsolescence of the *Aesthetics* follow from its date; after all, the *Philosophical Enquiry into the Origin of Our Ideas of the Sublime and Beautiful*, written three-quarters of a century earlier, is still pertinent, Burke having perceived the relationship between the beautiful and the erotic, and between the sublime and the desire for self-preservation—sex and anxiety, so to speak. Yet it must be said for Hegel's system that, in it, art together with philosophy and religion, is a necessity, a manifestation of Mind through which we transcend our existence, and a faculty innate in all human beings.

Georg W. F. Hegel and Ludwig van Beethoven were born in the same year. Beethoven created aesthetic objects, and of such appeal that many of us would part with almost anything else in preference. Hegel seemed to lack the capacity to understand Beethoven. But, conversely, would Beethoven have understood Hegel's *Aesthetics*, let alone its attempt to account for such a cosmic event as himself?

11. *Aesthetics: Lectures on Fine Art*, 2 vols., by Georg W. F. Hegel, translated by T. M. Knox (Oxford, 1975).
12. On Pater, for example. See *On Art and the Mind*, by Richard Wollheim (London, 1973), pp. 169–171.

THE DISCREET CHARM
OF THE BOURGEOISIE

He took out his fountain-pen and began to answer various items of his correspondence.

—Death in Venice

At Rutgers University's comprehensive symposium[1] commemorating the centenary of Thomas Mann, Hans Wysling, director of the Mann archives in Zürich, estimated that the novelist had written some 25,000 letters. Wysling attributed this epistolic prodigality to a variety of factors: the practical one of Mann's exile; his impeccable courtesy, even when conscious of being importuned to write letters for collectors; the substitution of letter writing for conversation; the constant need for literary exercise; the belief that his letters were a medium for his role as spokesman for the age. (At the same time, the written communication also enabled him to maintain distance and to preserve what others thought of as his aloofness.) Above all, according to Wysling, Mann regarded letter writing as a means to self-analysis, even to a "merciless examination" of himself. Yet one of the peculiarities of Thomas Mann is that the failure to see and understand his own character, as evidenced in the letters, could exist side by side with the powers of observation and analysis exhibited in his fiction.

—

The separate publication of the letters between two people is much less satisfactory than the inclusion of these individual

1. New Brunswick, New Jersey, April 10–12, 1975.

contributions in an integrated total correspondence. In order to view Mann from more than one aspect, it is necessary to compare his comments to different people, both concurrently and over a long period. The three new volumes of letters (to be considered in detail below) would have benefited by the fuller pictures afforded through references within an expanded collection. For example, in the letters to Kerényi concerning the transmutation of myth in *Joseph and His Brothers*, Mann's word *"umfunktionieren"* comes from Ernst Bloch, whose letters to Mann, along with Mann's references to this philosopher, are cited in a footnote, though the texts themselves are not provided. Unlike the only extensive selection of Mann's letters[2] that has so far appeared in English, however, these three volumes represent complete, two-sided exchanges.

Even Mann's most ardent disciples will look in the new collections for relief from the impersonality of his discourse. But precious few glimpses of his personal feelings are to be found in any of the published correspondence, which is less than a seventh of the letters so far counted, and only the earliest of these can be classified as bona fide private communications. Soon after his emergence as a writer the public persona eclipsed the private one, and the bulk of the available letters consists preponderantly of commentaries on public events. Indeed, the reader suspects that Mann would not have minded if much of his mail had been intercepted and printed in the "letters to the editor" columns of newspapers, the destination he sometimes seemed to have wished for it. The contrast with Kafka's letters is striking: in them it is virtually impossible to establish any orientation to the world without, even to the mention of the beginning or ending of a war, while in Mann's the reader searches, usually in vain, for so much as a peek at the world within.

But is there an "inner" Mann? The answer could conceivably

2. *Letters of Thomas Mann*, selected and translated by Richard and Clara Winston (New York, 1971). In fairness, it must be said that in the majority of cases, including that of the most voluminous correspondence, the one with Agnes Meyer, the unilateral restriction to Mann's contributions is probably a mercy.

lie in further publications of correspondence, surely to be anticipated, and in his diaries, on which the twenty-year seal is free
to be broken this year. If future installments of the letters do not
include more of those to his intimates and fewer to other public
figures, however, and if the examples from the diaries quoted in
The Genesis of Doctor Faustus[3] are indicative of what might be
expected from them, that "inner" life will remain an unsupported
conjecture. Most crucial for Mann studies would be the publication of the complete correspondence between Thomas and Heinrich,[4] since the love/hatred between these gifted brothers is the
darkest mystery in their lives, as well as an important unexplored
subject in contemporary literature.

—

Many Americans are surprised to learn that, outside the United
States, Heinrich Mann's stature as a novelist is recognized as the
near equal of his brother's, and that some German readers consider at least one book, *Zwischen den Rassen*, a masterpiece of
world literature greater than any single opus by the Nobel Prize
winner. The reasons for Heinrich's continuing obscurity in this
country are difficult to ascertain. Certainly, a quarter of a century
after his death, his "un-American activities" can no longer matter.
But the wonder is that the American academic machine could
have overlooked the rich thesis material in linguistic, stylistic,
statistical, and thematic comparisons of the brothers' works.[5]

The story of Thomas and Heinrich Mann is stranger than any
in the fiction of either writer, and Richard Winston's Rutgers
lecture on the subject was a revelation. Tracing the long history

3. *The Story of a Novel: The Genesis of Doctor Faustus*, by Thomas Mann,
translated by Richard and Clara Winston (New York, 1961).

4. It is remarkable that the centenary has failed to produce an English version
of the brothers' (incomplete) *Briefwechsel: 1900—1949* (Frankfurt am Main,
1968).

5. A comparison of recent publications of books and articles on Heinrich Mann
and Thomas Mann, in the latest volume of the MLA *International Bibliography*
—which is compiled from about 2,600 periodicals—indicates that Thomas
dominates the international scene and that, with a single exception, the literature on Heinrich is from Germany.

of fraternal animosity, Winston cited Thomas's confession, "My hostility to my brother was responsible for my worst hours," and concluded that Thomas was more at fault than Heinrich.[6] Winston reversed the accepted notion that Heinrich had simply attacked Thomas because of political differences, or gratuitously, or out of jealousy. Heinrich, of course, had bitterly opposed Imperial Germany, while Thomas defended it—in a preposterous, William F. Buckley-like polemic—actually calling the events of 1914–1918 "this stirring people's war."

But the war between the brothers had begun long before the Kaiser's. Thomas had insulted Heinrich, both covertly and pointedly, even going so far as to add barbs to unfavorable notices of his brother's work. Moreover, Thomas borrowed—or stole—from Heinrich's books, as in the case of the final phrase of *Royal Highness*, which had already been used by the older writer. Heinrich also borrowed—or stole—from Thomas, however, and it seems that the roots of the ambiguous relationship may have sprung both from ordinary sibling rivalry and from a strong family resemblance. A friend of both brothers in their Santa Monica period, describing her seventieth-birthday party for Heinrich, relates how, with sober mien and apparently no sense of pomposity, first Thomas and then Heinrich read lengthy speeches to each other.[7] Such behavior, it seems, was utterly characteristic of both of them.

—

Thomas was obsessed with the brother question, returning to it in almost every book. "The brother problem always stimulates me," he wrote. And apparently it did inspire him more than, for example, the subject of women, whom, as he once admitted in a letter to Heinrich, "I do not understand at all." But Heinrich understood them, and his erotic infatuations are sometimes flagrantly exhibited in his books. Nor did the sons-and-lovers

6. See the chapter on Thomas Mann in Heinrich Mann's autobiography, *Ein Zeitalter wird besichtigt* (Stockholm, 1946; reprinted in Düsseldorf, 1975).

7. See *The Kindness of Strangers*, by Salka Viertel (New York, 1969), pp. 250–251.

theme appeal to the brothers with the same intensity, for while Heinrich built an entire novel around their mother and the reminiscences of her early years in Brazil, Thomas made only a single chapter out of the same material.

Winston tentatively concluded that Heinrich possessed the larger talent and the greater originality, and that, unlike Thomas, he was unimpeded by an insistence on a rigid distinction between literature and life. Yet Thomas, the more careful artist, is ultimately the greater one as well. Heinrich's last novel concedes this superiority in a dialogue between two sisters (!), one of whom says: "You have defeated me, but is that a reason to hate me?" But in the very moment of congratulating his brother on having won the lifelong contest between them, Heinrich claimed that "In *Faustus* you have acknowledged your debt to my methods."

———

The memoir of Thomas Mann's widow,[8] compiled in her ninetieth year, does not illuminate the relationship of the brothers or offer any explanation for her husband's formality and traditionalism other than the influence of his North German burgher background. As in the case of other perfectly self-disciplined and tightly controlled people, it seems reasonable to suspect that some wayward attraction or propensity, what Jung calls the "shadow," must have required these constraints. Mann's social and moral upbringing was strict, as well as deep and enduring. And whatever the causes, such as a regard for the values of family and institutions ("Passion is like crime . . . it welcomes every blow dealt the bourgeois structure"—*Death in Venice*), he displays traits of suppressions and sublimations, though in a generalized and pervasive, rather than tangible, way.

All of which brings up the question of Aschenbach, and of "the love that dare not"—at least in 1911—"speak its name." Katia Mann unequivocally identifies her husband with his fictional character, explaining that Mann "stylized into extreme passion

8. *Katia Mann: Unwritten Memoirs*, edited by Elisabeth von Plessen and Michael Mann (New York, 1975).

. . . the pleasure he actually took in that charming boy." But can an "extreme passion" be "stylized" unless it has been experienced? And is it not possible that more of the inner Thomas Mann found a way into *Death in Venice* than into any of his other works? Moreover, is there not some connection between Tadzio and Joseph, since Joseph, too, was the pursued and not the pursuer?—though even this irreverent reviewer would not venture to suggest that the author had subconsciously disguised himself as Potiphar's wife.

Unfortunately, it cannot be said that Katia Mann brings her husband closer either as a person or as a writer. She adds helpful details: he worked slowly but with little rewriting; as a violinist he was at one time able to play Beethoven sonatas; Naphta was not intentionally modeled on Georg Lukács. Frau Mann also contradicts her spouse's officially publicized view of Theodor Adorno, whom they grew to dislike to such an extent that Mann did no more than allow his name to appear under a notice in *The New York Times*, actually written by his second son, of a book by Adorno and Horkheimer. But so brief a memoir should have been confined to personal reminiscences and not have included repetitions of such well-known stories as that of the triskaidekaphobic crisis surrounding Schoenberg's death, which occurred while the Manns were on a transatlantic steamer. "Schoenberg went upstairs to bed. . . ." In fact Schoenberg had not been downstairs for several weeks.

Katia Mann possesses considerable charm, bourgeois or otherwise, and even when made to speak in Vonnegutese:

And so it went until I was sixteen. . . . They drove to Italy and all over the place. . . . Somehow . . . Bert Brecht and my husband . . . just didn't click.

And, despite the shortcomings of the book, she endears herself to her readers in remarks like the following:

My husband always said that if he were born again he would like to be a conductor. I don't know if that will happen but you never can tell. . . .

Mann's correspondence with Hesse[9] and Kerényi[10] is presented from their respective sides and not from Mann's. In fact the foreword to the Hesse volume ill conceals a bias in Hesse's favor, while the Kerényi includes his preface and annotations. Only the correspondence with Kahler[11] is primarily for Mann devotees, but this is the least specialized and the least interesting. About halfway through their exchanges, and anticipating the reaction of future readers, Mann gives the game away:

> A deeper reason for our mutual not-writing-much may be the feeling that it is unnecessary. . . . We are on the whole experiencing the same things, and each of us knows fairly precisely what the other is feeling and thinking about them.

Yet he goes dutifully on, appraising world events and fulfilling his purpose, which would appear to be little more than that of returning the ball to Kahler's court.

One of the appendixes to the Hesse collection reprints his 1910 review of *Royal Highness*. Antedating his friendship with Mann, this offers more outspoken and more valuable criticism than the multitudinous compliments in the letters that follow:

> [Mann] lacks the somnambulistic sureness of the naïve genius. . . . A "pure," naïve writer . . . doesn't think about readers at all. A poor author thinks about them, tries to please them, flatters them. . . . [Mann] gives the average reader a certain feeling of superiority but in return cheats him out of all that is fine, serious, and really worth saying. . . .

9. *The Hesse/Mann Letters: The Correspondence of Hermann Hesse and Thomas Mann, 1910–1955*, edited by Anni Carlsson and Volker Michels, translated by Ralph Manheim (New York, 1975).

10. *Mythology and Humanism: The Correspondence of Thomas Mann and Karl Kerényi*, translated by Alexander Gelley (Ithaca, 1975).

11. *An Exceptional Friendship: The Correspondence of Thomas Mann and Erich Kahler*, translated by Richard and Clara Winston (Ithaca, 1975).

Mann's reply, which precipitated a forty-five-year correspondence, does not—could not—answer this, but instead shows that he either did not understand the depth of the criticism or was already impervious to unmanageable truths:

> Your shrewdly distrustful remarks have made me ponder the matter . . . and I can assure you that no calculation, no conscious flirtation with the public was at work.

Hesse's review might better have begun the book than Theodore Ziolkowski's foreword, which, describing the new Hesse-Mann "humanism," sets some kind of record in vacuity:

> It acknowledges all aspects of the personality—its good and its evil, the horror and the glory—and strives to reconcile them into a grand harmony that transcends all ideology.

It is true that Mann's pharisaism can be insufferable:

> When I received your letter yesterday at the post office, I had just sent off a banknote to a starving colleague.

And the same applies to his self-importance:

> I owed it to my fellow refugees to make a satisfactory statement . . . and I have shown that there is still something resembling character and conviction in the world.

Yet not even these and other objectionable qualities mandate the introductory *parti pris*:

> While Mann was savoring public adulation . . . Mann basked in public acclaim . . . the recipient of the Goethe Medal virtually eclipsed Goethe himself in the festivities . . . [Mann] never tired of reminding Hesse of the *grand monde* in which he [*sic*] moved so easily: he has just met Nehru, he recalls a visit with Roosevelt (the *first* visit . . . and therefore by implication not the only one). . . .

But this is unfair, since an encounter with Nehru in California was a far more conspicuous and mentionable event than it would have been in London or Paris, and since Mann's purpose was to compare Nehru's intellectual qualities with those (if any) of the American leadership (1949). Also, Mann's object in specifying the White House invitation as "the first" was to underscore the early date (1935) at which Roosevelt was giving private assurances of American intervention.

———

Mann's political vision was always astigmatic, and already in 1932 gullible Thomas was announcing that "the worst is over." Even so, his conduct is more laudable than Hesse's, who, a year later, declared that he still admired the "blue-eyed enthusiasm and spirit of self-sacrifice" in the Third Reich. Mann came charging back at this with

> the deceit, the violence, the ridiculous show of "historical grandeur," the sheer cruelty fills me with horror, contempt, and revulsion. I am no longer moved by the "blue-eyed enthusiasm" you speak of. . . .

Hesse later intimated that his position as a "notorious pacifist" had made him a martyr. But how long would pacifism, or that "philosophical detachment from German politics" which Mann respected in Hesse, have been tolerated in a Hitler world? Furthermore, soon after the war's end and the discovery of the crematoria, Hesse complained to Mann that "the sadists and gangsters in Germany are no longer Nazis and German-speaking, but Americans." One wonders how any informed person could seriously compare the crimes of the S.S. and the U.S.

The letters contain too little about the art of the novel, too much about public affairs. But when Mann adjudges *Steppenwolf* "in no way inferior to *Ulysses*," the reader is thankful to be spared further literary evaluations. Occasionally some clue to a true reaction inadvertently slips through the fulsomeness, as when Mann remarks that the style of *The Glass Bead Game* is "overgrown in shrubbery and rich in arabesques." Hesse, for his part, is quick to inform Mann of attacks on him in the press about which he might not otherwise have known.

———

Karl Kerényi introduces what is the most rewarding of the three collections with "the actual basis of our relationship was that [Mann] found me useful." It began in 1934 (while the novelist was writing *Joseph and His Brothers*), when the mythologist sent one of his essays on Greek religion to Mann. From then until Mann's death, with a four-year interruption during the war, Kerényi was the novelist's guide in mythological matters, instructing him, sensitively redirecting him, drawing his attention to parallels from classical literature (Potiphar's wife is a "new-born sister of Euripides' Phaedra"). But Kerényi is more tactful when writing to, rather than about, Mann, and some of his claims of influence on the novels could scarcely be termed self-effacing. "I was the observant, the warmer partner, he the creative, the colder," Kerényi writes, and he goes on to describe the writings of the "colder partner" as

the most reliable commentary possible on [his] mythological novel, an exceptional scholarly source for which there is hardly a parallel in world literature.

The "scholarly source" is too obviously not Mann, however, but his informant. No doubt the final Joseph books would have been different without Kerényi; whether he is justified in characterizing his effect on them as "the convergence of mythology with psychology" will have to await comparison of the novels with those of his writings that Mann is now known to have read.

The most challenging of the Rutgers lectures, Klaus Schröter's "Myth, Psychology and Society: The Changing Concept of the 'Joseph' Stories," postulated that *Joseph* was conceived as a work of art against its time and in accordance with Mann's current philosophy of the necessary discrepancy between the social reality and the work of art. Schröter (who was the first to uncover the association in 1895 of Heinrich and Thomas Mann with the reactionary and anti-Semitic review *Das 20. Jahr-*

hundert) then treated the development of the later parts of the book as reflecting Thomas Mann's increasing sense of political responsibility. Surely the "changing concept" theory will be further modified as a result of the publication of the complete Kerényi letters describing his "partnership."

———

Of the two correspondents, Kerényi makes the fuller and more valuable contribution, as Mann acknowledged when Kerényi published their prewar letters: "It is much more your book than mine." Kerényi's first entries disclose that he read English and was conversant with contemporary British writers unfamiliar to Mann—J. C. Powys, for one (*A Glastonbury Romance* and *Wolf Solent*), and D. H. Lawrence, "a poet who draws forth the positive from nature." Mann had scarcely heard of the former and found the author of *Twilight in Italy*, from which Kerényi quotes, less to his taste than Aldous Huxley. On the other hand, Kerényi inspires Mann to such literary-historical speculations as the possibility that Boccaccio might have been the bridge between the Greek novel and Cervantes, and mythology the bridge from Goethe to Wagner. Finally, some of Mann's best statements in any of the new books are addressed to Karl Kerényi: "My God, it is simply *sympathy* that must be the basis of everything . . . ," and, "One is always striving and wishing to get finished without noticing that in essence one strives for the sake of being finished and for death."

Almost every letter, beginning with Kerényi's recognition of Mann's partisanship toward Settembrini, pursues the meaning of "humanism." At one point Kerényi refers to his brand as *"religio Academici,"* which critics have attacked as "neither scholarship nor religion." Elsewhere he deepens the idea of *Humanitas* (*"anthropismós,"* which "occurs for the first time" in Aristippus) by characterizing his new book, *Prometheus*, as

the link between the *Hermes* and the "Socrates," between the figure who is able to live easily and the one who is able to die easily.

Once he ventures to define his "humanism" as "that state of progressive enlightenment that is part of the true progress of consciousness." Mann, too, believed in human progress at some level, the Bomb notwithstanding: "All in all, mankind has been pushed ahead . . . in spite of all signs to the contrary." Yet Kerényi failed to discern Mann's different attitude toward Freud, remarking, "You have definitely overcome the essentially disintegrating mode of analysis of Freudianism."

Then when Mann sent to Kerényi his Freud lecture—the same one that, out of blind egotism or a failure of a sense of the absurd, Mann had read to Freud himself—Kerényi took issue with the contents, and Mann rejoined, felicitously:

You put the seriousness of scholarship in the place of a half-playful etymology of convenience.

Aside from the Freud question, it is evident from Kerényi's reaction to *The Transposed Heads*—which will interest readers of Dumézil's *Mythe et épopée* more than those of Mann's "metaphysical jest"—that the mythologist was disconcerted by the novella.

In the second, postwar, half of the correspondence, Kerényi is too overtly continuing a good thing, and his writing becomes more self-conscious. He excitedly repeats a notice of the first half that compares the letters to those of "Erasmus and his friends," going on to quote from the piece:

It must be disheartening for [Mann and Kerényi] to write so many subtleties and allusions which presuppose enormous learning and great maturity, knowing full well that the succeeding generation will already be unable to understand them.

Though no blanket endorser of "the succeeding generation," this reviewer is inclined to believe that, this once anyway, it has been underrated. But the later letters also suffer from a divergence of interests. By this time Kerényi, having moved from Hungary to Switzerland, had begun his collaborations with Jung and immersed himself in the study of comparative religion. Mann's attention, meanwhile, had turned to the German problem, concerning which he declared that

> Goethe, like all our great ones . . . was, as a formative force, a dire fatality.

The "humanist" is a reader, Kerényi notes in a final provision, and he quotes from the Bibliothèque Nationale scene in *The Notebooks of Malte Laurids Brigge*:

> How good it is to be among reading men. . . . If you jostle a neighbor . . . he nods. His face turns toward you and does not see you. . . . I am seated and in possession of a poet. . . .

Kerényi writes to Mann: "I am in possession of a novelist, an epic fabulist."

———

Mann created no school. And, unlike Hesse, he is of no marked interest to the youth of today, perhaps because he was not an innovator, and because he held so firmly to dying values and middle ground. In spite of this, his "epic fables" are still studied in courses in "the contemporary novel" and are known to a substantial, if not exactly vanguard, readership. But some of his qualities, above all his powers of observation and his narrative technique, have seldom been surpassed. In the great story about Venice, for instance, he enumerates many characteristics of the people and the city which, at least to this reviewer's knowledge, are mentioned by no other writer. It would seem that Thomas Mann will continue to be read when much that is currently fashionable will have passed into oblivion.

THE *DOCTOR FAUSTUS* CASE

The career of Thomas Mann's modern Faust[1] is intended to illustrate the political, artistic, and religious dilemmas of the author's time. Yet paradoxically, the story of a former divinity student who bargains his soul and body to become a "musician of genius" is set in the wrong historical era. And the book's major flaw as fiction—counting as minor blemishes the discursiveness, and the imbalance between theory in the first half, story development and human variety in the second—may be attributed to conflicts between Mann's symbolic and realistic intentions.

Pacts with devils in human form, complete with "cold winds" and changing guises, are more appropriate to the sixteenth century than to the twentieth. Not that similar bargains with "the forces of evil" are uncommon today, being in fact the rule rather than the exception, but the agencies with which the contemporary kind are negotiated have been non-personal. And, apart from the Mephistophelian contract, the primacy in the novel of the theme of "sin," the importance of theology, and the space given to the subject of witchcraft belong more to the age of Martin Luther than to that of a "hero" dying in 1940.

———

Moreover, at the core of the book is the "German question," Mann's belief that the seeds of National Socialism existed long before Hitler, and the recommendation to reject "the myth of a 'good' and a 'bad' Germany, the bad [being] at the same time also the good." This postulate might have been presented to advantage in a more remote period; in any event, the portrait of

---

1. *Doctor Faustus: The Life of the German Composer Adrian Leverkühn as Told by a Friend*, by Thomas Mann, translated by H. T. Lowe-Porter (New York, 1948).

a moderately "conscientious" German inside the Third Reich in 1943–1945 is totally unconvincing, though the same character, Serenus Zeitblom, narrator and spokesman for the author, is credible at other times.

Mann, in California, writing in Zeitblom's name, is simply unable to arouse any sympathy for his fictional counterpart in the Germany of the latter part of the war. In a novelist so skilled at creating atmosphere and background, the failure to establish the sketchiest sense of what life must have been like in the collapsing Germany of 1945 is astonishing; Zeitblom's complaints about the aerial destruction of German cities, his fears of retaliations from the Russians, and his "consternation" at the Allied landing in Sicily are all unreal. Neither does he mention any privations, nor the presence of soldiers and movements of war matériel, nor even the effects of casualties on the families and friends. Furthermore, the voice behind his reflections on the German soul is transparently that of Thomas Mann, who provides Zeitblom with what are too obviously hindsights about the conclusion of the war. Finally, what could be more farfetched than a middle-European provincial's reference to occupied Paris as a "Luna Park" for New Order Germans?

Though Mann superbly evokes the main periods of the book— the decade in Munich before the 1914 war and, to a lesser extent, the 1920s, both of which he knew well—the 1930s are largely ignored. The reason for this is that the subject of Zeitblom's biography, the composer Adrian Leverkühn, could not have functioned in Hitler's Germany, and is therefore rendered non compos mentis during the entire decade. And since the tragic destinies of the Vaterland and of Leverkühn are bound together, neither could Mann's composer have joined all those German-refugee film-studio musicians in Hollywood. Because Leverkühn and Germany succumb concurrently to their respective insanities, and because the time gap between Leverkühn's mental collapse (ca. 1930) and the inception of Zeitblom's biography (1943) is not adequately covered, the plight of the artist confronted by Nazism does not arise, and the novel is the poorer for having excluded it.

Then, too, music, the representative German art, as well as a symbolic and actual subject of the novel, might have been treated more advantageously in the fifteenth or sixteenth centuries. For Leverkühn, music originates in theology:

> With Beethoven . . . music is a manifestation of the highest energy . . . almost the definition of God.

And in those earlier centuries not only did music derive inspiration from theology, but also its expressiveness was integral to its structure, which was itself theological. Jacobus Obrecht's *Sub tuum praesidium* Mass, for instance, exploits various doctrinal correspondences—in its twelve imitations of the *cantus firmus*, and between the seven voices of the *Agnus Dei* and the seven Marian chants, to mention only two details from the quadrivial (arithmetical, geometrical, musical, astronomical) aspect of the composition's inexhaustibly meaningful constructions. Mann, who was attracted to intellectual[2] contrivances of the sort, would have found more challenge in this number mysticism than in Schoenberg's comparatively simple "method of composing with twelve tones," a method governing only pitch, while Obrecht's Mass also includes the geometrization of tempo and rhythm. An objection to this translation to an earlier era would probably be that, following Schopenhauer's definition of music as a nonconceptual art, one of Mann's aims was to show that its mysterious power can be dangerous, as with Wagner; but Plato understood the potential subversiveness of music as well as did the nineteenth-century philosopher. Still another of Mann's intentions was to pillory a society's decadence in its music, but was this not also a purpose of the Council of Trent?

A further reason why an earlier century would have been preferable as a setting of Mann's Faust story is that the belief that

2. In a literal, noetic sense, for not all of the levels of Obrecht's symbols are aurally or visually perceptible.

disease may be a path to illumination has less validity in the scientific age—we prefer drugs—than in that of saints and stigmata; and though syphilis was one of the typological diseases of the Romantics—Nietzsche and Hugo Wolf were among Mann's models—a famous composer's death from it in 1940 seems somewhat anachronistic. Yet another argument for placing the narrative in an earlier century is Mann's predilection for archaic language, which then, at least, would have been appropriate. Both Leverkühn and the Devil speak a twisted scriptural tongue which is not only a tiresome affectation but also a considerable impediment to intelligibility—and which, readers be warned, makes another appearance in that cornucopia of incest, *The Holy Sinner*.

———

Mann's twentieth-century framework also leads to impossible complications when his fictional composer mingles with actual people living at the time. The idea is intriguing, and Mann's choice of which ones to include displays a real familiarity with the musical life of the age; Otto Klemperer, for example, would have been the perfect conductor for the premiere of Leverkühn's oratorio, *Apocalypsis cum figuris*, Maia de Strozzi-Pecič the ideal singer for his lieder, and Paul Sacher quite obviously the outstanding musician with whom to deal in Switzerland. To a fanciful reader, the matching of these people with Leverkühn's music might suggest something of its qualities.

But when Leverkühn attends the performance of *Salomé* in Graz in 1906, Mann does not mention that Mahler, Schoenberg, and Berg were there—naturally, for how could there be a great German composer who was *not* Mahler, *not* Schoenberg, and *not* Berg, or *not* Webern, *not* Pfitzner, and *not* Strauss? Leverkühn would either have to be a composite of all of these men, or he would have had to discover new musical territory unexplored by any of them. True, he does introduce experimental effects, including "howling glissandos," but his pieces depend on borrowed features. Thus the instrumentation of two songs for voice and string quartet, as well as of another chamber work, recalls Schoenberg's Opus 10 and Opus 29, and the "speaking choruses" suggest other Schoenberg pieces, though Mann had not actually heard them. The instrumentation and narrator-device in Leverkühn's puppet play are borrowed from *Histoire du Soldat*, while some of the *Apocalypsis* threatens to sound like Theodor W. Adorno's[3] idea of Stravinsky:

the parody of the different musical styles . . . Tchaikovsky, music-hall, the syncopations and rhythmic somersaults of jazz . . .

But the impingement of the actual on the imaginary must have become unmanageable, and therefore Leverkühn's public appearances had to be rare—surely a secondary reason why Mann crippled him with migraines as well as tertiary syphilis.

———

Besides the question of its misplacement in historical time, other features of Mann's vast novel demand criticism beyond the scope of this article. For example, something should be said of the many characters who enter the story at a late date, and who, though absorbing in themselves, are irrelevant to the development of the central theme. Frau von Tolna, Leverkühn's Madame von Meck, is one such, and so is the impresario Saul Fitelberg, *"Représentant de nombreux artistes prominents,"* whose analysis of career-making in Paris is diverting, but of whom Leverkühn and the plot have no need. Marie Godeau, on the other hand, does advance the story, precipitating a break between Leverkühn and one of his two principal attachments (both far closer to him than any woman); but Marie disappears as soon as this plot function has been accomplished, Mann apparently forgetting all about her, even though at one time Leverkühn had intended to marry the lady.

3. See the eminent Marxist critic's *Philosophy of Modern Music*, translated by Anne G. Mitchell and Wesley V. Blomster (New York, 1973). A prejudiced discussion of the book is included in this reviewer's *Prejudices in Disguise* (New York, 1974).

Mann's propensity for devoting separate chapters to the stories of each character may be responsible for the structural effect of a piling up of building blocks. Certainly this is true of his treatment of Leverkühn's biography, which is divided into the family background chapter, the discovery of musical talent chapter, the understanding teacher chapter, the Italian sojourn chapter, and so forth. And it is no less true of the discourses—on osmosis; on the Devil's casuistic argument that "in these irreligious times, in whom will you recognize theological existence if not in me?"; on the theory that the likeness of a certain two children to their father is greater than that to their mother "because her psychological participation when she conceived them was so slight"; on Kierkegaard's notion that genius is ipso facto sinful, and on Dostoevsky's that "the artist is the brother of the criminal and the madman"; and, above all, on Aristotle's "The acts of the person acting are performed on the one previously disposed to suffer them," this being part of the rationale for Leverkühn's deliberately contracting syphilis as "a means provided by the Devil to induce creativity."

As for the book's digressions, Mann deflects criticism by having Zeitblom anticipate their occurrence, not only mentioning his tendency to ramble but often reminding himself that he is writing a biography and not a novel. (But surely novels and biographies—*Marius the Epicurean*, for one—can be the same thing!) And, finally, for a digression by this reviewer, as far as critical perspectives are concerned, it might be interesting to examine Leverkühn, the remote and abstract, and Zeitblom, the humanistic, as extensions of their prototypes Naphta and Settembrini.

———

The Story of a Novel[4] divulges nothing of the actual writing of *Doctor Faustus* but simply collects Mann's comments on the people, the books, the journeys, the speechmaking, the illnesses that otherwise occupied his time while he was working on it.

4. *The Story of a Novel: The Genesis of Doctor Faustus*, by Thomas Mann, translated by Richard and Clara Winston (New York, 1961).

He refers to one excursus into public activity as "a visit to the world of humanity," as if the world of those who only stayed at home and wrote were not human. But in fact Mann did seem to consider artists, himself included, as somehow removed from "the world," which in his case the evidence in *The Story of a Novel* refutes. Yet the book is of greater interest to readers of the novel than the twelve-year delay in publishing the English edition would indicate. It reveals some of Mann's sources in literature, life, and even death—for the suicides of the fictional Clarissa and Inez were based on those of Mann's sisters, although he identifies only one of them.

Still another family suicide, that of Heinrich Mann's wife, occasions the first mention—nearly halfway through the book—of the older brother. This is all the more remarkable in that the two Manns were now Santa Monica neighbors. Thomas's account of the tragedy is distinctly chilly:

> A telephone call from my brother informed us of the death of her who had shared his life for so many years. The unfortunate woman had made repeated attempts to escape from life by an overdose of sleeping pills. This time she had succeeded. We buried her on December 20. . . . [Heinrich] spent the rest of the day with us and it goes without saying that, after the loss he had suffered, our ties became even closer.

But if the brothers had spent very many days together, and if ties had really been close, would Thomas have spoken in this way? A few lines later, describing a reading by Heinrich from *his* novel, Thomas remarks, somewhat contemptuously it may seem, that it came from a "tireless pen." But then, he is unable to convey, and no doubt even to see, anything significant about his brother.

The Story acknowledges the large collaborative role of Mann's "Privy Councillor," Theodor W. Adorno, but in musical matters only, although his influence on Mann's thinking, and even on his vocabulary ("niveau"), in social and political ones is apparent throughout the novel. Adorno's personality, however, remains as nearly impenetrable as his style, which Mann extravagantly

euphemizes as "pithy." At the opposite extreme, Arnold Schoenberg is vividly delineated in even the smallest scrap of conversation. When Mann asked the composer whether it is possible for
a capella choruses to sing in "untempered tuning," Schoenberg
answered affirmatively but did not add that most choruses achieve
this simple feat quite regularly!

An innate sense of form enables Mann to novelize his public
and social life, even to constructing a climax around his lung
surgery in Chicago in the spring of 1946. And as if to prove his
thesis about illness, in this episode his powers of observation—on
doctors and nurses, the effects of medication, himself as a patient
—are exceptionally acute:

> Overfastidiousness of the senses is characteristic of . . . [a
> certain] tender state of convalescence; sickness finds itself
> much too fine for many things that are quite acceptable to
> coarser conditions.

Told that when coming out of the anesthesia he complained of
having suffered during the operation, and then realizing that this
must have been impossible, he wonders if

> there still exist some vital depths in which, with all the senses
> shut off, one nevertheless suffers? . . . No one knows how
> dead [the organism] is before the actual dissolution; that fact
> might serve . . . as an argument against cremation. To put it
> in English once more, "It may hurt."

———

What apparently did suffer, and throughout a lifetime, was
Mann's ego; or at any rate this part of the psychic apparatus
seems often to have been in dire need of bolstering. And although
he was quick to detect malicious motives behind unfavorable
criticisms of himself, terming them "plainly impelled by private
rancours," he accepts at face value the favorable ones that
naturally follow his numerous public recitations of portions of
the novel:

The reading made an extraordinary impression; Adorno came up to me and said, "I could listen all night." . . . I expounded the plan of the novel to Neumann, who was stunned to amazement. . . . Read aloud from *Doctor Faustus*, the first three chapters. Was deeply moved . . . [My] reading of the lecture chapter. Intimacy with music gloriously confirmed. . . . "That is fascinating. . . . This may well be your greatest book."

No less concerned with posterity's view of him, he notes on the subject of people with striking personalities: "I think I am not one. I personally will be as little remembered as Proust" (as if Proust's personal idiosyncrasies had not generated some of the interest in his work). Finally, lest the Saint Peter at the portals of literary immortality fail to perceive the supplicant's minor virtues, he points out one instance:

I think I may well call myself a good colleague who does not look grudgingly at the good and the great things that are being done alongside him.

Turning to *The Story of a Novel* after *Doctor Faustus* itself, the reader is struck by the naïveté of the man in comparison to the sophistication of his work. The erudition, the irony, the psychological understanding, the self-mockery all seem to evaporate when the writer leaves the world of his imagination. For example, after registering his surprise that musicians do not recognize the Prelude to Act Three of *Meistersinger* in his description of a piece modeled on it, Mann nevertheless fails to see that this throws into question the value of all verbal descriptions of music. And with breathtaking ingenuousness, after calling a young man "good-looking," he then deems it necessary to inform the reader that "good looks are a pleasure, whether in men or women." Finally, in view of the complexity of mind exhibited in the dialogue with the Devil, most dismaying of all is the narrowness, in *The Story of a Novel*, of Mann's criticism of Flaubert's *Saint Anthony*:

A long review of the insanity of the religious world—and then, at the end, the countenance of Christ? Dubious.

But is it not a commonplace even among scientific positivists, and at least since William James, that the insanities, crimes, and cruelties of the Church do not invalidate the teachings of Christ?

—

Since its publication six years ago, Gunilla Bergsten's thesis on *Doctor Faustus*[5] has established itself as an authoritative as well as pioneering work on the subject. Though in no need of review, Mrs. Bergsten's book deserves to be re-recommended for its documentation, which presents excerpts from the novel and, in parallel columns, the passages from which they were derived. The latter range from musicological literature to Nietzsche's correspondence and Frank Harris on *Love's Labour's Lost*. Mrs. Bergsten explores such subjects as "further diseased geniuses," pursues countless clues to existing musical works in those of Leverkühn, and unearths many new links, including the novelist's markings in his copy of Stravinsky's autobiography, from which Mann borrowed some features for his Leverkühn portrait.

The definitive study of *Doctor Faustus* is still to come, and it is not the one by Patrick Carnegy.[6] The title, *Faust as Musician*, is misleading, since the book is merely a brief general interpretation and commentary. Mr. Carnegy does not concentrate on the extensive musical aspects of a novel, which, after all, is to music what *The Magic Mountain* is to TB. Nor does he investigate in sufficient detail Mann's claim that the book's structure contains analogies to music—in the use of leitmotifs, for instance, and in the emulation of musical time. The very first sentence is confusing:

5. *Thomas Mann's Doctor Faustus: The Sources and Structure of the Novel*, by Gunilla Bergsten, translated by Krishna Winston (Chicago, 1969; German version, Stockholm, 1963).
6. *Faust as Musician: A Study of Thomas Mann's Novel "Doctor Faustus"* (New York, 1975).

THE DOCTOR FAUSTUS CASE — 279

. . . *Doctor Faustus* is the imaginary biography of the German composer, Adrian Leverkühn, as told by his friend, Serenus Zeitblom.

In fact, it is the actual biography, in 510 pages, of the imaginary German composer, et cetera. Confusing, too, is the chapter which should have been the book's highlight, "Schoenberg and Leverkühn." Here the author observes:

Mann certainly did not enjoy Schoenberg's music and would seem instinctively to have distrusted its revolutionary aspect.

In truth, Mann had not heard enough of Schoenberg's music to know whether or not he enjoyed it, and of the revolutionary pieces—those composed with the "twelve-tone method," at least —he had heard none at all.[7] Though Schoenberg and Mann were Los Angeles neighbors,[8] the novelist was far more intimate with Bruno Walter, whose opposition to Schoenberg's music doubtless affected Mann. In short, Mann was not interested in the music of Schoenberg but only in his "twelve-tone method," and this through the proselytizing and intermediation of Adorno.[9]

7. This was because of the lack of opportunity, performances being practically nonexistent then, and recordings unavailable except for poor-quality private ones (and these only through Schoenberg himself or a few close associates who would have been unlikely to lend them to Mann). It is difficult today to realize how little known this music was in the early 1940s.
8. Schoenberg composed a "perpetual" four-voice canon cancrizans for Mann's seventieth birthday, June 6, 1945, partly, it would seem, to provide him with an example in a tonal idiom of one of the basic contrapuntal devices of the "twelve-tone method." Neither Mann himself, however, nor Carnegy, nor any Mann scholar mentions the existence of the piece. (It was recorded by this reviewer in 1954.)
9. Mann read Adorno's book (*op. cit.*) in draft form, but this could not have differed greatly from the published text, to judge from the more than thirty lines that the novelist quotes almost verbatim, and the more than one hundred others that he closely paraphrases. On Mann's instructions, the American edition of *Doctor Faustus* omitted one of the crucial passages that he had adapted from Adorno, thereby increasing the obscurity of the musical argument. This edition is in need of revision, incidentally, if only to eliminate such locutions as "seldom . . . more faultlessly played" (p. 199), "this twice-repeated unique event" (p. 417), et cetera.

Mr. Carnegy observes that

> Leverkühn's musical system and the use he makes of it differ
> considerably from those [*sic*] of Schoenberg . . . one reason for
> this being that Mann deployed his *ad hoc* version to air
> reservations about twentieth-century music. . . .

The latter part of this statement is true: Mann does give the
"system" a significance totally different from Schoenberg's. But
that has no bearing on the "system" itself. In essence the
Leverkühn-Mann "system" *is* Schoenberg's, and Mann's account
of it, as far as it goes, is correct:

> [It consists] of the twelve semi-tones, series of notes from
> which a piece . . . must strictly derive. Every note of the whole
> composition, both melody and harmony, would have to show
> its relation to this fixed fundamental series. Not one might
> recur until the other notes have sounded. . . . In addition to
> . . . a fundamental series . . . every one of its intervals is re-
> placed by its inversion. . . . One could begin the figure with
> its last note and finish it on its first, and then invert this figure
> as well. So then you have four modes, each of which can be
> transposed to all the twelve notes of the chromatic scale, so
> that forty-eight different versions of the basic series may be
> used in a composition. . . .

Even today, almost thirty years after *Doctor Faustus*, this shows
more of a grasp of Schoenberg's ideas than many professional
musicians have attained. Where Mann misrepresents Schoenberg
is in the statement, deduced from Adorno, that "There was no
longer any free note," which suggests a limitation that is not
real, the individual notes, even after satisfying the condition that
they follow their established position in the row, actually being
freer than they are in tonal harmony and counterpoint. Moreover,
Mann did not understand the true extent to which the Schoenberg method involves—as Zeitblom apprehends it—"composing
before composition." In fact this phrase is Adorno's, and it

constitutes his chief criticism of Webern, not of Schoenberg, to whom, in Adorno's view, it applies scarcely at all.

———

Not Schoenberg, then, but his disciple, Adorno, explained the workings of the "twelve-tone method" to Mann. And Adorno's exegesis was heretical: it contained built-in criticisms of the method's consequences that provided the basis for Mann's false analogy between the musical principle and totalitarian ideologies. Thus *Doctor Faustus* animadverted on Schoenberg and may continue to do so as long as the novel is read, which explains Schoenberg's shocked attack on Mann when it appeared. Nothing, however, will ever explain or excuse Mann's failure to acknowledge from the first that the method he had appropriated was Schoenberg's, a plagiarism which the broadest interpretation of literary license is unable to justify, and which remains one of the strangest incidents in modern literary history. No less mystifying is Mann's subsequent declaration that

> there is no point of contact, not a shade of similarity, between the origin, the tradition, the character, and the fate of my musician . . . and the existence of Arnold Schoenberg.

But is the "twelve-tone method" not a "point of contact" between Leverkühn and Schoenberg? And is Chapter 37's famous description of Leverkühn's rhythmic style not transparently based on that of Schoenberg? And did not both men come from the same Germanic tradition, similarly choose religious subjects for their largest works, compose music of initially almost unperformable difficulty, and suffer alike from neglect?

In later editions the novel contained a note that begrudgingly identifies Leverkühn's method as Schoenberg's, a note that bears witness to a highhandedness scarcely conceivable in someone of the stature of Thomas Mann. But fortunately this stain on his reputation does not detract from the great achievement of the book, whose données may be overambitious, but whose perspectives are both larger and deeper than those of his other books. But to compare *Doctor Faustus* and the realistic novels of, for example, Solzhenitsyn, is to recognize how much more limited in scope is the newer genre. In the sense of embracing the spectrum of humanistic, religious, and artistic themes, *Doctor Faustus* may be the last of its kind.

TV AND THE GREAT WORLD

IN THE MOUSE TRAP

I

"a . . . mouse [came] over with the . . . Conqueror."
—Alice in Wonderland

"Visitors from the real world," the Disney World receptionists say, and "real world" is a term of reference in Christopher Finch's[1] seven-pound book. But since Walt Disney World is a part of Florida, reality is hardly the issue. The Disney complex is simply another, albeit the ne plus ultra, Sunshine State resort. Peter Blake, who contributes a chapter on Disneyland and WDW, rates the hotel and motel architecture of the latter "considerably above Miami Beach standards." (*That* is a recommendation?) No doubt, too, WDW is not only technologically newer but also physically and morally cleaner than other amusement parks. Yet its outward aspect is no more incongruous in the Florida setting than are the derelict structures of World's Fairs along the traffic-jammed expressway to the New York airports.

What is more, the interior of WDW is primarily a shopping center whose "magicians" in the Magic Kingdom include such familiar entertainers as Gulf Oil, Goodyear, Eastern Airlines. "One purpose of WDW is to make money," Blake writes, as if he were revealing a well-kept secret. As for Fantasyland and Tomorrowland, these hold few surprises for a nation accustomed to stylistic agglomerations of the spurious old and the sterile modern, and to stultifying model communities of the past and future. In short, the borders of the real world, as distinguished from those on maps of the Disney enclave, may well have been crossed by society as a whole, and some time ago. And vis-à-vis

1. *The Art of Walt Disney* (New York, 1974).

this general schizophrenia, WDW is remarkable mainly as an attempt to establish an isolation ward.

The truth of Marx's argument that the economic life of capitalism is responsible for the secularization of society could hardly be more blatantly evident than it is in parts of Florida. Not that this state has a corner on the theory that the greatest public good derives from the greatest private selfishness, but the attempt to prove it is certainly more concentrated and apparent here. Wherever market value is both the determinant and the criterion, indifference to aesthetic quality—to say nothing of the disappearance of spiritual content and the alienation of the individual—is inevitable.

And what about the spiritual and cultural life in this materialist Eden? Surely the utter vacuity of both is without precedent in human experience. Regardless of the claims of the going religions on Man's Immortal Soul, it is the body that counts, and dead or alive. Yet by whatever name, death is unmentionable, which could hardly be the case in a gnostic civilization, and which is all the more hypocritical in this one, since mortality has created some of its liveliest industries.

Ante-bellum Greek-revivalist funeral homes (making a point about "gone with the wind"?) are everywhere, their pillared porches flooded with realistically cyanotic light. And, not surprisingly, these and other death-related businesses—of which the latest is the Audio-Visual Memorial, a substitute resurrection via sound film ("This *Was* Your Life"?)—are most cruelly conspicuous in the communities of the elderly. (The failure to find Ponce de Leon's fountain has resulted in a sociological problem of the 1980s, the shortage of gerontologists and the superfluity of pediatricians; in Florida, futurology, the science of predicting that what is will become more so, can already indulge in a backward look.) All of which is remote indeed from the Crucifixions stenciled on bus-stop benches—and in one case inscribed "Love is a many-splintered thing."

The state of culture on the peninsula can be gauged by the deterioration of language. Words, though often unrecognizable in the new orthography, are being adulterated to the extent that soon nothing will mean what it did only a generation ago. Syntax, too, has begun to disappear as the parts of speech become interchangeable. (Disney used "plus" as a verb, "to plus or not to plus.") And as a minor corruption, Floridian is now compulsively euphemistic and alliterative. Thus a garage is a "Collision Clinic," a furniture store a "Gallery" selling not tables and chairs but "Concepts" (though without explaining how one *sits* on a concept).

Some of this roadside epigraphy, moreover, is genuinely puzzling. What is meant by "The Frame Up," for instance? Fake paintings? And "Asterisk Incorporated"? Porn? Are "Mini-Adult Books" simplified porn? Some of the difficulty may be blamed on the proofreading ("Mery Xmas"), but who could be certain in the case of "Enter, Rest, Pay" on the door of a church? At family- and Boy-Scout-minded WDW—no youthquake types, no Bikini culture—hypocoristic language is inescapable, every name from "Amazon Annie" to "Zambesi Zelda," the principal jungle cruisers, being either cutely alliterative or wholesomely euphemistic. Thus a bartender, rare species that he is in these precincts, is a "Beverage Host."

The title of Christopher Finch's book is misleading. A more exact one would be *The Art of Hurter, Iwerks, and Others, and the Business Acumen of Walt Disney*. But the text is a gloss rather than a critical study, a mere puff written in publicity-release prose. Not that ideas are expected in the literature accompanying picture books of this sort, but neither is such fatuity as Finch's description of WDW—"The Versailles of the twentieth century but a Versailles designed for the pleasures of the people"—or Peter Blake's peroration on the Parks: "What a wonderfully ironic notion it is that in this turbulent century, urban man might, just possibly, be saved by a mouse."

Finch scarcely looks beyond the claims of the advertisements for any meaning in Disney's world, or even for the true nature of the Disney phenomenon in the century's cultural history. No hypothesis is proposed to explain the largest manifestation of anthropomorphism on record—an infantile one that uses the other mammals not didactically, to warn of moral, social, and political hazards, but simply as nursery toys. Finch also evades a discussion of the Disney mixtures of sentimentality and sadism, suppressed sexuality (apart from that of a censorship requiring udderless cows) and rampant, though apparently unconscious, Freudian imagery. As is well known, some adults seek to re-enter the child's world because their sexual desires are not then apparent to them as such. But ten million visitors annually, and by no means preponderantly children, entering not only a sexless but also a degenitalized (viz., the Polynesian statuary) speaking-animal kindergarten?

Finch also misses an opportunity to examine the animated cartoon gag, based as it is on maulings, murderous accidents, pratfall pranks. So conditioned is the laugh response to the sight of Donald Duck breaking his neck in a mishap, walking into an unseen abyss, being flattened by a boulder—though always sending up auras of colored stars—that one wonders if there is something innately hilarious about these painful disasters.

Disney's feature-length animations warrant even closer investigation of the subject, for they appear to have instilled permanent fears in many who were exposed at a too tender age. Thus the mother's death scene in *Bambi* left an emotional scar on some viewers, and no doubt Stromboli in *Pinocchio*, the yellow-eyed Satan in *The Night on Bald Mountain*, and other Disney villains—generally more successful than the Prince Charmings—would be identified as the anamnestic figures in the nightmares of later life. Finch is aware of this charge. The claim that *"Snow White* is excessively frightening," he says, "can be countered by pointing out that many episodes in the fairy tales of Hans Christian Andersen and the Brothers Grimm are far more terrifying." But can the Disney animations be compared to the books of Andersen and the Brothers Grimm? Bruno Bettelheim, in his defense of the fairy tale,[2] has argued that by giving each of the seven dwarfs a name and a personality, Disney

2. "Many young people [who] escape from reality into daydreams . . . were prematurely pressed to view reality in an adult way." (From *The Uses of Enchantment* [New York, 1976].)

seriously interferes with the unconscious understanding that they symbolize an immature, pre-individual form of existence which [the heroine] must transcend.

Yet the book's most glaring omission is that it does not analyze Disney's social philosophy as expressed in the films[3] and inside the gates of the Florida and California institutions, or show where his mid-American origins and modest early circumstances are basic to his conceptions. Of WDW's two utopias, one, EPCOT (Experimental Prototype Community of Tomorrow), represents the totally controlled technological future, the other the good old days in the shallow, complacent, and extraordinarily ugly towns of the Mid-America-the-Beautiful of Disney's childhood. The two are expressions of the "counter-identities" of an authoritarian personality that Finch, who boundlessly admires it, for some reason describes as "artistic":

Disney . . . would go to any length to ensure that a project was carried out exactly as he had conceived it. He would surround himself with talents of every kind, but at all times he was in complete control. The master plan was in Walt Disney's head. . . .

The real significance of the "New Art Form," Finch's first chapter, is that it reflects this personality in both the process and the finished product. Apart from the question of whether or not Disney's animated films are "art," they are undeniably totalitarian. No part of them has been left to chance, each of the 100,000 frames that are required for an animated feature film being drawn in every detail. The other elements are no less strictly controlled, from the synchronization of image and sound to the number of lines used in the construction of the cartoon figures. This may account for the sense of frustration that some people have felt in Disney's full-length animated movies (though

3. See *How to Read Donald Duck: Imperialist Ideology in the Disney Comic*, by Dorfman and Mattehart (Bagnolet, France, June 1975).

another factor is an inadequate spatial depth, something that even the use of the multiplane camera did not entirely dispel). Conversely, the same feeling could explain the relief that audiences have been known to experience in *Fantasia* as a result of a few moments of seeing a flesh-and-blood Stokowski or even Deems Taylor.

If the book's huge sales figures are attributable to its pictures, a few more examples of Disney's Studio Art at its best would have been preferable to the full-page color portraits of Dopey, the Blue Fairy, and the Big Bad Wolf. The color is not comparable to that of Disney's films, but fidelity of the kind required in photographing paintings would in any case be wasted on what is essentially an oversized souvenir album. Finch commends the Disney artists for the degree of realism they sometimes attain, but the book fails to place them in any historical perspective, or to suggest similarities and possible influences—apart from pointlessly dragging in Picasso—from the larger world of the graphic arts. The preliminary sketches for the *Pastoral* Symphony, for example, recall both Klimt and Moreau, while more than one forest landscape evokes Caspar David Friedrich.

The "New Art Form" chapter traces the technical development of animation, touching on the zoetrope; the kinetoscope; Edison's and others' experiments with motion pictures; the photographing of drawings to create the semblance of movement; and Earl Hurd's process of painting the animated figures on celluloid, thereby eliminating the necessity of drawing a complete picture for each frame when the background remained the same throughout a scene. By 1917 the adventures of such popular newspaper-cartoon characters as "Krazy Kat" and "Maggie and Jiggs" were available in animated-film form, a more consequential development than anyone foresaw, since this soon became a rut in which the subject matter of the animated cartoon has been stuck ever since.

What if Max Fleischer, rather than Disney, had dominated the animation field? Fleischer made an animated five-and-a-half-reel film, *Einstein's Theory of Relativity* (1923), years before Disney began work on the Oswald the Rabbit series (1927). Finch is too reticent about Fleischer's role, incidentally, for Disney seems to have borrowed back Fleischer's idea of combining live-action films with animation and his rotoscope method of filming actors to guide the animators. In 1927 Disney "completely abandoned his career as an animator to concentrate all his energies on the production side of the business." Yet Finch does not venture much of an appraisal of Disney's talents as a draftsman even during the brief period before the twenty-six-year-old artist's "retirement." He had had some training at the Kansas City Art Institute, as well as experience as a practicing commercial artist in the Missouri metropolis. While still a youth there, he met the most important person in his professional life, the Dutch artist and inventor Ub Iwerks. Disney later induced Iwerks to come to Hollywood, where he was principal draftsman, inventor-in-chief, and, in sum, house genius to the expanding Disney Studios. (It may be worth noting that in the Successful Man, business talent is dominant over artistic, a Mendelian law, no doubt; Iwerks left Disney for a time to establish a studio of his own, which failed utterly, even though his inventive powers were as strong as ever.)

Finch does not name the creator of *Oswald the Lucky Rabbit* (1928), but the metamorphosis from Rabbit to Mouse was so slight, graphically speaking, as to look like plagiarism. At the time, Iwerks was given sole credit as the designer of Mickey Mouse. Then, at a later date, the Mouse was described as resulting from a "collaborative effort" between Iwerks and Disney, the latter having contributed "the gift of personality." But to compare the facial expressions and even the gestures of the two animals (page 46 for Oswald, the cover for Mickey) is to be struck by the closeness of the resemblance, and in fact to suspect that the unlucky rabbit was a victim of artistic myxomatosis. Finch argues that "Disney's control over the situations in which the Mouse found himself allowed his personality to develop." But at what stage did attribution of authorship to Disney become necessary? Obviously he had a "thing" for the Mouse, even continuing to dub Mickey's voice for twenty years. Here Finch, for once, risks an uncharacteristic speculation: "Disney may even have viewed Mickey as his alter ego."

Disney's vision, entrepreneurial imagination, and intuition for making the right moves were evident in his every undertaking from the earliest years in Hollywood. To begin with, he understood the potential of his "artistic" property, nor was this simply blind conviction. No matter how hard-pressed, he resisted every offer to be bought out, and he survived partly because of consistently wise choices among distributors. Above all, he was quick to see the importance of each technical innovation, especially those of sound and color. And, almost alone among the studio moguls, he showed foresight in negotiation with television.

Like all great showmen, he knew his public ("Disney films are carefully designed for family audiences"), as well as the way in which to exploit the appetite that he had created for the new medium. Moreover, his timing was perfect. He sensed when both the industry and the public were ready for feature-length animated films, and, in later years, the advantageous moment in which to convert to live-action cinema. And, finally, he was lucky. *Seal Island* (1949), for example, was not one of his own projects, and at first the film failed to excite his interest. But, riding on the early tide of the ecological movement, it had an unexpected success, and Disney was rapidly alerted to the trend and quick to follow the film with *Beaver Valley*, *The Living Desert*, and other nature documentaries that are his most valuable legacy— just as the one worthwhile lesson of WDW is that men and animals can coexist to their mutual enrichment.

Disney was also a talented story editor, and, in the production of his films, more closely involved in this capacity than is generally realized. That he could both diagnose a script and prescribe for it is illustrated by his story conferences for *Snow White*— which bring Finch's readers closer to Disney the man than do the memoirs of his intimates. The minutes of these meetings display his absolute certainty about what he wanted and how to obtain it, as well as his hard-boiled, unsentimental language: "Snow White is stooped over, which gives you a swell position for the knife in the back . . ."

Though not musical, Disney had an ear for the box office ("Walt liked the way Julie Andrews whistled"), and, paradoxically, he played a more important role than any other producer in employing music and sound effects in films. The audio-visual puns in the *Silly Symphonies* may have degraded some kinds of music, but they also stripped some others of their pretensions. The Disney animators inadvertently became first-rate critics of second-rate music. Obviously a Beethoven symphony could not be satisfactorily pictorialized. But Ponchielli's *Hours* was a sitting target for the parody that the animators did in fact make of it. To this viewer, anyway, the ostrich and hippo ballerinas are the high point of all the animated cartoonists' inventions.

Disney also had a large part in increasing the awareness of the possibilities of stereophonic sound. *Fantasia*—1940, and far ahead of its time—was recorded on seven sound tracks and intended for thirty speakers, though this equipment was installed in only a few theaters, and hence the recorded sound, as conceived, was heard by only a few people. It might also be mentioned that whereas most soundtracks were recorded *before* the animators began their work, Disney insisted that the music could be made to fit the action in one very special case: Mickey Mouse.

II

Do not return. If you can bear it, stay dead with the dead.
—Rilke

With every automobile moving at the same speed, as if remotely controlled, driving to WDW during the energy crisis was more dreamlike than any experience in Fantasyland itself. But the landscape anticipates WDW—the Haunted Mansions, at least—in the thick draperies of Spanish moss, and in the weird gray forests of dead cypresses and live oak. "Mickey & Minnie Are Waiting for You," a billboard proclaimed, but the coastal-style neon language

ADULT MOVIE
Stop in if you are streaking by
No one under 18 admitted to ID

had phased out long before this.

At WDW's Polynesian Village Hotel, a sidewalk hostess cheerfully informed this reporter of a long delay before his reserved room would be ready and suggested waiting in one of two restaurants. In spite of People Movers, the Monorail, and a highly touted mass-transport system, every visit to WDW entails much queuing, waiting, and being told that this or that "attraction" is temporarily closed, not yet opened, or still on the drawing board. In what seemed to be the less disastrous of the two restaurants, the aforementioned reporter managed to question some of the waitresses: "Are you well treated here? Do you like the job? Are you well paid? What induced you to come?" Answers: "It is a thrilling place to be. I feel connected with a great thing. The money is pretty good. Everybody here is just great."

But the restaurant work seemed robot-like. And this proved to be one of the contradictions of WDW, that of people performing jobs that robots might be expected to handle very competently, and of robots accomplishing tasks that until recently were performed by people. Finch remarks the influence of Chaplin's *Modern Times* on the multiplication of the water carriers in Disney's *The Sorcerer's Apprentice* (1939), but the repetitive and monotonous labor of some people at WDW—in shutting the doors of every compartment of the Monorail at each station, for instance—might actually have been copied from the Chaplin film.

The WDW robots, or "audio-animatronic figures," are built, dressed, and made up to resemble human beings as closely as possible. The effect is like that of moving and speaking Madame Tussaud figures—or, worse, of galvanized fugitives from the Cosmetic Room at Forest Lawn. This reporter's first experience of the robots was in Tomorrowland's "Flight to the Moon," where, in a model of the NASA control room in Houston, several "scientists" were seated at computer consoles and other hardware, backs to the viewer. A guide, who might better have been a robot or recorded voice, spoke briefly, after which the figures began to move, standing and walking, and eventually turning around. Only then was it apparent that they *were* robots, and the realization was a shock. One of them, the closest to the glass panel separating the viewer from the control room, with furrowed brow and balding but hair-pieced head, a thoroughly lifelike appearance.

But why should a robot be made to resemble a human being? Surely a man-machine could be equipped with more, as well as more efficient, appendages than Homo sapiens. And what purpose is served by clothing imitation men—in surgeons' whites, in this case—like real ones? In fact, wouldn't it be wiser to make our imitation men as *un*like our real ones as possible, and especially at WDW, where confusion could so easily occur?

For the same reason, and some others, the "Hall of Presidents" is even more sinister. Finch reserves his highest accolade for it: "The most sophisticated attraction of all from a technological point of view." ("Sophisticated," used exclusively in the sense of "complex" and intended as a compliment—"a sophisticated drainage disposal," "a sophisticated soundtrack," "some highly sophisticated French-patented, double-ballasted automatic gates" —is the favorite adjective of both Finch and Blake.) As the Presidential roll is called and each of the nation's Chief Executives acknowledges his name, the thought occurs that one of WDW's minor educational values is in familiarizing school children with the succession of the many obscure holders of the country's highest office. When all are accounted for, Lincoln speaks, and his predecessors and successors nod agreement, an "uncanny effect" to Finch, an appalling one to this reporter— who by then, however, was more interested in the likeness of the present incumbent, and in discovering whether it was still intact or if the dismantling and "de-audio-animatronicizing" processes had already begun.[4]

Peter Blake claims that WDW is the "first urban complex . . . to be fully equipped . . . with a fast, efficient, and quiet mass-transit system." But if so, where *is* it? And where, for that matter, are the escalators and moving sidewalks from the department stores and airports of Yesterdayland? Blake counts not only the monorail in this system but also "two hundred watercraft," the

4. This was written in May 1974.

"electric cars and trains," and the "aerial transways." Yet all of these together are inadequate to transport even a well-below-average-sized crowd, since a seat on the Monorail *from* the Magic Kingdom, except at off hours, requires a wait of at least twenty minutes in cattle-style ramps and mazes. Anyone who can manage a pogo stick is advised to take it along.

Blake is still more ecstatic about WDW's sanitation features, especially the "tertiary sewage plant" and AVAC, the Swedish "pneumatic garbage system" which "inhales plastic trash bags through an underground network at sixty miles an hour." (AVAC is equipped with safety devices, but one cannot help imagining the accidental inhalation of a small child at that speed.) At the "tertiary sewage plant 97 percent of all suspended solids are removed. The effluent is chlorinated and fed into the swamp waters of the WDW nature conservatory. Some of the waste water is eventually channeled into the irrigation grid of the Living Farm." (From which it is "eventually" recycled into the "Orbit Burgers" and "Space Dogs" that are sold to the weary, after forty minutes in line, on Tomorrowland Terrace?)

Neither Finch nor Blake seems to be aware that the most repellent feature of the park for this visitor, noise pollution, is at danger level; loudspeakers blare indoors and out, medleys from the Disney films fill each "attraction" in 360-degree wraparound stereo, and even the lake is irrigated by underwater Muzak. And noise, not the quality but the decibels, provides the only terror of the Haunted Mansions, otherwise a kind of tunnel of love and something of a relaxation. Electronic reverberation and contortion vary the characteristics of the sounds from one primal scream to another, but the raw materials are the same old shrieks, detonations, ghostly organ music (all stops out, of course). The illusionist and spatial tricks here, and the antics of the animatronic hi-fi poltergeists, are probably ingenious, yet one's blood is chilled not by them but by the thought of the colossal waste of human, technological, and financial resources.

This should be said of WDW as a whole, except that its financial aspect is the most astonishing part of the story, uniting as it does old-time Robber Baronism and the methods of the

contemporary extortionist brotherhoods. In the first place, Disney
World is as independent of Florida as is the Vatican of Italy, the
"World" having its own government, with its own laws, police,
and even its own judges—in the sense that these are appointed by
a city council which is the elected body of a district owned by
WDW. But Florida's "Disney bill," an amazing piece of legisla-
tion, amounts to a charter for the secession of a principality, or,
rather—in view of WDW's political system and Neuschwanstein
Cinderella castle—of a kingdom.

The growth and financial structure of WDW are more "miraculous" than any of Disney's film fairy tales. An acre of the
surrounding land, said to have cost Disney about $167, has since
been valued at $500,000, and in one case sold for that. And
though WDW is a corporate enterprise, it only leases concessions
to "participant" companies and at such stringent terms for the
original franchise and the use of the brand names of the menag-
erie of characters from Disney films that no "participant" makes
money. Yet apparently all believe that the prestige is worth the
price.

The prestige of what? A self-erected monument to a man and
his movies, Disney World now exists to make money, and, despite
the publicity, to do little else. One feels sorry for the customers,
especially those from remote places (surprisingly few of whom
were Japanese; because of the superiority of their own mechanical toys?). Everyone whom this pollster questioned gave the
name of a Midwestern or Southern state as his residence, and
how this American heartland must have throbbed when, after
sunset, a calliope began to play, the lake to churn (thanks to a
"surf-making machine"), and a fire-breathing sea monster to
emerge and to threaten the "World"—until exploding into three
very red-white-and-blue flags.

Disney World challenges many fundamental values. In small
instances, it does so in a street full of plastic flowers or in a
shrub sculpture of an animated cartoon animal, and, in a larger
one, in the whole cretinous cult of Mickey Mouse, whose sacred
image is displayed by all true pilgrims on pins, balloons, articles
of clothing (and reverently, *not* on boobs or seats of pants).

Any demonstration of mass mindlessness is depressing. What makes this one all the sadder is that children are so greatly in need of good models, wise teachers, examples of beautiful and inspiring works of art. There is no more pernicious and powerful force against all three than WD and his WDW.

HAZARDS
OF THE FOURTH OF JULY

Thursday, July 1. Will the efficiency of a high-rated New York hospital be seriously affected by the general paralysis of the Bicentennial Independence Day! I enter Lenox Hill for "hernia repair" this afternoon with increasing qualms, not about a possibly unfavorable outcome of this question, but about the limits of newspaper assignments and whether this one is going too far. I am not an "action reporter," after all, and the surgery is postponable.

Seventy-five other patients are sworn in at the same hour, a process no doubt slowed by actuarial complexities resulting from the malpractice crisis. In fact the patient leaves "Admissions" with the feeling that his identification bracelet manacles him to a "no-fault" system in which a fatal mistake, such as the transfusion of incompatible blood, becomes a "therapeutic accident." One of the new non-liability contracts which must be signed states that "the charges incurred represent the fair and reasonable value of the services rendered." But, one might ask, how can this be known in advance?

Certainly my cramped room is not worth the "charges incurred," with its shower but no tub, towel rack but only paper towels: blotting the entire body is one of the more peculiar experiences of the assignment. Worse still, the centrally controlled air conditioning, set at 55°, is not modifiable by the thermostat, and the frigid drafts from a vent along one rim of the ceiling are reminiscent of those in window seats of some airplanes. Also, the bed seems to be extremely narrow, especially when the railings are up, though no one can manage these without an amount of trial and error, just as no staff member can immediately find the right cranks for raising and lowering the head and feet, each move invariably beginning in the wrong direction; the secret of the 'knee break" segment remains undiscovered—and that part of the bed uncomfortably elevated—throughout my stay.

I am requested to exchange my clothes for the open-back, knee-length, immodest hospital gown, and to "prepare for tests." But first comes a detailed inventory of personal effects, which includes the question of whether my teeth are part of me or detachable—rip-offs of dentures reportedly being on the increase. Then follows the taking of blood pressure, pulse, temperature, and of specimens for the laboratory. The electronic digital thermometer registers to two decimals until a "beep" signals that the correct degree has been determined. But whereas the machine is faster and more accurate than mercury in glass, it also produces more anxiety, the patient realizing that the longer the interval before the noise, the higher the fever.

Technology has not changed the method of ascertaining pulse, which is still done by human fingers on radial arteries. In my case the nurse looks alarmed and asks if my beat is normally only forty-eight. No, I say, and suggest hopefully that this evidently failing rate may be due to "vagus inhibition." Continuing to grasp at this straw, I mention the thermodynamics calculation by which the heart's lifetime energy expenditure is equivalent to that required to build the pyramid of Gizeh, and I explain that while sympathicotoniacs usually complete their pyramids, and vagotonics rarely reach the pinnacles of theirs, the "vagos" generally live longer. Ignoring my optimistic fumblings, she simply enters the pulse on the chart, but my metronome readings are recorded every hour thereafter.

Another consequence of rising malpractice insurance rates is that all patients must be accompanied on each intramural excursion, lest they trip, fall, be kidnapped, or otherwise disappear. My escort, an elderly volunteer, watches me like a bailiff during the journey to Radiology, where I join a queue of women wearing bathrobes and worried expressions (no doubt from the mammogram scare). But my own consternation must also show, since I still fear the deleterious effects of shoestore fluoroscopy of three decades ago. In Cardiology, afterward, the line and the wait are still longer, despite the three-woman team, one dabbing the jelly, another attaching the clamps and rubber bands, and a third running the ticker tape. From here I try to slip back to my room unescorted but am apprehended and made to join a convoy of wheelchairs.

The next step to prepare me for the operation is the shaving of "Hesselbach's triangle" and the perineal and inguinal areas. The indignity of this is exacerbated by the tonsorialist's too evident relish in the symbolic emasculation, and by his pun about peotomies and his ribald remarks concerning future itching and the impossibility of scratching in public. Even the soreness from the dry razor on the genitalia is a lesser affront than the manner in which he manipulates their centerpiece—like a barber pushing a nose to the side while scraping an upper lip. But however ridiculous the newborn look, the episode serves to loosen proprieties and to reduce the embarrassment, moments later, of being penetrated with a clyster by a teen-age girl—instead of by the more or less male nurses of my past experience. Referring to what feels like a substantial inundation, she orders me to "Hold it ten minutes."

———

July 2. At 6 a.m. I am awakened by a remarkably cheerful anesthetist shaking my shoulder and asking about my allergies, reactions to sodium pentothal, carbon dioxide, or ethyl chloride, as well as about details of previous operations (a childhood tonsillectomy, a fractured elbow seventeen years ago!). He says that I will receive "tranquilizing medication" in my room about an hour before the operation, which, however, has had to be postponed until midafternoon because of an emergency. Intravenous feeding is begun—after three unsuccessful attempts to find a vein in the left wrist—and, at about 3:30 p.m., I am given two gluteal injections. I try to resist the numbness and grogginess, the euphoria and the shimmering vision, the oblivescence and dissolving time sense, and the feeling of increasing isolation from friends who have come to see me "off." Nor am I "out" when the masked figure in Shinto green, rubber cap, gloves, and galoshes, comes for me with his stretcher. The drugs have not "taken," I protest, but perhaps inaudibly, for I hear my "*bons voyageurs*" whisper "He is fading"—words that hardly reassure.

The I.V. apparatus being part of our procession, an onlooker might deduce that my vehicle is propelled by the bottled fuel. Despite my semi-comatose condition, I am aware that the elevator is bumpy and not smoothly aligned on either floor. On the higher one I begin to whistle, not out of bravado, or "in the dark," but rather because of a desire to know if my "inner" and "outer" ears are hearing the same thing (they are), and thereby to confirm my consciousness. Since no one else notices this music, however, it may be that only the visual memory can be trusted as real and not imagined. Perhaps, too, the operating theater is not really as cold as it seems (for cryosurgery?), or the crossing of the threshold comparable, in the sense of temperature, to a ferrying over the Styx.

Wheeled to the center of the room and transferred to a table— no signs of previous carnage—I lie in lonely splendor before a large green lamp (my day in the limelight). Green cylinders of oxygen are visible, and other, human figures—sacerdotalists, to judge from the solemn, ritualistic-sacrificial way in which they approach me. All wear the same green uniforms and all are masked. As they close in on me, one of them outstretches and straps down my I.V. arm, another strips me, a third announces that "after this injection you will go to sleep." I do, and, mercifully, in a place without darkness or dreams.

———

"Time to wake up," strange female voices are saying (four and a half hours later), and I am aware of being again on the same conveyance, this time guided by four laughing Philippine nurses. (Or are they demonic pallbearers, and have I been reincarnated on a different plane?) Suddenly I find myself talking to one of my friends (in voluble but incoherent French, I am told later), and am aware of being hoisted to my bed ("upsy-dazy"), trembling from burning head to glacial feet. "Anti-embolism stockings," white like British naval officers' summer hosiery, are pulled over my shanks; but a note on the wrapper, *Seamless stockings are contraindicated in cases of gangrene, heart failure, extreme deformity of leg,* tickles my sense of "sick humor," and a giggle makes the fire in the left side of the abdomen burn more intensely, until doused by a hypodermic of morphine. When consciousness returns in the night—with some far-off detonations, premature fireworks, probably—I feel a wet-paint stickiness on my left hand. The I.V. needle has been dislodged, perhaps as long as an hour before, since the *sang* on my fingers is already *froid.* An intern tears off the tapes (and patches of hair), then carefully reinjects the feeder.

———

July 3. The pain is sharp this morning, the anesthetics having worn off, and I make my way to the bathroom at a step a minute, clinging to an Amazonian nurse. Here the I.V. comes loose again, but I realize it only when I see a pool of blood around my feet. This time the artificial feeding is abandoned and a light diet prescribed, yet as soon as I am again decubitus, and even before the blood is mopped up, a lab assistant has extracted his daily vial from the other arm. Now, too, the rantipoling head nurse threatens me with the catheter unless I "pass urine." But the receptacle's cold steel and bull-size neck are strong deterrents: I ask for a faucet to be turned on, close my eyes, and eventually *think* forth a satisfactory flow, the one instance during the week when mind triumphs over matter.

My physician, making his rounds, reports the discovery of a prehernial lipocele, larger than the rupture itself; he explains that this was the reason for the extraordinary length of the operation, more than double the surgeon's expectations. Biopsy shows that the tumor is benign, but this is only partly comforting since I remember hearing that lipomas are famous for returning in the same place.

———

July 4. The surgeon enters the room this morning like a three-star general on a tour of inspection, asks how I am, departs in less than ten seconds. Concern is expressed over my pre-operation pulse, nevertheless, and another cardiogram has been scheduled; owing to the holiday, however, several hours pass before someone is located to administer it. Finally, at 4 p.m. I am pushed along to Cardiology, where a truculent technician allows me to remain in my chair only because, or so I suspect, the arm and leg straps remind her, as they do me, of an execution.

By late afternoon, too, my temperature has mounted, a reaction, in all likelihood, to the Presidential (and other) platitudes pouring all day from the television. But a further cause may be the thought that a society in which medicine is practiced for the profit motive, and which permits its physicians to accept retainers from the rich to be assured of being given priority, has no right to mouth the equality formulas of the Philadelphia manifesto.

At midnight, a new doctor wakes me to say that "a cardiogram has been arranged for tomorrow." But I have had one only eight hours ago, I reply. Has no one read it? He has not, at any rate, and knows nothing about the matter, or why my bandage has not been changed in the more than fifty hours since surgery. On the premise that the higher temperature is being caused by a pulmonary infection, he sends for a "blow bottle," a plastic vessel consisting of two containers, one filled with water, the other empty. In order to force the patient to breathe deeply, he is made to blow through a hookah-like stem and to displace the water from the one bottle into the other. Since the transfer becomes progressively more strenuous, however, it seems that the exercise might easily cause a new hernia. Yet every two hours I am aroused from sleep to play Aeolus with this Sisyphean toy.

———

July 5. Today my surgeon's profile is even lower: no visit at all. My chief pains now are gastric, for which the cure is to drink ginger ale and to burp like a baby. Otherwise I feel almost back-to-normally bad and am able to shuffle through the corridors along with the other nonagenarians. Doing so in my blue hospital skirt, white support socks, and green slippers, and thus in some measure resembling an emperor of China, I am undoubtedly regarded as undergoing "psychiatric evaluation."

———

July 6. At 7 a.m. a new nurse arrives with an electrocardiograph. "Have you ever had an EKG in this hospital?" she asks, before adding to the already considerable collection. A staff doctor then describes the mattress-suturing technique that was used on me, removes the bandage with one pull, and exclaims: "A perfect job of mending." He has me look at the incision, whose red, yellow, and purple cross-quilting makes me queasy, and he says that after he returns with the surgeon, I can be discharged. But neither of them appears—this, I hope, for the benefit of cases more serious than mine.

Nor is there any shortage of these, of course, either here or elsewhere. (At home, where charity is said to begin, I sometimes watch the dog-walkers, the well-dressed women, and the retired-executive types as they pass the derelicts asleep on the bench below and across the street from my window. The misery and dire need of these people is obvious, yet few ever so much as glance in the offending direction. And myself? Do I go down and offer help? I do not, being exactly *comme les autres*.)

———

July 7. At 8 a.m. the same staff doctor peeks at my scar and again promises to "see me later." At $400 a day, however, deciding that it is already too late, I dress, pack my bag, walk to the elevator, descend and pay the bill, taxi home.

———

July 8. The hospital telephones. Someone has discovered that the patient in Room 8606 is AWOL.

———

August 21. At Pompano Beach, where I come to complete my recuperation, gilded youth is greatly outnumbered by Senior Citizens and Golden Agers, and in the barbershop nearly all of the customers are bald. On the beach itself workmen are performing "hair transplants" with palm trees, placing them in front of a new condominium, then bending them for that natural blown look. And on the beach, the last Two of the Seven Ages of Man are far more conspicuous than the first Five, thus raising the thought that perhaps beach-wear should be restricted to the under-thirties—which I say risking the wrath of age-lib. Ages Four and Five definitely would benefit from the revival of whalebone corsets—which I should not say, having signed a petition to "Save the Whale." The latest fashion among Age Three females is to stretch the natal cleft and exaggerate the dichotomy of the derrière.

And the Second Age? "Jesus loves them, this I know." Still, one imp, with a toy mine detector, auscultates the sand near me for buried treasure, while another refuels a gull in flight, flinging crumbs into the air and attracting a flapping, squawking, excreting flock. Prejudiced by Alfred Hitchcock, I am relieved when they fly away on a mission elsewhere. A buzzard, looking like the eagle on a Reichsmark, hovers *hors concours*, even higher than the airplane advertisements for *Deep Throat*.

The sight of a jogger, Fifth Age, obese and puffing, turns one's thoughts to the oxygen respirator in the Beach Patrol Tower. But the Tarzan in Kelly-green sweatsuit who normally roosts there is out sprinting—past lollygogging lovers, recumbent bodies glistening with embrocations guaranteed to patinate with the perfect tan ("under the influence of sunlight, Vitamin D synthesizes in the skin"), and even past the gasping jogger.

ELEGY FOR
MARY HARTMAN,
MARY HARTMAN

Formal sociological studies of the once phenomenal popularity of *Mary Hartman, Mary Hartman*[1] will undoubtedly appear in the professional journals, but until then perhaps an amateur fieldworker may hazard a few observations. The first of these, from admittedly limited samplings, is that the program in its initial months provoked immediate partisanship. While some viewers found it to be no more than a puerile comedy in bad taste and recoiled from its assaults on their cherished ideals and modes of behavior, devotees would rush home of an evening in time for the latest encounter between the staff psychiatrist of Fernwood Receiving Hospital's mental ward and its celebrated inmate, "The Number-One Typical American Consumer Housewife."

Like other programs, this one appealed or repelled in accordance with social, generational, regional, and other biases, none of which, however, accounted for the vehemence of the responses. Madeleine Edmondson's and David Rounds's *From Mary Noble to Mary Hartman*[2] contains several pages on the almost violent controversy that the program generated (*Time*: "Silly, stupid, silly, stupid"; *The New York Times*: ". . . fascinating departure . . ."). Marriage counselors, social anthropologists, educators and theologians, all of similar backgrounds, strongly disagreed about its entertainment as well as documentary value, and even the common assumption that "liberals" liked and "conservatives" disliked the program proved unreliable. Guessing which friends

1. For an account of the background, see *The Mary Hartman Story*, by Daniel Lockwood (New York, 1976).
2. New York, 1976.

and public figures were *Mary* watchers was fast becoming a new parlor game.

What was *Mary Hartman, Mary Hartman* originally? In exploiting the humor of ludicrous circumstances, it resembled sitcom, but, unlike those situations contrived to produce a succession of jokes—in, for example, *The Jeffersons*—many episodes of *Mary* were, by intention, not funny at all. *Mary* was also partly soap opera, and no less addictive, though fans preferred to think of *their* program as realistic in contrast to the soporific fantasizing of the daytime serials. Nevertheless, *Mary* followed the soap-opera form of several rotating and suspended plot lines, and used the same subject matter of marital and family problems. But again, the differences, especially in novel ways of treatment, were greater than the similarities.

For one thing, soap opera has no comedy element, certainly none of the black humor that was *Mary Hartman*'s essence. And, for another, while "the suds" adhere to dramatic conventions, *Mary* was haphazard, without conspicuous over-all plan or consistent development—a television theater of the absurd. Moreover, the people in the afternoon dramas—doctors, lawyers, executives, and their women—are played by mannequins and glamorous actors—the embodied dreams of what the viewers wish they could be and of whom they would like to marry. The people in *Mary*, on the other hand, belonged to the working class and were ordinary-looking, without benefit of orthodontia or *haute couture;* Charlie Haggers, Grandpa Larkin, Chester Markham— the endearing lunatic who planned to blow up Ohio—and even Mary herself would never be offered jobs on *Search for Tomorrow.* Then, too, while most of the social life in soap opera takes place in well-appointed living rooms, *Mary*'s was in the kitchen. Spectators with the drabbest lives could hardly indulge in daydreaming identification with *MH* characters.

But *Mary Hartman* at the outset satirized the genre even while belonging to it, beginning with the pleated lampshade and fringed curtains of the enclosing-frame backdrop, the syrupy signature tune, and the sentimental organ interludes. Exaggeration was the principal element, used especially in calamities. Thus while the personae in the soaps suffer rare and mysterious diseases such as amnesia, subdural hematomas, and unexplained forms of paralysis, death in *Mary* came from drowning in chicken soup and choking on a TV dinner. Another aspect of the parody was the difference in the duration of these catastrophes, which drag on for years in true soap opera but were precipitate and brief in *Mary*. The mortality rate, too, could be compared to that in a Western, a feature of the series having been the truncated life-spans of some of the most original and best-delineated roles, those of Officer Dennis Foley and of the eight-year-old Reverend Jimmy Joe Jeeter. Some of the disappearances could be explained by practical considerations such as ratings, exhaustion of material, and child-welfare regulations; nevertheless, the audience had become attached to these characters and now misses them.

The charge was brought that *Mary* made fun of the factory-working class to which the Hartmans, Shumways, and Haggers belong—and to judge by their homes and appliances, the men of the Fernwood Assembly Plant are members of a strong union. The badges of class are unmistakable: lumber jackets and baseball caps; lunch pails, peanut butter, "chicken-fried steak," Twinkies, beer and soft drinks; bowling, sports on television, country-western music. (The higher social level of Annie—"Tippytoes" —a temporary interest in Tom's life, was indicated by her taste for Vivaldi and the *Sonnets from the Portuguese*, but she was obviously slumming.) None of these blue-collar workers appeared to be concerned about money—a troubling inconsistency, for when Tom lost his job, and when he and Mary were separated, their thoughts should immediately have turned to financial problems. Otherwise the portrayal of the social stratum was remarkably accurate.

But the targets of the original *Mary Hartman* were larger and more important than a social class, being in fact nothing less than contemporary schizoid America and its purely commercial values, disintegrating human relationships and hollow inner life. Out of this broad range two subjects have been most effectively attacked, television itself and the psychology and psychotherapy establishments. The characters' ideas (platitudes), language (jargon), and creed (dogmas of advertising) derive almost wholly from TV, which also fixes the standards for nearly every other aspect of living. This was emphasized when Mary wanted to be discharged from the mental ward and was advised to "sit and look at television to show them that you are normal." No program has gone so far as this one in ridiculing the medium, as well as in warning of its power to reduce its habitués to followers of herd philosophies. The point is made symbolically when a TV set causes the death, by electrocution from a television wire in the bath water, of a divinely inspired child (Jimmy Joe Jeeter), "for," as Loretta Haggers says, "the sins of the six-thirty news."

More fundamental than this in *Mary Hartman*'s critique of television is the program's deliberate confusion of the medium with reality. Thus some viewers may have wondered whether the child actually expired before their eyes—like Lee Harvey Oswald—simply to oblige the networks (and as human beings have recently been photographed doing in Beirut, Belfast, and Johannesburg). And when Zoning Commissioner Rittenhouse strangulates while taking part in a televised panel discussion, his fellow participants do not notice his plight until long after the TV audience, one of whom, our Mary, rushes to the screen, pounds on it, and yells instructions for saving his life. (This is similar to what happened when Aldous Huxley's Hollywood house was burning down, and the television cameras arrived before the fire trucks.) *Mary Hartman* has been criticized for episodes like these two televised deaths, but such incidents expose the growing acceptance of, and indifference toward, the increase of live horrors in our news programs.

Finally, Mary's own emotional collapse, the most potent scene in the series, occurs on, and as a result of, television, when she succumbs to the relentless questioning of three experts on "The David Susskind Show"; the introduction of this de facto TV venerable, of course, is another device in the blurring of real and tele-real. To compound the irony, the audience interprets her breakdown as part of the entertainment, indeed as a spectacular performance, for which she receives congratulations during her subsequent hospitalization. At the moment when her mind snaps, she regurgitates chauvinistic slogans, screaming, as her underpinnings give way, "I believe in America." The advertising blurbs and *Reader's Digest* truisms that fill her mind fail to sustain her in this crisis and are the ultimate factor in her psychotic seizure.

While the "nervous breakdown" episode is serious, the spoofings of psychotherapeutic malpractices are funny. In a particularly droll incident between Mary and the company psychologist, this charlatan claims "to have heard everything" and "to understand and accept" all manner of aberrations. But when she tells him about her affair with Dennis in his hospital bed, the therapist reacts with shock, declares this to be the most disgusting behavior that he has ever known, and refuses to continue seeing her. Worse still, he betrays this confidence to her husband Tom, thereby temporarily destroying her marriage and ruining her life. In sum, her first counseling interview is to a considerable extent responsible for her eventual commitment to a mental ward.

Mary is later assigned to a "religious sex therapist" whose technique for eliminating repressions and puritanical attitudes is to read enigmatic passages from the Bible—which mystify Mary as they would anyone, sane or insane. Then, in order to overcome her husband's impotence, the "healer" supplements his scriptural examples with a Masters-and-Johnson-type exercise. But the whole freak-cure racket—group encounters, self-help, EST—is brilliantly lampooned in STET (Survival Training and Existence Therapy), from which even gullible Mary has the sense to flee.

Institution psychiatry is also attacked, primarily for its profit-making motives. Thus the chief administrator of the mental ward, determined to keep Mary in his hospital for as long as possible because of her publicity value, overrides the doctor's decision to discharge her. The methods of treating disturbed people in this asylum are the usual shock therapy, dosing with tranquilizers, and the diverting, with Pollyanna responses, of all serious discussion of patients' problems. It should be said that the inmates and staff are well conceived and cast—though playing a catatonic should not require exceptional histrionic talents, and though it is unclear at first that Nurse Gimble's broken neck and multiple injuries are due to mistreatment by her sadistic husband, rather than being job-related or a result of exceptional accident-prone-ness. The effect on the viewer of Mary's experiences with psycho-therapy in all of its ramifications is that he or she prays never to require such services from similar persons or organizations. In fact the real mystery concerning *Mary Hartman* is the failure of the American Psychological and Psychiatric Associations to have lodged complaints against the producer.

At first the series developed from character rather than from plot and circumstance, which may be the main reason for that sense of reality which was the program's distinctive and superior quality. The best-drawn characters were complex, and the mere caricatures, such as Mary's nitwit mother, a situation-comedy type, were stylistically alien. The viewer felt the action to be spontaneous, happening rather than unfolding, with the charac-ters ad-libbing what they did as well as what they said. This partly accounts for such crudities as the disjointedness and abbrevia-tion resembling those of a comic strip, the faulty timing, the illogicality of the sequences, the many loose ends, the incon-sistencies (such as Loretta's continuing residence in the old Fernwood neighborhood after having made a recording and a nationwide television appearance), and the general shapelessness of the half-, or, rather, quarter-hour; few other programs seem to be interrupted by so many commercials—possibly another aspect of the satire.

Mary's eccentric, *jeune fille* appearance is the first clue to her character, this mother of a thirteen-year-old dressing in a younger manner than her daughter, as well as in that of an age before slacks and jeans became the universal uniform. Bangs and pig-tails, puffed sleeves and knee-length skirts make Mary a suitable companion for Orphan Annie, Dorothy and Toto, Rebecca of Sunnybrook Farm. This get-up signifies not only Mary's inno-cence but also her lack of development, for she is the prototype of the unintegrated personality, a conglomeration of not-yet-assimilated ingredients. She is aware of the "in" attitudes and gimmickry of her milieu, but the flotsam never falls into place, surfacing in free association and veering away from the intended meaning. Consequently, and no matter how often Mary repeats her pathetic comments ("Isn't that interesting? . . . Oh that is so *interesting*"), she fails to communicate anything except anxiety feelings that the audience recognizes but that are probably not often articulated in American families. These interjections are entertaining and more acceptable because they come from a bewildered, perpetual little girl.

Mary's honesty, openness, and good intentions are insufficient to compensate for an almost total dependency. But how could she be other than dependent with a father and mother like George and Martha Shumway, neither of them any more equipped for parenthood than Mary herself? Martha, rattling on blithely and irrelevantly, never really listens to the troubles of her confused elder daughter, or to those of Kathy, Mary's anonymously pregnant sister. And George—before he vanished into the rear view of a mirror—is accurately described by Grandpa Larkin as the person to whom Kathy should turn for advice, since "That is what he is for even though he won't know what to say."

Mary's reactions when she leaves the mental ward on a weekend pass illustrate the eagerness with which she will clutch at any new straw to help her "cope." As her daughter Heather appears in the kitchen, wearing heretofore forbidden platform shoes and putting her foot up on a chair, Mary berates her, as in the past, but stops short when she remembers one of the child-psychology doctrines learned in the hospital, namely that it is wrong to try to control such behavior or to place good manners ahead of "freedom of expression." Then, revoking what she has just demanded, she begs Heather to return her foot to the chair. The mental ward also seems to have disoriented Mary's time sense, for Heather's sudden increase in height leads her mother to suppose that she must have been away for a long time.

While Mary is a bizarre though real character, Tom, a mixture of appealing and frustrating qualities, is unexceptional. As illprepared for marriage as his wife, he is more at ease with male friends than with her, and although convinced that he wants their relationship to last, and that he is doing his share toward this end, he soon turns every reconciliation into a fresh quarrel.

He and Mary are adolescent, and together they typify the American marital syndrome: husband looking for mother, wife seeking father. Neither of them having found the parent image in the other, Tom's present adventure with an older woman will undoubtedly alter his life.

The marriage between Loretta, aspirant to country-western superstardom, and Charlie, hard-hat worker and his wife's manager, would seem to be a mismatch in age, appearance, talents, and intelligence. A girl as pretty, gifted, and exuberant as Loretta could hardly be expected to spend a lifetime with a man whose main attraction is a prodigious sexual capacity. Now that this is gone, the incompatibility is beginning to show, and obviously she will be put to a severe test. Faithful wife and loyal friend, forthright, extroverted, unspoiled, Loretta—who "psychologicates" and senses when adultery is "glomping" about—has the strongest moral character of anyone in the story. Her stability and healthy outlook are rooted in her simple, Bible Belt religious beliefs, and though it is not safe to predict anything about this erratic series, it seems unlikely that she will follow Mary into a mental institution.

The attitude toward Loretta's religion is one of the puzzles of the first year of the *Mary Hartman* show. A naïve, literal faith such as Loretta's would normally be the butt in a generally sophisticated approach such as this program formerly had, and offended viewers from fundamentalist America evidently thought that her religion *was* being ridiculed. Curiously, the aim was not satire but rather a true portrayal of character. Furthermore, her wholesome and sympathetic qualities are placed in contrast to the rigidity, pedantry, and self-centeredness of three "intellectuals," the women's libber, the sociologist, and the sexologist, who so brutally interrogate Mary on "The David Susskind Show." Granted that they are stereotypes, yet it is their insensitivity which pushes Mary over the brink, while the kindness and protectiveness shown by Loretta help to restore her. The implication that a religious background can be desirable is surprising in a production of this kind.

No generalization is made, of course, about the virtuousness of *all* followers of the Lord, and the apparently pious Merle Jeeter arouses distrust; he is too smooth, too good-looking, and his means of livelihood—touring with his evangelistically and psychically precocious son—is suspect. Merle also has an acknowledged weakness, for he frequents whorehouses and even attempts to rape Loretta. But a transformation comes over him after the death of his little Jimmy Joe, and Merle continues to pursue his "Condos for Christ" movement, while planning to run for President of the United States.

Some of *Mary*'s minor characters were among the most original on television. One of them, much regretted in his absence, is Dennis, the least "pig"-like law-enforcement officer on any screen, as well as the most resourceful of Don Juans: his infinite patience while laying siege to Kathy, Mary, and the STET recruiter (among others) is already legendary. Grandpa Larkin, too, is a refreshing cynic, optimistically resigned to his place on the refuse pile to which America consigns its elderly.

Some audiences have complained about the prominence and the "off-color" treatment of sex in *Mary Hartman*, and a reason for this reaction is that the sexual naturalness is so different from the coyly euphemistic references to the subject that pervade television's talk-and-variety shows. Sex is neither material for jokes nor a peripheral amusement in *Mary*, lying instead at the core, and generating much of the action. Objections have also been made to the language, though this is candid, rather than coarse. True, Loretta and Charlie are explicit in word and gesture about their hyperactive love life, which is "vulgar," but in the dictionary sense of the word, "of the people." The progressive attitude toward the homosexuals, Howard and Ed, conveys both the validity of their desire to marry and the prejudices of a society that prevents them from doing so. But the frankness in dealing with sex opposes present-day prurience, and in this sense *Mary Hartman* actually seems to stand for conventional virtues and morality.

In its first year *Mary Hartman*, though exasperatingly uneven, was sometimes a remarkably perceptive instrument for puncturing the hypocrisies of American life. It was also a welcome antidote to those "comedy" half-hours, such as *The Mary Tyler Moore Show*, which say, in effect, that the U.S.A. can be a pretty nice place and lots of fun, at least on an executive's salary. The original success of *Mary Hartman* may be explained by the existence of two, sometimes overlapping, audiences, one for whom it was merely an entertainment with a peculiar heroine, another for whom it was unique social criticism. But the new series is very disappointing and now can be described only as $99^{44}/_{100}$ percent pure soap opera, late-night. The social class level is changing, and everyone has moved far out of character; Grandpa Larkin, for instance, recently referred to "the two Pablos, Picasso and Casals." Also, in recent programs the pace has slowed, the satire is no more, the improbabilities are of the wrong kind, and none of the new characters offers much promise of development.

Though former devotees can now stay for the last act of the opera or theater, or retire to bed somewhat earlier, they do so nostalgically, asking "What ever became of Mary Hartman?"

EDVARD MUNCH:
SELF-PORTRAITIST
(Notes from a Diary)

December 1, 1975. Oslo. From my hotel room the pedestrians in Karl Johansgate seem to be walking as they do in a Munch picture, at approximately the same pace and without glancing to left or right, but whether they are also silent and grim-looking is impossible to tell in the midnight-dark of midmorning. I am constantly being struck by scenes that remind me of Munch vignettes, and my discovery of the realistic element in this "subjective" painter is expanding in several directions. Thus the sightless windows in an old house seem to resemble those in *The Red Vine,* the sky to evoke the palette of the early *Starry Night,* and the blank expressions to recall some of Munch's people, though I have yet to see one of his entirely featureless faces—like that of a holdup man, or guerrilla, with a stocking over the head. Munch-like, too, is the unhopeful sky, which in early afternoon turns a deepening blue, with a squint of cold pink just before the abrupt "lights out." An acquaintance with the artist's physical world, and with its psychological effects on the inhabitants, must broaden the understanding of his work, yet Munch is more than a regional painter. The best of his creations are universal by virtue of both themes and artistic mastery.

———

December 2. On any itinerary the Oslo National Gallery should precede the Munch Museum. The older institution not only owns more of the artist's greatest paintings but also provides examples of contemporaneous work, notably by Hans Heyerdahl, whom Munch admired, and by Christian Krohg, whose classes Munch attended. A visit to the National Gallery reveals that Munch was not a totally isolated phenomenon, at least in his beginnings, and that a related style and recurrent subject matter already existed. Furthermore, his apparent preoccupation with illness and death becomes less morbid in the context of so many other sickroom and deathbed scenes—which indicate a high incidence of tuberculosis in the Christiania of the time. Finally, the gloomy, creaky-floored old building suggests the atmosphere of the artist's early years, while the passionate posturings of the Rodinesque sculptures in halls and on landings are evidence of the repression of a society in which Munch was exceptional only because of his genius.

The Munch Museum, at the other extreme, offers comfortable seats, is better lighted (even by an occasional sunbeam), and presents its collection in ample, uncluttered space—one aspect of an architecture that is incongruously neutral if not in actual conflict with the turbulent emotions of the art. An attraction of the museum is that the paintings are surrounded by lithographs, woodcuts, and drypoints of the same subjects, thus providing supplements, clues, variations, simplifications, all of inestimable importance in Munch's case. Once this is said, however, it is necessary to add that his graphic work should be considered not merely as ancillary, but for its intrinsic merit—*The Frieze of Life* series, for example, being more nearly complete in engraved than in painted form.

Not many of Munch's more than seven hundred graphics exactly duplicate the paintings, if only for the reason that the compositions are reversed. An example of a difference between a canvas and a lithograph is seen by comparing the painting *Puberty* (probably suggested by Félicien Rops's *La plus belle Amour de Don Juan,* 1886) with *The Young Maiden,* which is the same picture executed in the other medium a year later. Here the expression of the nude girl with hands crossed in her lap— "to cover the object of her fear," Thomas Messer[1] believes—is transformed to indicate feelings that anticipate the erotic curiosity of Balthus's *Georgette.*

———

December 3. I rehearse the Oslo Philharmonic in the Aula, the University's assembly hall and site of Munch's celebrated murals (1909–1911).[2] With a single exception these face each other on the sides of the rectangular room in symmetrical architectural frames. Having seen the tableaux only in photographs, I am astonished by their magnitude, by the resemblances to Max Beckmann in two of the murals, by the debt to Gauguin in one of the harvesting women and in the figure of the girl in *The Chemistry.* The exceptional, unforgettable picture *The Sun* stands by itself at the end of the room, behind and above the orchestra. Broken rays of color, like spokes from an aureole, emanate from a white, borealis disk, for which Munch's first sketch was "a

1. *Edvard Munch* (New York, 1970).
2. See *Edvard Munch: The University Murals,* by Johan H. Langaard and Reidar Revold (Oslo, 1960).

pillar of naked men climbing toward the light"—like his 1902 lithograph of a pillar of naked women bearing a coffin high over their heads. Whether, as Messer claims, *The Sun* is "perhaps the greatest achievement of modern mural painting," it is the most arresting picture of the artist's post-breakdown, rehabilitation period.

———

December 4. An after-concert party in the hotel. Do the stolid countenances of the guests conceal tempestuous emotions like those of the people in the sculptures in the National Gallery? The conversation, at any rate, centers on the scandal of Fru Ø. who has deserted her husband and eloped with Å., the director and actor. Gossip about this liaison predicts that it will not last, other women having preceded Fru Ø. in what is said to be Å.'s "pattern." But apparently such affairs flourish in the isolation of this country, where the climate limits the culture and confines life to the indoors.

———

December 6. By coincidence I am invited to the home of Å. and Ø. on Holmenskollen Hill, above the ski jump and next to a lodge belonging to King Olav. (Ø's aunt is His Majesty's cook here, and according to her the King is so lonely that he sometimes comes to the kitchen and dries the dishes.) After the inevitable aqvavit, smoked salmon, and sweet brown cheese, I go for a walk in a Munch winterscape, wearing fur-lined stovepipe boots that might have been designed as leg-weights for Siberian convicts— though they also help to prop me up. But without ear baffles and a face guard to deflect the sub-Arctic wind, I can remain outside for only a few minutes.

———

December 7. I spend the day reading books about Munch and revisiting the gallery and museum. The most formidable obstacle in all of the publications is the radical difference between the color photographs of each picture, as well as between these and the paintings themselves. Thus the white-ish head in blue-ish space, a detail of *The Scream* on the cover of Reinhold Heller's monograph,[3] is reddish brown in the Messer, Selz,[4] and other books, and even in the corresponding part of the picture reproduced inside the Heller; but in every case the tones are utterly different, and no photograph is true to the actual painting. Heller defends the use of black and white for another picture included in his illustrations on grounds that its colors defy the camera. But though this is undoubtedly so, his verbal descriptions of tints and shades here and elsewhere are even less helpful than distorting photographs, since colors and their relationships are an essential instrument of Munch's composition and one on which the meaning of a painting may depend.

Nevertheless, the quality of the reproductions is vastly superior to that of the texts. As might be expected of the director of the Guggenheim Museum, Messer's choice of pictures could scarcely be bettered—except, perhaps, by having included an example from the earliest period. His technical analyses, too, are occasionally apt, as when he explains that the "airy, vibrant surface" in *Self-Portrait in a Blue Suit* (1909) is achieved by the white spaces between the long, parallel brushstrokes. Above all, his thesis of the decline of Munch's art after 1909 is to me the only tenable one, while the demonstration of it in this same *Blue Suit* is perceptive:

the reliance upon an axial order with horizontals and verticals largely supplant[s] free form, and . . . the use of pure colors [gives] an easily legible relationship between advancing and receding picture planes.

Few today would dispute the statement that when Munch was cured of his illness—and of his tensions, paroxysms, hallucina-

3. *Edvard Munch: The Scream* (New York, 1973).
4. *Munch,* by Jean Selz, translated from the French by Eileen Hennessy (New York, 1974). See also *Edvard Munch* (Basel, Editions Galerie Beyeler).

tions—he was also cured of his genius.[5] But Messer's language is banal.[6] And it is misleading. Referring to *The Scream*, he says that

> the gloomy hues and . . . concentrically enlarging lines . . . define and ultimately embrace land, sea, and sky.

But these hues and lines *are* the land, sea, and sky, while the "enlarging" is *ex-* not *con*centric. And he has a habit of introducing mysteries where none exist. Thus in *Self-Portrait with a Wine Bottle* he sees

> three, distant, almost featureless and half-averted creatures fac[ing] empty tables,

even though two of these "creatures" are unmistakably waiters in what is clearly a restaurant, while the third, seated, "creature" is almost certainly a customer.

Reinhold Heller is concerned with sources, influences, and the psychological back- and foreground. Apropos the blood-colored evening sky in *The Scream*, he notes that the sunset hour was thought to be the favored time for suicides until Durkheim's study

5. For the contrary view, see *The Oxford Companion to Art* (New York, 1970).
6. "[As a young man Munch] would pursue his off-beat ideas. . . . *The Frieze* grew out of the Norwegian's deep commitment to significant content." Still worse, at times it is quite impossible to understand what Messer is saying, since the referents to his pronouns and even some of the subjects of his sentences are indeterminable:

> Despite its poetic strain, *Girls on the Jetty* is a literal translation of a scene at Asgaardstrand. Now, some seventy years after its original conception, the visitor to this spot at Oslo Fjord will find . . .

Finally, a whole manual of misusages could be compiled from the book. Messer says that, in one picture, woman

> picks the fateful apple—an act translatable to the jealous mind of the brooding foreground figure as apprehension in flagrante delicto. . . . [Caught in the act of apprehension?]

And a chair in another picture is described as "a focal point for the six dramatis personae who turn to it," though only one dramatis persona is visible.

disproved the notion. Heller has evidently borrowed some of his material from Werner Timm,[7] who, in turn, derived it from Rolf Stenersen.[8] But while the latter two scholars merely mention the artist's 1928 discovery of the similarity between some of his early emotional experiences and those described by Kierkegaard in *The Concept of Dread*, Heller explores the connection, going so far as to say that Munch

> constantly stood at the edge of Kierkegaard's precipice and felt the dizziness of that external reality he freely chose to let test its might against him. . . .

But the idea of Munch exposing himself to the "elements" to determine how much he could endure is almost as ridiculous as the one that he could "freely choose," especially at the time of *The Scream*.

Kenneth Clark also appears to have underestimated the gravity of the artist's psychological state, writing that "Munch was a deeply neurotic man."[9] But in spite of difficulties of definition, and the lack of clear categories and boundaries, would it not be more accurate to describe his symptoms as psychotic ones, or as those of a schizophrenic of the paranoid type, characterized, according to Arieti, by "unrealistic, illogical, hallucinatory thinking, and by bizarre delusions of being persecuted"? In fact, Arieti's example of hallucinatory symptoms in paranoids might have been suggested by *The Scream*: "The individual [reports] 'voices' that no one else seems to hear, but the 'reality' of which he accepts."

7. *The Graphic Art of Edvard Munch*, translated from the German by Ruth Michaelis-Jena and Patrick Murray (Greenwich, Connecticut, 1969).
8. *Edvard Munch: Close-Up of a Genius* (Oslo, 1969). See also *Edvard Munch: Masterpieces from the Artist's Collection in the Munch Museum in Oslo*, by Johan H. Langaard and Reidar Revold, translated from the German by Michael Bullock (New York, 1964). This book contains even more color photographs than Messer's but is marred by such fatuous remarks as "[Munch's work sprang] from his quite personal feelings for life."
9. *Edvard Munch*, catalogue of the exhibition by The Arts Council of Great Britain, forewords by Sir Kenneth Clark and Knut Berg (London, 1974).

Clark says, also, that

> writers on Munch maintain that he was not disturbed by [his] breakdown; . . . I find that it affected him profoundly. . . .

But how could it not affect him? And surely a breakdown that did not disturb would be a contradiction in terms.

If Munch were no more than "deeply neurotic," the following statement would be perfectly acceptable:

> [After Munch's nervous collapse] he seemed afraid that the symbols which had haunted him so long were like a dangerous magic, and might again upset his mental balance: so no more devouring women. . . .[10]

But if, on the other hand, he were schizophrenic, the capacity for deliberate choice implied here is not plausible. And are not these symbols manifestly the symptom, not the cause, of the illness? Clark here appears to grant to Munch powers of direction over his mind and of distinguishing between subjective and objective that this sadly disoriented brain did not have. Furthermore, the women *did* return, for example in the hair-fetishist *Weeping Maiden* and *Womanly Act*, both of 1920.

While Clark at least always views Munch as an artist, Heller asserts that the "paintings were created . . . to act as non-verbal symbols. . . ." But were the paintings not created as paintings, as compositions of forms, colors, lines, textures? And how can Heller even have glanced at *Anxiety* and still say that

> the eyes which stare at [the viewer are] the eyes of modern city-dwellers alienated from the majesty of nature and accustomed to being constantly confronted by ugliness[?]

Surely the subject of *Anxiety* is loneliness, the isolation of people from each other, rather than the preoccupation of Oslo's residents with the city's aesthetic shortcomings.

10. Clark, *op. cit.*

Messer and Heller disagree in their interpretations of *The Scream* (1893). "Nothing external gives a clue to the horror that impels the outcry," Messer writes, although the sky is both external and bloody, which might be thought sufficient provocation to cry out. He also says that "The subject [is] apparently a woman," despite the bald head, so different from the abundant tresses that typify Munch's females. Heller, on the other hand, refers to

the sexless, emasculated figure [which] . . . takes on the art nouveau curvature of the landscape rather than retaining human form.

An emasculated figure is still male in appearance, however, and the form of this one, while skeletal, is still human—and not, say, werewolf. Finally, Munch's confession that the experience had been his own suggests that the "subject" was a representation of himself. The sunken cheeks are strikingly similar to those in his self-portrait as John the Baptist.

William S. Lieberman, for whom *The Scream* is Munch's "most vivid image,"[11] argues that through translation to a graphic medium, the picture

gains effectively in expressiveness. The colors are reduced to black and white. The sinuous curves contrast with the diagonals of the bridge over the railing. . . . A couple continues to promenade. . . .

In fact the lithograph is superior to the painting in two ways, the higher intensity of focus on the screamer, achieved by eliminating (not "reducing") color, and the greater distinctness of the promenaders, which supports the theory that the cry, if not merely imagined, is unheard. But the contrasts, not only between "sinuous curves" and diagonals but also between them and the

11. "Edvard Munch as Printmaker," introduction to the catalogue of the exhibition of Munch's lithographs, etchings, and woodcuts at the Los Angeles County Museum of Art, 1969.

newly introduced verticals, are almost academic, or at any rate too obvious, compared to the vertiginous—swirling and enveloping—"Nature," which is one of the marvels of the painting.

Surprisingly, no investigation of Munch's abnormal personality and ultimate breakdown has yet appeared, and the commentaries purporting to examine his mental state attempt to relate his numerous aberrations to his work but not to each other or to physical causes. Thus Messer discusses the evidence of agoraphobia in Munch's treatment of space and in the way in which his crowds huddle together. But one might add that their closeness to buildings and the extreme foreground position of individual figures are additional signs of this phobia. Rycroft (in *Anxiety and Neurosis*) believes such a condition to be due to excessive fears of reality, of death, and of leaving the mother, and Munch was undeniably subject to all of these. His mother died when he was five, an event that he seems to have portrayed in the horrifying etching *The Dead Mother* (1901), in which the child, though dressed as a girl, could be Munch; her clenched hands at the sides of her face, moreover, are reminiscent of the subject in *The Scream*.

The question of Munch's relationships with women is usually approached as if it were a separate matter. Messer, for instance, echoes the remark, repeated in every study of the artist, that

with women [Munch] was influenced by ideas derived from the popularization of Schopenhauer

—as if the mere reading of a misogynist could have inspired the artist's very real terror of women, or have filled him with guilt about his sexual behavior, or have helped to drive him to what would seem to be at least latent necrophilia (*The Madonna* being conceivable as an expression of this brand of desire[12]), all of which constitute some of his feelings about women in his sexually

12. "No doubt he had some strange experiences with the opposite sex," Clark writes. One might add that no doubt the opposite sex had some strange experiences with Munch.

obsessed art. As for the lithograph of *The Madonna,* in which the woman is even more cadaverous than in the painting—or more adept at playing dead—it is difficult to agree with William Lieberman that

> The figure appears as eternal womanhood. . . . The woman, albeit haloed, is not an object of devotion. The embryo and the fluid border suggest the equivocal irony born of a scientific age. . . .

The woman is indeed not an object of devotion but of sex, while the embryo is a fetus, the "fluid border" a stream of spermatozoa.

"Munch was exceptionally handsome and never married," Clark writes, but if an allusion to homosexuality were intended, the word would have to be understood in the sense of the artist's flight from women, rather than of his attraction to men. True, his bisexuality is implied in the self-portrait as a sphinx with female breasts and in his inscription on a drawing, done under psychiatric supervision, of an electric device

> inducing positive male power and negative female power in the painter's weakened brain.

But in Munch's depiction of the relation between the sexes, woman is generally man's destroyer, and she is nearly always so in his self-portraits, such as *Under the Mask of a Woman,* which seem to say that he is in hell as her victim and through no fault of his own.

Munch's frequent rear-view presentation of women may be part of his obsession with long hair (*Young Girl on the Shore,* 1896; *Summer Night,* 1907), and with the threat of being drowned in its coils, as in the waves of the sea. But much more remains to be explored on the subject, from Munch's fantasies of masochistic abasement and his use of the symbols of Salomé and Charlotte Corday to his fear of losing his identity in women —made explicit when the lips of his kissing couple form a single ugly snout.

What Kenneth Clark may have meant, and what is incontestable from Munch's work—still the primary source of knowledge about the artist—is that the painter was deeply "narcissistic." This could have originated in ego bruises dating from infancy, or from his mother's death, and developing rapidly when he began to exhibit his pictures, in which case the "narcissism" would have been a protective response to the feeling that his art was under attack. He tells of entering an Oslo gallery in which people were laughing at one of his pictures, and, in the street afterward, of hearing himself called "fake painter" by the most esteemed artist of the day. "I was subject to unusual persecution," he writes, and obviously he thought of the critics as being in league against him. In one pathetic diary entry he expressed the hope that a particular enemy "doesn't imagine that I take any notice of him."

Munch's persecution feelings led to violent episodes. A woman with whom he lived attempted to shoot herself after his refusal to marry her, and, intervening, he accidentally mutilated one of his fingers. Even in his seventy-first year he was involved in a drunken street fight with a younger colleague.

But the persecution was balanced by the fascination with the face in the mirror. It is difficult to estimate the number of his self-portraits—overt, hidden, incipient, transferred—but the proportion must be among the highest in the *catalogue raisonné* of any artist. While still young, Munch pictured himself with a skeleton arm—in a lithograph that might have appealed to John Donne. And even as an old man, Munch was still painting his portrait in the nude. His self-absorption may be the most important fact about him, since his breakdown was the consequence —apart from all of the other physical and parataxic causes—of his inability to see the world except as it pertained to himself.

———

The film *Edvard Munch*[13] shows an understanding of the painter's personality, in his apparent diffidence, impassivity, and failure

13. In Norwegian. 167 minutes. Directed, and with English titles and narration, by Peter Watkins; distributed by New Yorker Films.

to respond appropriately, for he remains a silent observer in scenes of discussions where others react with animation and spontaneity; but then, volcanoes smoldering beneath immobile exteriors are not cinematic. In sum, no protagonist in a three-hour film can have had fewer lines to learn or less histrionic range to display than the actor who plays Edvard Munch.

More than a third of *Edvard Munch* is devoted to the artist's childhood and youth, thereby enabling the director to dwell on the Norwegian social background; on Munch's guru, the anarchist Hans Jaeger; and on the harsh pieties and gruesome maladies of the Munch family. But the scenes of the artist's consumptive sister frothing blood at the mouth, and of his own pulmonary hemorrhage at age fifteen, must convince the viewer that the blood-smeared skies in *The Scream* and in *Anxiety* are related to these traumatic experiences.

The film's researchers claim to have uncovered new facts, the most crucial being that the painter's grandfather had syphilis. This could account for the insanity (paresis?) of another of Munch's sisters, as well as raise a question about the likelihood of the same disease in the artist himself: though if he did not have it congenitally, he might well have contracted it during his early "free-love, Bohemian" years in Oslo, or, later, during a debauch in Berlin; no one seems to have considered that a possible reason for Munch's early resolution never to marry could have been the fear of transmitting venereal disease. The film identifies Dagny Juell as the model for *The Madonna* (heretofore erroneously believed to have been the violinist Eva Mudocci), attributes an influence on Munch's color symbolism to the phrase from the *Iliad*, "Blue death closes the eyes," and reveals that he was given naphtha injections, presumably to relieve his coughing spells and stridulous breathing.

Apart from these and other matters of fact, the narration contains questionable judgments (*The Sick Child* is "the first great expressionist picture in modern art"); debatable interpretations (Munch's early withdrawal into himself is "signified by the veiled eyes in a *Self-Portrait*"); and misstatements ("Perspective vanishes from Munch's pictures," the commentary says, though it has not done so in those chosen for illustration). At one point the audience is told that Munch is in Paris, but he is not shown there, nor are such of his Parisian pictures as the *Rue Lafayette*, whose elongated balcony with leaning figure is an important motif repeated later with railings of bridges. In films it is not unexpected that the creation of works of art is secondary to stories of love affairs, though here this emphasis gives the impression that to escape from them was Munch's primary artistic motivation. As for the act of painting, this is limited to some glimpses of the artist setting up his easel, posing a sitter, and briefly applying pencil and brush—which, however, make chipping and scratching sounds like those of scaupers or incising tools. Toward the close of the three hours, the camera begins to stray to the lakes and forests of Norway, thereby betraying Munch's creed that nature and art are enemies.

The movie ends as Munch is about to enter a psychiatric clinic. No doubt the reason for this conclusion is to exploit the irony of the artist's finally receiving his country's recognition (a knighthood in the Royal Order of St. Olav) at the very moment of his mental breakdown. Shortly before this he enumerated the priorities in the creative process, but the truth of this order is unchallengeable, at least for Edvard Munch:

Art is the form of the picture that has come into being through the nerves, heart, brain and eye of man.

INDEX OF NAMES

Abert, Hermann, *W. A. Mozart*, 38, 39
Adams, Henry, 231
Adorno, Theodor W., 246, 254, 261,
    273 and *n.*, 274–7, 279 and *n.*,
    280–1
    Versuch über Wagner, 74
Aeschylus, 146, 147, 151–2, 219, 220
Agoult, Marie, Countess d', 171, 172
Andersen, H. C., 168
Arendt, Hannah, 251 *n.*
Arieti, Silvano, 321
Aristophanes, 217
Aristotle, 115–16, 274
Auden, W. H., 222
Austin, J. L., 246
Avalle, D'Arco Silvio, 75 *n.*
Ayer, Sir Alfred, 246

Bach, Johann Sebastian, 47, 198, 199
    The Art of the Fugue, 9
    Mozart and, 9–10, 11 and *n.*
    The Well-Tempered Clavier, 9, 11
Bach, Karl Philipp Emanuel, 199
Bacquier, Gabriel, 62
Baer, C., 48 *n.*
Balakirev, Mily Alexeyevich, 174
Barbarossa, Friedrich, 76
Barbier, Jules, 65 *n.*
Barry, Michael, 241
Barth, Herbert, 99 *n.*, 100 *n.*
Bartók, Béla, 180 and *n.*
Batley, E. M., *A Preface to "The
    Magic Flute,"* 44–5
Beaumarchais, Pierre-Augustin Caron
    de, *Le Mariage de Figaro*, 49–51,
    54–5, 57

Beck, Martin, 82 *n.*
Beckmann, Max, 317
Bedford, Steuart, 49 *n.*
Bedford, Sybille, *Aldous Huxley*, 234–
    44
Beethoven, Ludwig van, 9, 198, 255
    Mozart compared to, 8
Berg, Alban, 129 and *n.*, 202
    Lulu, 68, 83
    Wozzeck, 67, 130
Berg, Knut, 321 *n.*
Bergman, Ingmar, 67
    The Magic Flute (film), 35–8
Bergson, Henri, 114–15
Bergsten, Gunilla, *Thomas Mann's
    Doctor Faustus*, 278
Berlin, Sir Isaiah, 252 and *n.*
Berlioz, Hector:
    Benvenuto Cellini, 169 *n.*, 182
    Symphonie Fantastique, 177
Bernardete, Seth, 217 *n.*
Berry, Walter, 137
Berlati, Giovanni, 25 *n.*
Bettelheim, Bruno, 288–9
Bignen, Max, 65 *n.*
Blake, Peter, 285, 287, 295, 296
Blegen, Judith, 137
Bloch, Ernst, 257
Blomdahl, Karl-Birger, *Aniara*, 67
Blumer, Rodney, "The Characters in
    Der Rosenkavalier," 140–1 *n.*
Bluthaupt, Heinrich, 18–19
Böhm, Karl, 16–17
Boissier, Valerie, 173 *n.*
Boito, Arrigo, 63 *n.*, 65, 106, 116–20
Bormann, Martin, 154

Boulez, Pierre, 84, 89
  on Wagner, 99–102
Brahms, Johannes, 159, 174, 198
Brecht, Bertolt, 261
Britten, Benjamin, *The Turn of the
  Screw*, 67
Brosses, Charles de, 82
Budden, Julian, *The Operas of Verdi*,
  107–8
Burke, Edmund, 255
Busch, Hans, 106

Caballé, Montserrat, 114, 136
Cairns, David, 182
Carlsson, Anni, 262 *n.*
Carnegy, Patrick, *Faust as Musician*,
  278–9
Carlyle, Thomas, 71
Carré, Michel, 65 *n.*
Cassirer, Ernst, 75 *n.*
Chailley, Jacques, 39, 46
Chaplin, Charlie, 294
Chopin, Frédéric, 179
Clark, Sir Kenneth, 321, 322, 324 *n.*,
  325, 326
Condillac, Etienne Bonnet de, 185
Cossotto, Fiorenza, 113–14
Cowell, Henry, 213

Dallapiccola, Luigi, *Il Prigioniero*, 67
Da Ponte, Lorenzo, 19, 22, 24, 25, 27,
  33, 49 *n.*, 57
da Vinci, Leonardo, 162
Debussy, Claude, 90–1, 151, 176, 177,
  191, 212
  Le Martyre de Saint-Sébastien, 191
  n.
  La Mer, 188–9
  Pelléas et Mélisande, 83, 91
Del Mar, Norman, *Richard Strauss*,
  131–3, 146 *n.*
Dent, Edward, *Mozart's Operas*. 22
  and *n.*, 25 and *n.*, 28, 38, 39, 43,
  45–6, 55–6
De Romilly, Jacqueline, 219–20

Disney, Walt, 288–93
Domingo, Placido, 113–14
Dorfman, 289 *n.*
Dostoevskv. Fyodor, 274
Dupin, *see* Sand, George

Edmondson, Madeleine, 306
Einstein, Alfred, 25–6
Ellinwood, Leonard, 165
Eliot, George, 172
Eliot, T. S., 211, 223–34
Ericson, Eric, 35 *n.*
Eschenbach, *see* Wolfram von
  Eschenbach
Euripides, 146, 219, 220
Everding, August, 80

Fassbaender, Brigitte, 17
Fellini, Federico, 67
Finch, Christopher, *The Art of Walt
  Disney*, 285, 287–92, 294–6
Fischer-Dieskau, Dietrich, 82 *n.*, 153
Flaubert, Gustave, 49, 54, 277–8
Fleischer, Max, 290–1
Forte, Allen, 196 *n.*
Fraenkel, Hermann, 219
Freni, Mirelli, 62
Freud, Sigmund, 32, 230, 267
Frick, Gottlob, 82 *n.*
Frijerio, Ezio, 59 *n.*

Gadamer, Hans-Georg, *Hegel's
  Dialectic*, 245
Gauguin, Paul, 317
Gazzaniga, Giuseppe, 25 *n.*
Gedda, Nicolai, 17, 66
Gellner, Ernest, 246–7, 250–2
Ghislanzoni, Antonio, 106, 109–12
Giesecke, Carl Ludwig, 43–4
Goebbels, Joseph, 154
Goethe, Johann Wolfgang von, 251,
  268
Gombrich, Sir Ernest H., 222 *n.*

Gossett, Philip, "Verdi, Ghislanzoni and 'Aida': The Uses of Convention," 109–10
Gounod, Charles, *Faust*, 65–7
Grist, Reri, 17
Gruber, Gernot, 46 *n.*
Gunzel, Klaus, 76 *n.*
Gutman, Robert, 82 *n.*

Hafner, Philipp, 44
Hagopian, Viola L., 163 *n.*
Hands, Terry, 63 *n.*
Harding, Lawrence, 43 *n.*
Haydn, Franz Joseph, 9, 40
Heard, Gerald, 240, 241
Hegel, Georg W. F., 244–55
Heidegger, Martin, 251
Heine, Heinrich, 172, 175
Heller, Reinhold, *Edvard Munch: The Scream*, 319–23
Heraclitus, 220
Herder, Johann Gottfried von, 251–3
Hesse, Hermann, 262–5
Heyerdahl, Hans, 316
Hitler, Adolf, 92, 94–8, 101, 103, 154, 155
Hobbes, Thomas, 115
Hoffmann, E. T. A., 24, 29, 30
Hofmannsthal, Hugo von, 135
Elektra, 145–52
Der Rosenkavalier, 136, 138–42, 144–5
Hölderlin, Friedrich, 251
Honegger, Arthur, 194
Horkheimer, Max, 261
Hotter, Hans, 82 *n.*
Hume, David, 222
Hurd, Earl, 290
Huxley, Aldous, 234–44
Huxley, Laura, 242–4
Huxley, Maria, 237–42

Isaac, Heinrich, 159
Isherwood, Christopher, 241
Ives, Charles, 211–14
Iwerks, Ub, 291

Jahn, Otto, 43
James, Henry, 29, 230–1
Janina, Countess Olga, 171, 172
Janowitz, Gundula, 17
Jefferson, Alan, 152–4
Jerome, Saint, 127
John the Baptist, 127
Josephus, 126
Juell, Dagny, 327
Jung, Carl G., 74

Kafka, Franz, 15, 257
Kahler, Erich, 262
Karajan, *see* Von Karajan, Herbert
Kaufmann, Walter, 101, 246–9, 252
Kélémén, Zoltan, 82 *n.*
Kelly, Michael, 23–4
Kennedy, Michael, 154–5
Kerényi, Karl, 76, 257, 262
Kermode, Frank, 223–4
Kerner, Dieter, 48 *n.*
Kierkegaard, Søren, 25–7, 30–3, 247, 274, 321
Either/Or, 30–1
Kirkpatrick, John, 213
Kirkwood, Gordon, 219
Kleiber, Carlos, 14
Klemperer, Otto, 155
Klindworth, Agnes, 171, 183
Kollo, René, 82 *n.*
Komorzyński, Egon von, 44
Kratz, Henry, 84–5
Krauss, Clemens, 137
Krogh, Christian, 316

Laforgue, Jules, 127
Landini, Francesco, 159, 162–6
Langaard, Johan H., 317 *n.*, 321 *n.*
Lavelli, Jorge, 65 *n.*
Lawrence, D. H., 240, 242, 266
Lehár, Franz, 145
Lemaître, Georges, *Beaumarchais*, 55 *n.*
Levi, Hermann, 100 *n.*
Levine, James, 137–8
Lichtheim, George, 245 *n.*

Lieberman, William S., 323, 325
Liszt, Franz, 168–83, 198
   Dante Symphony, 169 *n.*, 175, 176,
     179
   Faust Symphony, 179
   First Concerto for Piano, 179
   Hamlet, 178
   love affairs of, 171–3
   Ce qu'on entend sur la Montagne,
     178
   Perényi's biography of, 168–73, 175,
     179, 181–3
   piano works, 180
   Les Préludes, 177–9
   Réminiscences de Don Juan, 175
   sacred music, 175–6
   Second Concerto for Piano, 179
   symphonic poems, 177–9
   Totentanz, 180 and *n.*
   Von der Wiege bis zum Grabe, 176,
     177
Lockwood, Daniel, 306 *n.*
Louÿs, Pierre, 134
Ludwig, Christa, 82 *n.*
Ludwig II, King of Bavaria, 100 *n.*
Lukács, Georg, 246, 261
Lully, Jean Baptiste, 135
Luzio, Alessandro, *Carteggi verdiani*,
   106

Machaut, Guillaume de, 159–63, 165–8
   La Louange des Dames, 162–3
   Le lay de la fonteinne, 167
   O livoris feritas, 160, 168
Mack, Dietrich, 99 *n.*, 100 *n.*
Mahler, Alma, 95
Mahler, Gustav, 95, 175
Mallarmé, Stéphane, 127 and *n.*, 128,
   190–1
Mann, Heinrich, 258–60, 265–6, 275
Mann, Katia, 260–1
Mann, Michael, 260 *n.*
Mann, Thomas, 256–82
   Adorno and, 261, 273 and *n.*, 275–7,
     279 and *n.*, 280–1
   Death in Venice, 260, 261

Doctor Faustus, 260, 269–82
   Heinrich Mann and, 258–60, 265–6,
     275
   Hesse and, 262–5
   Joseph and His Brothers, 257, 265
   Kerényi and, 257, 262, 265–8
   Royal Highness, 259, 262
   Schoenberg and, 261, 271, 273, 276,
     279–81
   The Story of a Novel: The Genesis
     of Doctor Faustus, 258, 274–8
Mann, William, *Richard Strauss*, 131,
   132
Marcuse, Herbert, 246
Mark (apostle), 126
Marrocco, Thomas, 163
Martini, Padre Giambattista, 10
Mary Magdalene, 88–9
Marx, Karl, 85 and *n.*, 248, 252, 253,
   286
Mattehart, 289 *n.*
Matthew (apostle), 126
Matz, M. J., 108 *n.*
Mayer, Hans, *Richard Wagner in*
   Bayreuth, 98–9
Meisl, Karl, 38 *n.*
Mendelssohn, Felix, 251
Menotti, Gian-Carlo, *The Consul*, 67
Meredith, George, 115
Messer, Thomas, *Edvard Munch*, 323,
   324
Metzler, Johann Georg, *see* Giesecke,
   Carl Ludwig
Meyerbeer, Giacomo, *Les Huguenots*,
   108
Meysenbug, Malwida von, 99
Michels, Volker, 262 *n.*
Moberly, R. B., *Three Mozart Operas*,
   45
Molière (*pseudonym of* Jean Baptiste
   Poquelin), 26
Mondor, Henri, 127 *n.*
Moore, Douglas, *The Ballad of Baby*
   Doe, 67
Morgann, Maurice, 116 *n.*
Mortimer, Raymond, 235
Mozart, Anna Maria (Pertl), 7
Mozart, Constanze, 7, 42

Mozart, Leopold, 3–7, 10, 33–4
Mozart, Maria Anna (Marianne), 4
Mozart, Wolfgang Amadeus, 3–63,
113, 144–5
  Adagio and Rondo for Glass
  Harmonica (K.617), 12
  Bach's influence on, 9–11
  childhood and adolescence of, 3–8
  Così fan tutte, 16–24, 47
  Don Giovanni, 24–34
  Fugue (K. 401), 9
  Fugue in C Minor (K. 426), 11 n.
  fugues by, 9–10, 11 and n.
  The Magic Flute, 19, 34–48
  The Marriage of Figaro, 7, 16, 47,
  49–63, 66
  Mass (K. 139), 10 n.
  Mass in C Minor, 10, 11, 46
  Requiem, 46
  The Seraglio, 47
  Sinfonia Concertante (K. 364), 12–
  13
  Sonata for Clavier and Violin (K.
  402), 10
  Violin Concerto in A Major (K.
  219), 20
Müller, Max, 75 and n.
Munch, Edvard, 315–28
  Anxiety, 322, 327
  Edvard Munch (film), 326–8
  The Madonna, 324, 325, 327
  The Scream, 319–21, 323, 324, 327
  Self-Portrait in a Blue Suit, 319
  The Sun, 317–18
Mustard, Helen, 84 n.
Muti, Riccardo, 113 n.
Myers, Rollo, 125 n.

Nehru, Jawaharlal, 263, 264
Nestroy, Johann, 43 n.
Newman, Ernest, 170–1
Nietzsche, Friedrich, 90, 272

Obrecht, Jacobus, 271
O'Hearn, Robert, 49 n.

Opern in Deutschland, Die (history),
42–3 and n.
Ophuls, Marcel, 94
Orel, Alfred, 46 n.
Orenstein, Arbie, Ravel: Man and
Musician, 185–7, 191
Osborne, Charles:
  The Complete Operas of Verdi,
  107 n.
  Letters of Giuseppe Verdi, 105 n.

Paganini, Nicolò, 172
Paisiello, Giovanni, 56
Palestrina, Giovanni Pierluigi da,
Stabat Mater, 159
Panerai, Rolando, 17
Passage, Charles, 84 n.
Pavarotti, Luciano, 136
Perényi, Eleanor, Baroness, Liszt:
The Artist as Romantic Hero, 168–
73, 175, 179, 181–3
Piaget, Jean, 222 n.
Pindar, 220
Plasson, Michel, 65 n.
Plato, 245
Plessen, Elisabeth von, 260 n.
Ponchielli, Amilcare, 293
Ponte, see Da Ponte, Lorenzo
Poulenc, Francis, 67
Prey, Hermann, 17
Price, Margaret, 61–2
Proudhon, Pierre Joseph, 85
Puccini, Giacomo, 112

Raabe, Peter, 170 n.
Rank, Otto, The Don Juan Legend,
32–4
Rauschning, Hermann, Hitler Speaks,
88 n.
Ravel, Maurice, 184–95
  Une Barque sur l'océan, 189
  Boléro, 184, 194
  childhood world of, 187–90
  Daphnis et Chloé, 184, 188, 190,
  192, 193, 195

Ravel, Maurice (*continued*)
  L'Enfant et les sortilèges, 185, 187–90, 192
  L'Heure espagnole, 185, 189–91
  Histoires naturelles, 190, 193
  Ma Mère l'Oye, 185, 187, 188
  Menuet antique. 189
  orchestrations by, 191–2
  Ouverture de Shéhérazade, 191
  Pavane pour une infante défunte, 192
  Piano Concerto in G, 192–4
  Pictures at an Exhibition (Mussorgsky's orchestrated by Ravel), 189
  Rapsodie espagnole, 190, 191 and *n*.
  Le Tombeau de Couperin, 184
  Trois poèmes de Stéphane Mallarmé, 190–1, 193
  La Valse, 184, 194
  Valses nobles et sentimentales, 184
Remedios, Alberto, 136
Rennert, Günther, 17, 49 and *n*., 50
Revold, Reidar, 317 *n*., 321 *n*.
Ricks, Christopher, 233, 234
Rilke, Rainer Maria, 293
Rimsky-Korsakov, Nikolai Andreyevitch, 174
Rolland, Romain, 125, 133–5
Roosevelt, Franklin D., 263, 264
Rops, Félicien, 317
Rosen, Charles, 56
  Arnold Schoenberg, 196, 200–10
Rossiter, Frank R., *Charles Ives and His America*, 211–14
Rostand, Claude, 171–2
Rostand, Edmond, 30
Rounds, David, 306
Rubinstein, Anton, 174
Rycroft, Charles, 324
Ryle, Gilbert, 246

Sackton, Alexander, 225
Salieri, Antonio, 56
Sand, George (*pseudonym of* Amandine Aurore Lucie), 170, 171, 173

Satie, Erik, 103
Saussure, Ferdinand de, 75–6
Sayne-Wittgenstein, Princess Carolyne (née Iwanowska), 171, 173, 183
Scheel, Walter, 103
Schelling, Friedrich Wilhelm Joseph von, 87
Schikaneder, Emanuel, 41–5
Schmalhausen, Countess, 171 and *n*.
Schoenberg, Arnold, 129 and *n*., 160, 170 *n*., 195–210
  Erwartung, 83, 91, 203–10
  Five Pieces for Orchestra, 91
  Mann and, 261, 271, 272–3, 276, 279–81
  Moses and Aaron, 73
  Obbligato Recitative, 151
  Pierrot Lunaire, 204, 210
  Style and Idea, 195, 197–200, 207 *n*.
  Verklärte Nacht, 83
Schonberg, Harold C., 60–8
Schopenhauer, Arthur, 271, 324
Schreier, Peter, 17
Schröter, Klaus, 265–6
Schubert, G. H., 76 *n*.
Schumann, Robert, 169 *n*.
Searle, Humphrey, 170, 178, 181
Selz, Jean, 319
Servais, Franz, 171, 183
Shakespeare, William, 115, 120
  Henry IV, Part One, 116, 117
  Henry IV, Part Two, 117
  Macbeth, 126
  The Merry Wives of Windsor, 116–18
Shaw, George Bernard, 30, 183
Siegmund-Schultze, W., 10 *n*.
Smith, Patrick, 67
Solti, Sir Georg, 59–60, 62, 63 and *n*., 82 *n*., 83–4
Sophocles, 89, 219, 220; *Elektra*, 145–8
Squarcialupi, Antonio, 164
Starobinski, Jean, 75–6
Stein, Leonard, 195 *n*.
Stendhal (*pseudonym of* Marie Henri Beyle), 55
Stenersen, Rolf, 321
Stolz, Teresa, 112

Strauss, Johann, 145
Strauss, Richard, 97
  Ariadne auf Naxos, 136
  Le Bourgeois Gentilhomme, Suite
    ("Lully"), 135
  Der Rosenkavalier, 136–45
  Elektra, 125, 129, 138, 139, 145–55
  lieder, 153
  Salomé, 124–35
Stravinsky, Igor, 21, 91, 135, 151, 175,
    278
  The Rake's Progress, 67
  on Ravel, 191 *n.*, 194–5
Strawson, P. F., 246
Strehler, Giorgio, 59 *n.*, 60–1, 63
Svoboda, Joseph, 63 *n.*
Swieten, Baron Gottfried van, 9, 42
Syberberg, Hans Jurgen, *Winifred
    Wagner* (film), 92–8, 103
Szabolcsi, Bence, 170 *n.*

Taylor, Charles, *Hegel*, 245–54
Tchaikovsky, Peter Ilyich, 179
Thales, 220
Tietjen, Heinz, 97
Timm, Werner, 321
Tippett, Michael, *The Midsummer
    Marriage*, 67
Treece, Henry, 225
Troyanos, Tatiana, 136, 137

van Swieten, *see* Swieten, Baron
    Gottfried van
Varnhagen, Rahel, 251
Verdi, Giuseppe, 58 *n.*, 104–24, 145
  Aida, 106, 109–14, 118
  Un Ballo in Maschera, 108
  correspondence of, 105–6
  Falstaff, 114–24
  Giovanna d'Arco, 114 *n.*
  new and forthcoming books on,
    106–11
  Otello, 63–5, 118, 119
  Rigoletto, 105
  La Traviata, 118
Viertel, Salka, 259 *n.*

Vincent, Dr., 186
Vogler, Georg Joseph (Abbé), 5
Von Karajan, Herbert, 52
Voss, Egon, 82 *n.*, 99 *n.*, 100 *n.*

Wagner, Cosima, 92–3, 99
  Diaries, 98, 100 *n.*
Wagner, Gottfried, 99
Wagner, Richard, 58, 71–104, 159, 197
  Barbarossa, 85
  Boulez's views on, 99–102
  Götterdämmerung, 73–4, 77, 79–80,
    86
  Hitler and, 92, 94–8, 101, 103
  on Mozart, 18, 19
  "The Nibelungen: World History as
    Revealed in Saga," 76
  Parsifal, 77, 82–92, 96, 100 *n.*, 101–
    3, 179
  Religion and Art, 88, 101
  Das Rheingold, 73, 77–9
  Der Ring des Nibelungen, 14, 66,
    72–81, 85
  Siegfried, 73–4, 79
  Siegfrieds Tod, 77
  Tristan und Isolde, 15, 19, 77, 80–1,
    178
  Die Walküre, 73, 77–9, 149–50
Wagner, Siegfried, 93, 95, 98–9
Wagner, Wieland, 77
Wagner, Winifred, 92–8, 103
Wagner, Wolfgang, 73, 74, 77, 93
Wagner, Wolf Siegfried, *The Wagner
    Family Albums*, 98
Walter, Bruno, 279
Watkins, Peter, 326 *n.*
Weaver, William, *Seven Verdi
    Librettos*, 107 and *n.*
Weber, Carl Maria von, 9
Weber, Max, 164
Webern, Anton, 159, 198, 202
Wechsberg, Joseph, *Verdi*, 108–9
Weisgall, Hugo, *Six Characters in
    Search of an Author*, 67
Wellesz, Egon, 206 *n.*
Welting, Ruth, 136
Werfel, Franz, 95

Wesendonck (Wesendonk), Mathilde, 77, 81
Weston, Jessie, 84 *n.*
Wilde, Oscar, *Salomé*, 124, 126, 127, 133–5
Wilder, Thornton, 43 *n.*
Wilkins, Nigel, 162 *n.*
Williams, Bernard, 54–5
Williams, Winifred, *see* Wagner, Winifred
Wilson, John Dover, 116
Winston, Clara, 257 *n.*
Winston, Richard, 257 *n.*, 258–9
Winter, David G., 32
Wolf, Hugo, 272

Wolf, Johannes, 165 and *n.*
Wolfram von Eschenbach, 84–6
Wollheim, Richard, 255 *n.*
Wood, Christopher, 241
Wood, Michael, "The Struggles of T. S. Eliot," 223–4, 232–3
Wysling, Hans, 256

Zimmermann, Bernd Alois, *Die Soldaten*, 67–8
Ziolkowski, Theodore, 263
Zuckerman, Elliott, 81
Zweig, Stefan, 155
Zylis-Gara, Teresa, 137

A NOTE ON THE TYPE

This book was set on the Linotype in Bodoni Book, so called after Giambattista Bodoni (1740–1813), son of a printer of Piedmont. After gaining experience and fame as super-intendent of the Press of the Propaganda in Rome, Bodoni became in 1768 the head of the ducal printing house of Parma, which he soon made the foremost of its kind in Europe. His *Manuale Tipografico*, completed by his widow in 1818, contains 279 pages of specimens of types, including alphabets of about thirty languages. His editions of Greek, Latin, Italian, and French classics are celebrated for their typography. In type designing he was an innovator, making his new faces rounder, wider, and lighter, with greater openness and delicacy.

Composed by
The Maryland Linotype Composition Company, Inc.,
Baltimore, Maryland

Printed and bound by
The Haddon Craftsmen, Inc.,
Scranton, Pennsylvania

Typography and binding based on a design by
Clint Anglin